# BIAS IN THE NEWS

# BIAS IN THE NEWS

Network Television Coverage of the 1972 Election Campaign

C. RICHARD HOFSTETTER

OHIO STATE UNIVERSITY PRESS : COLUMBUS

*Library of Congress Cataloguing in Publication Data*

Hofstetter, C. Richard
  Bias in the news.
  Includes index.
  1. Television in politics—United States.
2. Television broadcasting of news—United States.
3. Presidents—United States—Election.  I. Title.
HE8700.7.P6H65            070.4'49'329023730924            76-40272
ISBN 0-8142-0268-3

FOR TRUMAN E. AND ETHEL E. HOFSTETTER
AND FOR PHYLLIS, PHILLIP, AND ANDREW HOFSTETTER

# CONTENTS

# List of Tables

# Preface

The Television Election News Coverage Project (TENCP) was born of a desire to investigate systematically and rigorously a variety of assertions about national network bias in coverage of political events. The idea was to apply scientific methods to the analysis of this controversial issue so that policy implications concerning bias could be drawn forth. It was hoped that this information would be helpful in stimulating more informed discussion of news dissemination and its quality in America.

The 1972 presidential campaign was selected for analysis because it was the most recent instance of intensive campaign coverage. Although no explicit policy recommendations are made, the report hopefully will be important because of its findings about the role and character of mass communications during the 1972 election, and also because it will serve as a model for the kinds of considerations that are necessary in assessing news coverage of important events of our times.

The TENCP was organized in two phases: (1) an analysis of the content of news coverage on weekday evening network news programs; and (2) a series of national surveys of the public, political campaign leaders, and news personnel. This volume encompasses analysis based on the first phase. The second phase—concerning beliefs, values, attitudes, reported behaviors, and estimates of the impact of the network news programs—will be forthcoming shortly. The content study was designed to be an extensive, multimethod inquiry into questions of bias in television news reporting. It is unfortunate that space does not allow a more complete explanation of the many methodological and technical considerations that underlie the content analysis in this volume; however, a series of working papers and technical documents that elaborate the broader concerns are available to interested readers from the author.

The study reflects the imprint of many people. Howard Penniman's inspiration, ingenuity, patience, and encouragement have been invaluable. Charles S. Hyneman has had a major impact on my thinking, and his influence is reflected throughout the study. Lyle Nelson (study director and chairman of the Advisory Committee) and Richard C. Snyder (member of the Advisory and Technical Advisory committees and a colleague and friend) provided innovative ideas and excellent criticism. Many members of the Advisory Committee (Daniel Patrick Moynihan, Douglass Cater, Seymour Martin Lipset,

Irving Kristol, Charles Colson, and John Stewart, in addition to the aforenamed) made helpful comments during the design and analysis phases of the project.

A special Technical Advisory Committee was also appointed. Its membership was of immeasurable aid in more specific questions of design, measurement, and interpretation. Members included Michael J. Robinson, John P. Robinson, John H. Kessel, Klaus Krippendorff, Donald Roberts, in addition to Richard C. Snyder. John P. Robinson and John H. Kessel were particularly patient and helpful in the work, as were my colleagues Stuart J. Thorson, George I. Balch, and Randall Ripley. Personal conversations with Brian P. Emmett (head of audience research for the BBC) and Jorgen Westerstahl (University of Göteburg) were most informative and helpful to me. The impact of each is apparent in this report.

It is not possible to acknowledge adequately the aid of the large number of staff members who worked on the project in a personal way. Over one hundred people participated in various phases of television content and survey coding at one time or another. Mary Jane Judge directed television content coding, and Helena Czepiec Landers directed survey coding; both participated as well in project design and development of instrumentation. Karen Conrad contributed greatly by coordinating clerical activities and making a number of helpful suggestions, as did Shirley Adams. Gary Malaney, Deborah Rock Evans, William S. Oiler, Warren P. Yarnell, Catherine Rudder, Paul S. Strand, Cliff Zukin, and James Upton made particularly important contributions to the project. I am grateful to Leanne McLaughlin and Regina Reid for helping put the manuscript in a more readable form. Warren P. Yarnell conducted an extensive technical review of the entire manuscript in its final form. Anonymous referees made many helpful comments that greatly improved content and style. The patience, tolerance, and support of Phyllis J. Hofstetter contributed greatly to this effort. The same must be said for Phillip T. Hofstetter.

Several institutions were of invaluable aid in doing the study. The Vanderbilt Television News Archive (James P. Pilkington, Director) made it possible to conduct the study. Videotapes of evening news programs from 10 July 1972, to 6 November 1972, were made available to coders at the Ohio State University at nominal cost. The study encompasses the period from the first day of the Democratic National Convention through the Republican National Convention through election eve. The research reported here would simply not have been possible without the services of the Television News

Archive. Coding was conducted in the Polimetrics Laboratory, Department of Political Science, and computing was performed on the Instruction and Research Computer Center computer at the Ohio State University.

It was a privilege to work on a study of this nature in these highly politicized times without political pressure of any kind being brought to bear on any aspect of the study.

# BIAS IN THE NEWS

# 1. Bias and News Programming

This study describes and evaluates the coverage of the 1972 presidential election campaign by the three major television networks. The analysis focuses on weekday-evening news broadcasts from 10 July to 6 November 1972, a seventeen-week period of the most intensive election campaigning. Two objectives form the foundation of the study: (1) to identify and explain discernible patterns of campaign news coverage; and (2) to show how these patterns or policies of treatment relate to the candidates, issues, parties, and campaign activities, how they relate to each of the networks, and how they persist or vary as the campaign progresses.

This investigation was undertaken because of a growing apprehension by some Americans that the nation's news services are not to be trusted. Experienced practitioners and serious students of the subject have voiced uncertainties about the adequacy and reliability of news programming. In recent years prominent public officials and candidates for high office have charged newsmen with bias. Television has been the prime object of attack and may well be the principal object of public distrust.[1]

## BIAS IN NEWS REPORTING

After the 1968 presidential campaign former Vice-President Agnew unleashed a spirited debate, charging that network television news programming reflected the views of an effete, snobbish, liberal New York–Washington elite who played the role of "nattering nabobs of negativism" when reporting news about American society and politics. The Agnew speeches focused criticism on American journalism, but it is unlikely that his strictures aroused a ground swell of opinion hostile to network news. Many people already distrusted television news and a variety of other information-carriers.[2] The speeches, however, did sensitize both the general public and social scientists to the possibility of pervasive bias in social and political reporting. They stirred thoughtful people to contemplate the blurred line separating indefensible deception from unintentional errors that stem from editing, interpreting, and fitting facts into a broader context.

Bias is a helpful term if we are careful of how we use it. In both lay usage and scientific writing "bias" encompasses many meanings. The layman uses "bias," along with such terms as "slanted reporting" and "coloring the facts," to put a wide range of practices into one package. These practices may include outright falsehood at one extreme. "Bias" may also include analyses and evaluations that the newsman will defend as legitimate expressions of personal judgment. The scientist finds the word helpful for directing the reader's attention to a precise area of inquiry. This report always uses "bias" to denote partiality in news programming

In order to determine the incidence of bias, describe its forms, and appraise its significance, the investigation is of necessity directed to particular motivations, particular practices, and particular responses to news policies. To prepare for this analysis, the study focuses briefly on three principal complaints that lead to charges of bias. Lying, distortion, and aggrandizement of values are sufficiently descriptive titles.

### Bias as Lying

Many viewer complaints are based on the suspicion or the conviction that a news report is marked by untruthful statements or made with the intent to deceive. The newsman says that X occurred; some members of the audience think something else took place. If a viewer concludes that a departure from truth is due to incompetence or laziness, he calls the newscaster an ass and labels his output as rubbish. If he concludes that the news-bearer was aware of an untruth, the viewer calls the journalist a liar and says that the news service is shot through with bias.

To support a charge of bias in this sense—as deliberate, purposeful deception by assertion of untruths—two requirements must be met: (1) there must be a source of knowledge about reported matters that is independent of the reporter under scrutiny and is regarded as authoritative; and (2) there must be evidence that the reporter (or someone who participated in the news story's production) was aware of a difference between the authoritative version and the account under scrutiny.

Patent, provable lying is a rarity in news broadcasting.[3] However, if lying *ever* occurs, there is too much of it. Social scientists have neglected to investigate the frequency of lying and its effect on the public, if and when such falsehoods occur. In any case, it is not a high priority on the agenda of science at this time.

Disputed charges of deception present difficulties. There is no reasonably complete version of an event that disputing parties mutually accept as authoritative. It is rarely possible to prove whether a reporter has been ignorant or has consciously set out to be deceptive in recounting an event. The ordinary citizen's own observation may be the only account he can accept as authoritative. He heard a candidate make a speech, and he thinks he "knows" that the candidate said he would stop the war right away and get the troops home in a hurry. But the television newsman says the candidate talked in other ways about stopping the war. And the few feet of film showing the speaker before the audience caught the candidate saying that baffling logistical problems would hamper the withdrawal of troops and he would stop at nothing to defend the men until they were safely on the way home. Viewing and listening to the tape recording of the entire speech should settle all disputes as to what words and sentences were actually spoken, but the outraged citizen who thinks his candidate was wrongly presented in the evening news is not likely to do this.

Even if citizen and reporter sit together to monitor the tape, they still might furiously dispute the "plain implication" of the speech taken as a whole. Who can say authoritatively that the candidate is ready to sacrifice important national interests for an immediate end to hostilities? Or that he considers certain terms of settlement a *sine qua non* for peace? Or that he does not know what ought to be done, and by announcing an attractive goal and citing obstacles, he hopes to keep himself free to choose the best course when he finds himself in a position to act for the nation?

Finally, even if a dozen reporters tell the story alike, their agreement is not proof that they tell the story correctly and that others who tell it differently give a false account. One may be a sharper observer than the rest or in a better position to observe. Even if the twelve reporters are found to be right, this is not proof that the man who supplied the untrue account is lying. Honest error and careless oversight probably occur far more frequently than palpable falsehood in news accounts. When several reports are compared, skepticism about the divergent report puts the lone reporter on notice to marshall his evidence and reasoning with special care. Proof that his reporting is purposely false, however, must meet the two requirements cited earlier.

### Bias as Distortion

Distortion occurs when the impact of a news account is affected by unjustifiable omissions of significant facts; underemphasis or overemphasis of certain aspects of an event; or suppression or exaggeration of parts that fit together to make a whole story. It can occur when reporters describe an incident or assemble many materials to provide a frame of reference for ongoing events. Distortion can appear while discussing progress or retrogression, or explaining the significance of affairs that are too complicated for ready comprehension. Like untrue statements, it can be purposeful or inadvertent.

Think back to the presidential candidate who wants to end the war but is conscious of problems that make instantaneous peace impossible. He summarizes his intentions by labeling his goal "peace with honor." He lists concessions to the enemy he will make to secure an early peace. He surveys major obstacles besetting his efforts to reach agreement with the enemy on points that must be negotiated. He declares himself confident that a peace can be effected during his first year in office, if he is elected.

Perhaps the only way to give an unquestionable version of the speech is to quote it verbatim, but then something may be lost through the inability to reproduce the emphasis, color, and sense of purpose supplied by the speaker's delivery. A summary necessarily omits some of the speaker's words. One that is short enough to be read on the evening news can only touch main points and reduce the rest to general language that the speaker never uttered. The speech, in the summary process, is unavoidably transformed, and perhaps not even a master of summarization expects to escape charges of altered meaning. The term is useless if every departure from the original is branded as deception. The extent of the departure and the significance of the transformation determine whether distortion takes place.

Every charge of suppressing, twisting, altering appearance, and changing meaning must be studied in context. The news story may purposefully concentrate on only one aspect of a complicated matter. It is appropriate for a news reporter to examine the views of a candidate (or two or more candidates) on the probable hindrances to peace. If this focusing of a news story is made clear, the reporter may pass over, without offense, the candidate's views about the importance of defending national honor or the disastrous consequences of continuing the war much longer. Distortion occurs if reasonably attentive and intelligent listeners can be expected to reach wrong conclusions about the significance that the candidate attaches to obstacles he perceives to beset the crusade for peace.

Distortion in its most flagrant forms borders on outright falsehood and can be established by the rules for determining falsity cited above. A descriptive account can be made just as deceptive by omitting essential facts as by misstating them. Thus, in reporting a badly managed troop movement, failure to say that the mission was finally accomplished may twist truth as much as a false statement that the men never arrived at the munitions depot they were instructed to destroy. Ordinarily, it will be harder to prove that particular items in the account have been wrongly told. When reporting attempts to analyze and to evaluate, social scientists may find it impossible to prove distortion because there is no model to test the report against. The analytic or evaluative report is built up by a series of decisions to mention, to stress or not stress, to ascribe this significance or a different one. Each decision tests the skill and sound judgment of those who prepare the story. If all analyses and evaluations coming from a number of sources were identical, one would suspect a conspiracy in which the citizen is defrauded. If they vary, as social scientists expect them to, the prospect recedes for a model version against which other versions can be judged.

And yet, the citizen must appraise each news service critically, deciding which networks and which broadcasts are entitled to his confidence and attention. He can ponder evidence and read signs. If he is a persistent and attentive listener, he can construct his own version of the facts and their location in time, events, and conditions. If particular reporting does not jibe with the general run of stories, the viewer is wise to be dubious about the divergent account. It is easier to believe that one story is wrong than that many have been wrong. But there is risk in this rule for judging because the shrewdest, most insightful account will always be exceptional, and the story one suspects to be in error may possibly be different because it is marked by fuller investigation or superior analysis. To prevent falling into this trap, the viewer must be sensitive to signs. Does the broadcaster have the bearing of an honest and judicious person? Do his remarks suggest sensitive observation or shrewd reasoning? Do other persons, thought to be worthy of trust, have confidence in the network or the newscaster whose reports are in question? Most importantly, what is the underlying political and social philosophy of the broadcaster? This is bound to significantly affect his perception of events and his evaluations of newsmakers.

### Bias as Value Assertion

The world a person inhabits is in large part his own creation. If the climate is "beastly" in one man's view and "not so bad" in the view of his neighbor, the difference lies in the standards they set for judging. If A likes the town because people are "friendly" and B abhors it because people are "impolite and aloof," the difference in view may be due to popular acceptance of A and rejection of B.

7

But it may also be the case that A looks for smiles and sees them; cynical B expects to encounter grumpiness and never misses any manifestation of bad humor. And it could be that A just likes people and B does not like anybody much, including himself.

News reporters, because of their training and the necessity of pleasing a wide variety of people, may be more objective than the average citizen in sizing up the environment. The world they observe and comment upon, however, is a world compatible with their respective psychological and philosophic dispositions. They may differ from one another in position (supposition, conviction, judgment) and hold different opinions of who is important. They may argue about whose character and action ought to be made public. What is good conduct and what is bad? When should approval or derogation be bestowed? What are the most estimable ideals and goals for the nation? What elements of its tradition ought to be extolled and extended? And so on and on. Rooted in this welter of ingrained belief, studied conclusion, and raw prejudice is the inevitability of a restricted view of reality. There is a constant invitation to seduce or cudgel the audience into accepting the newscaster's test of good and evil: approving his judgments, bestowing praise, questioning acts and policies, viewing with alarm, and condemning others for shortsightedness, stupidity, weakness, or wrongdoing.

Instant complaints are expected from viewers whose underlying beliefs and standards for passing judgment on events are violated. What the offended reader or listener cannot charge off to carelessness or incompetence, he will charge to newsman bias. When classified, such charges differ enormously in character, and when examined, many of them are wholly incontestable. The most sweeping charge a few years ago was that of the Negro who claimed his race was all but totally unnoticed by the white-controlled communications media. Blacks might make up a half of the city's population, he argued; but if one depended on the newspapers or radio for information, the audience could conclude that black people were never born, never married, never died, and never made any contribution to the life of the community except to pay fines and go to jail. Here was a colossal astigmatism, only partially corrected today. If properly called bias, it is a bias of the white population and neither a bias of news reporters in general (who offend no more than white ministers or white college professors) nor of particular reporters and commentators (though some may surpass others in their disdain for the black race). Bias of this order, reflecting class disposition, includes disregard of women in affairs viewed as the male's terrain; regional preferences (the East Coast is up, the Deep South is down, and the Southwest is rarely mentioned); class preferences (the rich are mentioned for their dress, but a life of sacrifice and heroism will not win notice for the poor); and the elevation of big city life over the small town. To charges of bias on these counts, the newscaster replies with a demurrer. It is his job to report the news, and news is what a large-sized audience will pay attention to. If a large audience wants to know whether the jet set is going by air or by yacht this year, the newscaster must find out and tell them.

The individual news reporter also holds a personal, interrelated set of expectations, beliefs, and preferences that one may refer to as ideological, giving that word one of its more inclusive meanings. Ideological holdings may be rigidly structured and zealously propounded. In sharp contrast, they also may be tentatively held, laxly connected with one another, and subject to continuing revision. Doctrinaire Marxism and extreme laissez faire individualism illustrate rigid and religiose ideology. Mixtures of liberalism and conservatism, characterizing the center of political controversy, illustrate tentative and compromising ideology. Ideologies dominating public debate in America today are varied and cannot be ordered on a single continuum. Particular persons have different mind sets. Some persons are more or less abhorrent of poverty; more or less tolerant of big rewards for distinctive achievements; more or less committed to ethnic mixing. Some viewers are more or less attracted to grand-scale planning and governmental enterprise; more or less conviced that merit is concentrated in one political party; more or less sympathetic to the idea that the "less enlightened" party ought to be given a fair chance to rule when it does succeed in capturing enough votes. These ideological components come packaged in every conceivable combination. Every news commentator finds some listeners to bless, and several times as many to scorn, his most earnest thoughts.

The newscaster's ideology will affect every judgment he makes not wholly controlled by immediate sensory impressions. Liberal and conservative broadcasters will see the same words in the posted "Order of the Day." Their reports will begin to vary when one notices that expected things are not in the order (he finds hidden meanings). The reports may vary immensely when the newly announced program of activities is related to previous actions and strategic goals (the facts are interpreted). As the report or comment strays further from its factual base, ideology intrudes more certainly and starkly. One reporter will ordinarily repress his own conclusions and inclinations, acknowledging uncertainty where reasonable people might make different readings. His personal convictions may be stored up for presentation on those occasions when he is billed to speak "As This Reporter Sees It." With another newscaster, every report is: "As this reporter sees it looking through stereoscopic glasses; turn elsewhere for hints as to how other intelligent observers may see and interpret the course of events."

Ideological commitment probably accounts for most television newscasting that has created charges of bias in recent years. There is probably a conscious motive for provable falsehood, if such occurs, and distortion that verges on falsehood. Overlooking a failure or an error of judgment, or chiseling the sharp corners off of an unpleasant fact, may be hard coin in which past favors are paid for and future favors are purchased. If the reporter has proved himself to be "eminently fair," "understanding," "disinclined to take his pound of flesh," the senator, general, or high-ranking official will see to it that he does not miss any important piece of news in the future and perhaps gets an advance tip-off once in a while. There appears to be no reason for thinking that venality and unethical cutting of corners is a trait more characteristic of liberals than conservatives, or vice versa. If liberal reporters are thought to indulge more generously than conservatives in slanting their reporting of military campaigns, the conclusions may be warranted because more liberals than conservatives may be in the news-reporting business. If conservative reporters are thought to exaggerate the evidences of increasing street crime, the impression may result because conservative reporters may attach more importance to crime and mention it more frequently.

Think back to the indictment discussed at the beginning of this chapter. The most impressive attack on the broadcasters' objectivity and fairness was filed by former Vice-President Agnew, a Republican who is popularly labeled a conservative in politics. He did not charge that television newsmen of all ideological attachments overexpose their preferences and their prejudices. He asserted that liberals, by grossly outnumbering conservatives, dominate the presentation of television news; that prominent liberals in news-broadcasting are unrestrained in their display of personal favoritism and antagonisms; and that they are bold, if not vulgar, in their disdain for the political sense of the common man. The former vice-president's allegations did not set the bounds or emphasis of this investigation, but his allegations were addressed, dramatically, to issues of fact that must be studied in any comprehensive inquiry into the incidence of bias and the way bias may be expressed in reporting political campaigns.

*Fairness and Balance*

Fairness and balance[4] may be ideals of television newscasters, but fairness has no precise referent. Positive attributes or components of fairness cannot be listed easily because they include everything that a competent and honest journalist ought to feel free to report. In judging a reporter's fairness, one does not ask how closely he came to doing everything a good reporter might do. One only asks whether he did anything that a good reporter would not do, or failed to do something that a good reporter is obliged to do. What is viewed as unfair because it ought not to have been said depends on the standards of the man who makes the judgment. There is no code of good journalistic practice that defines a forbidden land of malpractice.

The goal of reporting balance also evades simple definition. The word in physics usage suggests equal proportions, but equal attention cannot always, and perhaps ought not usually, be a goal in news reporting. A sense of due proportion exists, however, and conscientious reporters try to avoid criticism of favoring one candidate by giving his opponent some notice that the reporter doubts he is entitled to.

A sense of equal proportion and fair treatment overall may also lead network managers to give a candidate more attention than he gets from the reporters. Minor parties and their candidates get little notice during prime news time because most listeners want to hear about candidates who stand a chance of winning. In a national television audience, however, many persons are interested in the third-party candidate and his cause. They want to know what the candidate has been saying and how voters respond to his appeals, even if they assume he cannot possibly win a single electoral vote. This is a legitimate claim to information. If the audience is believed to be substantial in size, the networks will respond to the demand, though they may not satisfy it. This special attention for the third-party candidate and his cause may come in a special report—"Meet the Press," "Face the Nation," "Issues and Answers," or other news features outside prime television time. The attention a presidential candidate receives in such a manner will not be noted in this report on the 1972 campaign because the investigation is restricted to evening news broadcasts.

The right of candidates to fair treatment or the right of citizens to full information does not call for the allotment of equal time in reporting what the candidates say and do; attachment of equal significance to the candidates' arguments and promises; or equalization of the impacts that news reports make on popular evaluations of the candidates. This becomes evident in the case of a candidate who says he will wage a front-porch campaign. Perhaps he is the incumbent seeking reelection. He says he stands on his record and his record speaks for itself; he will issue a statement or make a speech only when he thinks the public needs to be reminded that he is still a candidate for a second term.

In this imagined campaign, candidate A will say very little about the campaign issues and where he stands. He may say nothing at all about his opponent's position and the probable fate of the country if his opponent is elected. Candidate B, in contrast, gives the newsmen a steady stream of statements to report and analyze about four years of failure, the nation's plight, and the promise of a New Day if the White House has a new tenant.

### Scope of Attention

Election year is a time for the voter to ponder what the country needs, what government could do to improve conditions, and what candidates for public office promise to achieve if given control of the government. The communications media provide information to stimulate and nourish the voter's thought. But collectively, the media do not attempt to give anyone a complete political education. Ideally, the process of citizen education is continuous, and election year is a time for particular emphases. It is a time to focus attention on those problems that candidates and other political leaders proclaim to be issues in the campaign. It is a time to study the candidates' statements on the issues, their fitness to assume the responsibilities of the office they seek, and the records of both parties during periods when each was in power.

Matters immediately relevant to public choice are the media's prime concern in an election year. News reporters will pay little attention to a third-party candidate unless such a candidate stands a chance of winning or is thought likely, by his attraction of votes, to have a critical effect on the major-party candidate who will capture the office. If a third-party candidate, with no chance of affecting the outcome of the election, injects important issues into the campaign, his policy proposals may be generously publicized on television, but not at the cost of crowding items of more lively public interest out of the news. In 1968 George Wallace, nominee of the

American Independent party, had appeal that might have thrown the choice of president into the House of Representatives. Accordingly, Wallace was mentioned frequently in the news-reporting of 1968. In 1972 newsmen saw no prospect that the party Wallace founded would significantly influence the outcome of the election. Consequently, only less than one percent of the news stories dealing with presidential candidates were about the AIP nominee, John Schmitz; approximately 53 percent were about Democratic candidate George McGovern and 46 percent about Republican candidate Richard Nixon.

Without question, the television attention minor parties receive affects their success on election day and their chances of evolution from minor- to major-party status. The neglect that the minor-party supporter perceives leads him to charge newscasters with bias. A more generous treatment of candidates, who have no chance of winning, is just as good a cause for alleging bias. The newscaster distributes his attention according to what he thinks his audience wants to hear and the kind of subjects that will enlarge that audience. As he glosses over a matter of social importance, he sidesteps an opportunity for citizen education. But it is equally true that, if he molded reports and commentary to what he thinks the citizenry ought to be interested in, he would be liable to the charge of trying to mold the nation into his own image.

No effort was made in this analysis of newscasting in 1972 to fix the maximum and minimum limits of appropriate attention to minor-party candidates. The number of third-party stories is given, and the content is noted. No judgments are offered, however, as to whether third-party candidates were sufficiently or insufficiently noticed.

Judgments about news value control coverage of third-party candidates. News value also regulates the telecaster's notice of particular issues that are debated in the campaign; particular statements of the leading candidates; and particular incidents and occurrences that might, if publicized, have an effect on the vote count. The newsman has a responsibility to inform the public of anything he thinks the public ought to know, with due consideration for other things that merit attention, of course. But it is not the news reporter's responsibility to harangue the public until it sees the matter as he does. The presidential candidates, not the reporters, bear the main responsibility for determining what issues will get most attention in campaign time; what candidate weaknesses and mistakes ought to be exposed; what light previous experience throws on the candidates'

13

sincerity; and the likelihood that one or the other candidate will be able to deliver on the promises he sincerely makes. If neither candidate has anything to say about farm policy during the campaign, the newscaster can hardly be charged with bias if he fails to point out that the platform of the Democrats promises more for the farmers than the platform of the Republicans. If the Democratic candidate promises the farmers more than he can possibly hope to deliver, and his opponent lets him get away with it, the reporters who cover the campaign can hardly be blamed for not dwelling on the extravagant language that the opposing candidate neglected to expose. If the two candidates join in vigorous debate on appropriate farm goals and feasible policy means, then particular reporters become liable to charges of bias if they fail to give something approaching equal treatment to both candidates, regardless of the reporter's view on which one made the better argument.

In this study of television coverage of the 1972 campaign, observations were made of each network's allotment of attention to the candidates, the issues, and the campaigns. The study measured the frequency of mention and duration of attention for each network, and compared figures for the three networks. Interesting differences from network to network are reflected in the figures for frequency and duration. Differences of judgment as to what candidate statement or other event had the most news value probably accounted for the most variance. If anything properly classified as bias occurred, it is more likely to be found in the content of news stories and the aura of the broadcast than in the figures for frequency and duration of mention.

### Accuracy and Truthfulness

The difficulties certain to be encountered in identifying false statements and departures from the whole truth have been noted. This investigation did not attempt to construct model (wholly true and sufficiently complete) accounts of important incidents and events and then compare the broadcast accounts with the models in a test for correctness and adequacy. Even if resources had permitted this procedure, it is not clear that such a testing program could be administered with trustworthy results. Tip-offs to error and abuse were available, however. All three networks' evening newscasts during seventeen weeks were reviewed and analyzed in a number of ways. The study looked for striking differences in the reporting of strictly factual matters; however, no significant disagreements in facts that could be attributed to falsehood were found. Emphases in political reporting did vary, of course, but these differences appeared to be well within the bounds of truthfulness.

### Breadth and Depth of Analysis

News commentary was thoroughly examined and elaborately analyzed. Bias, as a manifestation of conscious purpose or the unwitting consequence of ideological position or party attachment, was not the primary point in this report on news commentary. Instead, the central objective was to observe whether what was said—the verbal statement and the visual material shown in connection with it —seemed to favor one candidate or one party over the other. The probable impact of such comments on the listener, not the motivation of the commentator or the art and effort in his words, was the major concern. This did not preclude a constant watch for opinions and judgments that could only be accounted for by the commentator's own predilections, social philosophy, or personal preference for a candidate, a party, or a cause.

This chapter was drafted with the considerable aid of Charles S. Hyneman. The entire study owes much to the conceptualization by Jorgen Westerstahl in "Objective News Reporting," mimeographed (Göteburg, 1972).

1. A mosaic of the conflict is summarized in Edward W. Knappman, ed., *Government and the Media in Conflict: 1970-74* (New York: Facts on File, 1974). A recent report on Americans' views concerning institutions is presented in Subcommittee on Intergovernmental Relations, *A Survey of Public Attitudes*, Part 1, *Confidence and Concern: Citizens View American Government* Washington: Government Printing Office, 1973).

2. B. Roper, *A Ten-Year View of Public Attitudes toward Television and Other Mass Media, 1959-1968* (New York: Television Information Office, 1969).

3. Peter M. Sandman et al., *Media: An Introductory Analysis of American Mass Communications* (Englewood Cliffs, N.J.: Prentice-Hall, 1972).

4. Perhaps the best available technical discussion of these attributes appears in Westerstahl, "Objective News Reporting."

# 2. Studying News Coverage of the 1972 Campaign

INTRODUCTION

There is great diversity in the many ways "bias" is commonly used, in both laymen's discussions and scientific jargon, suggesting that one must be careful to define the term each time. News reports may be "biased" in relation to any or all of these varied definitions, although one would not expect several kinds of bias to appear frequently in professional American journalism. The audience does not want false or distorted news coverage in the important American news media. One might expect, however, to find considerable *selectivity*, favoring one side or another in disputes, one candidate or another in elections, or one theme in preference to other possible themes.

News reporters always select certain facts from a much larger pool of facts in putting together their stories. The reporter selects facts he thinks are relevant and important and excludes details he presumes to be of less value. If we assume that distortion or falsehood do not occur, how is the selection of facts performed and what effect does this selection have on viewers of the news program? To what extent is partisan bias—selection that favors one of the sides in a conflict—present?[1]

This study is concerned with the manifest *content* of election year television news programming about politics and with the impact that this programming has on the American electorate. The implications of media bias and the stakes of the conflict over bias and objectivity in news reporting are very different, depending on the extent to which television news makes a difference in the way people conceptualize and evaluate the political scene. Therefore, the way people learn from television news and conceptualize political life must be taken into account when formulating general categories used in a study of the news.

METHODOLOGICAL CONCERN

Canons of science are applied in this study and analysis of election coverage. Consequently, this report reflects a search for knowledge rather than an attempt to indict or vindicate television news programming. In this sense the research goal is not too different from what a good reporter tries to do in telling the facts of a public affairs story to a network news audience. The analogy, however, should not be carried too far because the social scientist and news reporter work under different conditions. The social scientist has time to be more precise and careful in drawing conclusions; he can be more rigorous in performing analyses than the news reporter, who is constantly confronted with immediate deadlines. Nevertheless, certain parallels can be drawn between what the good reporter and the good social scientist do when they analyze an event.

The social scientist and the reporter are confronted with two frustrations as each seeks to reconstruct important aspects of the events they report: (1) frustration grows out of the necessity to make statements about the world (in this case, the world of television news) in the face of uncertainty; and (2) frustration grows out of the necessity to deal with error in all aspects of the scientific or the reporting process. Both the social scientist and the news reporter try to apply a microscope to one small part of reality in order to understand it better. In doing this, both ignore much of the rest of the world when formulating general conclusions. Some uncertainty remains; thus both are never completely certain whether conclusions are absolutely and irrevocably true. However, by looking more closely at a small segment of television news programming, researchers hope to reduce uncertainty concerning the extent of political bias found in the news and to know more about it. Social scientists, just like reporters, try to draw conclusions from the best evidence that is available.

Both the social scientist and the news reporter are continuously aware that error is possible when drawing conclusions from what is observed. The reporter develops expertise based on prior experience with a subject, and the social scientist depends on theories and research that others have done or he has done at some earlier time. Both have ideas about what is going on. Both sift through facts that are related to what they are observing because the cost of drawing incorrect conclusions are high in either case. Both the social scientist and the news reporter try to deal with error by testing the conclusions they have garnered from what has been observed. Both have hunches about what is happening; and both test those hunches by checking deeper and deeper into the facts.

The social scientist and the reporter differ in the way their theories, methods, and techniques of analysis are made explicit. The social scientist constructs abstract theories that serve to guide general kinds of research, whereas the news reporter is more interested in specific events. Neither completely ignores the domain of the other: The news reporter holds theories about the way events occur just as surely as the scientist take individual occurrences into account. The social scientist uses formal methods and statistical techniques to make his observations more precise and his work more comprehensible to other social scientists. The reporter relies on intuition to a greater extent and uses less formal techniques of investigation. But a scientist needs some intuition, and a reporter needs some analytic capabilities. Thus the parallels between good social science and good news reporting are marked.

LEARNING AND THE POLITICAL MIND

This analysis of news content is geared to the perspectives of individual Americans, who are confronted by political news on the one hand and by a variety of groups competing for elective office on the other. The average citizen carries images around in his head that are assumed to be shaped by television news in large part, although the shaping may not be as simple and straightforward as the average viewer might suppose.

Studies about the impact of television suggest that learning takes a variety of forms. On the one hand, learning from television is based on observation and imitation rather than on trial and error.[2] Overt practice is not necessarily involved.[3] Learning is also passive rather than active, changing the salience and perceived importance of issues.[4] Learning from television, moreover, creates an "image" of reality that may be more or less accurate, but it is perceived to be a mirror of reality.

Television produces a "secondhand reality" because the images selectively broadcast comprise the reality of an event or a sequence of events as far as viewers are concerned.[5] Most of the viewing public have never directly experienced the events depicted on television news. Yet they "see" events unfold before their eyes, usually with little idea of the film editing and text revision used in producing the story once a reporter has selected the facts he assumes are important. If a viewer were able to observe a story unfolding from a reporter's perspective, he might well "see" different facts than those reported on the evening news.

Passive learning occurs when people watch news with little personal involvement. Attention focuses on what happens on the screen. Many viewers may not approach the evening news with the same high motivation to learn that the more optimistic university professors attribute to their best students. News may be seen as important, and a person may make every effort to pay rapt attention; but many people use the news, just like other television programming, as entertainment. A fact here, an impression there, an interruption when a distraught wife shouts for the husband to take the dog for a walk, are probably what many viewers experience as they watch the evening news. It is also likely that the nearly accidental acquisition of certain facts and impressions results in glacial change rather than sharp and rapid changes of opinion during a campaign.

Network news coverage of McGovern's difficulties with organized labor throughout the 1972 campaign illustrates how different citizens might have acquired different information from the same programming. This coverage also illustrates the kinds of story content that was of concern to the study. It will be recalled that the Democratic standard-bearer was viewed with considerable distrust by the top ranks of the AFL-CIO during the campaign. McGovern, nonetheless, acquired some labor backing after his nomination in July, although then incumbent and opponent Richard Nixon was supported by leaders who represented a far greater number of union members. The Democrats gave a great deal of attention to campaigning for union votes and backing despite initial opposition of the leadership.

Assume that news coverage reflected each of the above phenomena. Some stories focused on difficulties that McGovern had with a particular union; others focused on successes that he had in winning support of a union; and still others focused on intra-union disagreements about what should be done to extend or withhold labor support. TV news also touched on Republican successes and failures in GOP incursions into the usually Democratic ranks of organized labor. This was especially true when coverage concerned the upper echelons of the AFL-CIO and when it touched on issues such as Vietnam or military preparedness. A few longer stories provided composites of each of these themes. Others reviewed the traditional support given to the Democrats by unions.

Assume that a viewer has not regularly followed campaign news reporting. He is a strong Democrat, a strong "union man," and does not belong to the union that is being covered in a story he is watching. The story describes a lack of support for McGovern by a union. The story also asserts that Nixon received the backing of leaders representing the 29.4 million (of 35.4 million) union members. In the absence of other information, he might hold a somewhat less favorable attitude toward the Democratic standard-bearer, candidate McGovern, than before. The story might suggest to him that McGovern is losing the support of labor, even though labor supported other Democratic contenders. The general impression might be that, try as he might, McGovern will not be able to overcome the non-support of labor (although this possibility is suggested in the last paragraph of the story). But if the viewer "sees" that leaders who represent an overwhelming proportion of union membership (29.4 million of 35.4 million) back the opposition, then his feelings for labor unions might cause him to withdraw support for McGovern that might otherwise be present. The story might also suggest that labor-related issues are more important than the viewer would have believed them to be in the campaign had he not seen the broadcast. A simple reminder that the top echelons of organized labor do not favor McGovern is significant to make a viewer who is sensitive to labor matters draw a connection between the candidates and labor-related issues in the campaign. Perhaps the relationship between organized labor and McGovern had not previously crossed the viewer's mind. Television news may have effectively "established an agenda" for our viewer that now includes concern for labor's fate under a Democratic administration.[6]

It is important to consider, moreover, that a news story, such as the story broadcast by CBS that ostensibly supplies the same information to all viewers, may stimulate very different thoughts among individuals who are sensitive to politics and political events in different ways.[7] Quite clearly, the labor partisan will derive different implications from the above story than will the individual who is hostile to organized labor. Similarly, intense supporters of former President Nixon may come to damn exposure of Watergate affairs as being anti-Nixon, but strong Nixon detractors may regard television news reporting of Watergate affairs as an attempt to cover up information by giving the government a "whitewash."

To appreciate the way passive learning and stimulation to think about particular topics (agenda-setting) may work, one should note that television news may "fill in" information in an existing set of attitudes.[8] The television news story may provide new information that relates to preexisting attitudes. We may dislike the former president initially, but once we hear about Watergate, we will be able to cite even more reasons why we dislike Nixon than we could previously. These reasons reinforce our preexisting dislike, making it even more intense. This "I told you so" response to electoral defeat by many anti-McGovern Democrats provides yet an additional example.

In most cases the sheer amount of exposure given to political and social issues proscribes the total amount of information about issues available to the public. The media act as gatekeepers, determining what is and is not news. Since most people, most of the time, receive the bulk of their information about public affairs through the media, the amount of exposure that is given to an issue effectively determines how much citizens can learn about public affairs.

In cases where different sources of information exist, and at least one source represents each issue viewpoint, a viewer's dependence on a single popular source, such as television network news, is not as crucial as in situations where sources representing a variety of important viewpoints do not exist. When many different and often-conflicting sources of information are present, citizens can weigh different arguments, assess conflicting information and come to conclusions on their own in a meaningful way. The availability of many possibly conflicting news sources about public affairs, therefore, appears to be a necessary condition for meaningful citizen participation in popular government.

Although diverse sources of information exist in the United States, television news remains the most popular source of national political information used by citizens to assess public affairs.[9] Many Americans are dissuaded from actively seeking information from other sources because of the personal costs involved. Indeed, it is difficult for most normally active people to find the time to search out very extensive information about any socially significant topic. Although many sources produce voluminous information about most topics, public events are usually quite complex. The citizen may have neither the inclination nor time (to spare from his job, family, or other concerns) to conduct scientific investigation on his own. Thus *de facto* reliance on television information about public affairs, coupled with production decisions to cover or not to cover an event, places a fairly effective limit on the range of affairs many citizens have a chance to learn about. The impact of these facts on shaping particular views about news events is tremendous.

Two indicators are used to measure opportunity for exposure (and thereby the opportunity for people to be influenced by the news) in this study. The first indicator is a simple count of the number of distinct stories about campaign events, revealing the frequency of various kinds of stories. Figures are then calculated on the percentage of stories about particular topics. The second indicator is the length of stories (in minutes); it reveals the total amount of time assigned to each kind of story. Length of exposure is as important as frequency of exposure to evaluate television news, a time-conscious medium. Longer stories, as this study will show, are qualitatively different from shorter stories. Certainly longer stories provide a better opportunity to convey more information in greater detail about a topic than do shorter stories. But frequency and repetition are important factors when broadcasting messages. In general we assume that the more often something is reported in a particular way, the more likely it is to have an impact on public views. Each indicator discussed above leads to somewhat different answers concerning the nature and extent of network coverage of political and social issues.

### The Dynamics of Political Behavior

Various voting studies suggest that persons conceptualize and evaluate political life and then vote for candidates for a fairly specific set of reasons.[10] Television news, and particularly whatever partisan biases that may be present, become relevant to election outcomes to the extent that they influence some or all of these reasons. Television also becomes relevant to the quality of political life, in a much broader sense, to the extent that television programming affects more general conceptions of politics.

Identification with one of the two major parties is an important long-term "cause" of partisan voting, but party identification is not the only determinant of partisan voting.[11] Party identification organizes a cluster of attitudes about the parties and it influences perceptions of candidates and issues.[12] Citizens tend to see candidates and issues associated with "their" party more favorably and those associated with the "other" party less favorably.

But most people also receive other information, in addition to the facts that they accumulate prior to the campaign. This information may alter long-term attitudes to a certain extent, and it is even more likely to influence voter perceptions of major-party candidates. One learns that McGovern and Nixon are associated with this group or with that group, or take a supportive position on certain issues and oppose others. Information that one candidate favors an issue that the voter intensely opposes may cause the voter to change his mind about the candidate he previously supported. Television is likely to be the public's most important source of additional information. Issues are important because most persons hold strong views on at least some socially relevant concerns, even if the range of these concerns is great, and few partisan issues evoke strong feelings from large proportions of the public.[13]

Campaign efforts and perceptions and attitudes about candidates, issues, and parties combine to form the imagery that many people use to evaluate electoral campaigns and political life in a general sense.[14] Longer-term attitudes, especially stable and central attitudes about parties, have a tremendous influence on the images of politics and government that persons hold. Information also influences, complements, bolsters, or undermines images about politics. Television news is assumed to be one important source of this information; this study tries to be sensitive to candidate, issue, and party reporting.[15]

## DESIGN OF THE STUDY

### The Sample of Broadcasts

This study scrutinized CBS, NBC, and ABC weekday evening network news programs between 10 July 1972 and 6 November 1972. Videotapes of the news programs were obtained from the Vanderbilt Television News Archive, Joint University Libraries.[16] Various ways to sample program content were considered before deciding to include all weekday news programs in the study. It was assumed that it was more important to eliminate the possibility of error by selecting from the eighty-nine broadcasts for each network in the period of study rather than by extending the coverage to days earlier in the primary phase of the campaign. A "saturation sampling" of broadcasts was used to prevent the exclusion of crucial campaign events from the study. These considerations should not be interpreted to mean that the character of news during the primary period is unimportant.

It is important to note that inferences can be drawn directly from observations in this study without the normal strictures applied to statistical "significance." All of the relevant news stories that were carried by the three networks during the period of the study were included in the analysis; no sampling of stories was involved. Therefore, errors associated with sampling are not a factor; any differences are significant in a statistical, if not necessarily theoretical, sense.

In this research an attempt was made to avoid some of the problems for which others have been severely criticized.[17] All stories, for instance, even remotely related to public affairs are included in the analysis. Rules and conventions for story content classification were explicit,[18] and great pains were taken to ensure that coding of material met standards of reliability acceptable to social scientists.[19] Any measure that purports to be scientific must be reliable in the sense that it must provide accuracy in measuring what it is designed to measure. In operational terms, accuracy is usually tested by re- peatability.[20] Can more than one investigator given similar settings, resources, materials, and rules or procedures come to the same con- clusions that another investigator has reached? Results that are not reliable in this sense are worthless, since different observers would be measuring different things.

Content analyses are particularly susceptible to criticism when information about the reliability of measurement is not included in reports (because rules for classifying the presence or absence of many of the more interesting traits in a story are difficult to de- fine in clear and explicit ways). It is particularly difficult to define coding rules and conventions clearly and completely when entire stories are evaluated. Many of the stories in this study were classi- fied, for instance, according to whether the Republicans or the Democrats were favored. It was exceptionally difficult to make what appears to be such simple, straightforward judgments in a reliable way. Reliability was greatly improved when "neutral" or "am- biguous" categories were added to the classification scheme and when coders were instructed to be particularly wary about jumping to conclusions concerning the extent to which a story favored one side. There are a variety of statistics that can be used to compute reliability coefficients.[21] Only very simple ones were used in this study.

Coder reliability was tested by comparing production classifica- tions of story content that were completed by each coder with the classification of the same story content by the staff coding super- visor for a sample of stories. The objective was to attain agree- ment between the production coders and the supervisor on no less than 80 percent of the content classifications made. Percentages of agreement between coders and supervisor were computed for indi- vidual items and for sets of items (e.g., items about candidates, about parties, and about issues). Most items and all groups of items reached the proposed goal.

Production coding was planned so that no single person (coder) would exclusively code material from a single segment of the cam- paign (or other extended period) in order to eliminate spurious "trends" in news content due only to coder idiosyncracies. The total number of weekday broadcasts from 10 July 1972 to 6 Novem- ber 1972 were divided into thirds in a sequential manner. Each coder was assigned one-third of the broadcasts, so that he was responsible for coding every third day on each network. Coding forms (in addition to coders) were also rotated as each coder completed one-third of the broadcasts, so that each coder would have coded each of three sets of coding forms (classifying various kinds of story content) for each one-third of the broadcasts.

Overall, coders were in agreement on 87 percent of the judgments that they made in coding news story content in coding global content of news stories in the study. In general, "harder" indicators (i.e., indicators for which judgments were easier to make because criteria were more explicit and more easily understood) had considerably higher levels of reliability; "softer" indicators had considerably lower reliabilities. Reliabilities met criteria that are generally accepted in content analysis studies.

Edith Efron's analysis has been criticized because it focused on stories broadcast during the last seven weeks of the campaign, rather than dealing with a lengthier segment of news coverage of electoral politics. Critics suggested that the style and substance of campaign news reporting may differ during various stages of a presidential campaign. They argued, moreover, that campaigns build to a climax just prior to the election, and that campaign issues are most sharply drawn at that time. It is also clear that the public's attention is most sensitive to politics—but probably least susceptible to influence by the media—during the final stages of the campaign. Ideally, one would want to scrutinize news coverage during the entire inter-election period. Studies that encompass longer time periods might well discover biases in news reporting that would not be so evident late in the presidential campaign.

Feasibility and cost, however, are major reasons why any study can encompass only a limited portion of the total news coverage during a campaign. This study assumes that it is more important to focus a study of campaign coverage on the latter portion of a campaign precisely because election campaigns are designed to build to a climax just prior to voting day, the time that people are most sensitive to political events and public affairs.

Consideration was given to including news programs that are broadcast on weekends and at times of the day other than the evening dinner hour. Thought was also given to including programs of a sometimes political nature other than formal news broadcasts, such as the "Today" show on NBC, and programs of a usually political character, such as "Meet the Press," "Face the Nation," or "Issues and Answers." Such programs may well provide even more information about politics and have an even greater impact in shaping basic political views on select publics than do the formal newscasts, because they may focus more intensively on a very limited set of political issues.

A decision was made to exclude all non-news programs from the study (except campaign advertisements sponsored by the respective campaign organizations) because of the relative size of the audiences for these special programs, the focus of the debate concerning political bias in the television news, and feasibility. Although many particular programs are very popular among highly select special audiences, it is likely that the news—in particular, the evening network news broadcast at the dinner hour—has the largest audience.

The news, moreover, and not special public affairs programs or talk shows, has been the focus of the controversy concerning political bias. Few have been critical of the political implications of talk shows, interview-based programs, and general non-news fare. Finally, it was decided to investigate a limited set of information more intensively rather than make a limited effort to study a wider variety of programming. With a limited set of resources, this decision seemed most judicious. Strictly speaking, all generalizations in the study apply to the most widely viewed news programs that are broadcast during the dinner hour; generalizations that go beyond the news programming included in this report must be based on other observations.

### Stories as Units of Analysis

The news story was selected as the basic unit to be analyzed because it is the smallest completely self-contained message in a news program. Analysis was conducted by relating different characteristics of the news stories about candidates, political issues, parties, and campaign efforts to other characteristics of these stories. Why make the news story the primary unit of analysis? It was assumed that stories were popularly perceived as unified wholes rather than smaller bits and pieces. Indeed, television news producers, editors, and reporters produce news stories as if they *were* unified wholes, or "packages" of information.[22]

The number of stories included in the sample of eighty-nine weekday news programs on each network was quite large, 4,349. All news stories at all relevant to American politics (in a very inclusive sense) were included in the study. Explicitly non-political, "human interest" stories (e.g., a North Carolina frog race and a Florida worm-pulling reported by Charles Kuralt on "On the Road") and most sports stories were excluded. News reports about terrorism at the Olympic games in Munich were included because the terrorist acts were political in nature and had overtones for American politics. Finally, headlines read at the beginning of a broadcast were not included, since a headline did not constitute a story in itself. The fact that headlines might well sensitize a viewer to story content was taken into consideration. Researchers did code whether or not a story was introduced by a headline as a characteristic of the story.

One particularly vexing problem encountered in this study was specifying where one story stops and another story starts. The problem was acute when stories dealt with different aspects of the same general topic. In most cases, the problem was handled by trying to maximize the number of stories contained in each broadcast. It was assumed that characteristics of smaller, more homogeneous stories could be coded more reliably and more meaningfully than characteristics of larger, more heterogeneous units.

Fortunately, it was obvious where most stories ended. In cases where story endings were not so obvious, decisions about where to end a story were based on changes in the subject matter. Subject changes occurred by these rules when, obviously, a reporter in the studio stopped discussing Vietnam and began to talk about the Nixon campaign in Oregon. Less obvious cues included: changing tones of inflection used by reporters to shift from one topic to another, the pregnant pause accompanied by a change in camera angle, shifts from action to location or to studio settings, and changes in background graphics behind a studio reporter or anchorman.

Many stories involved less obvious delineation. Consider, for the sake of illustration, the following coverage. NBC carried two adjacent stories about the Committee to Re-Elect the President at one point in the campaign. In one story, Martha Mitchell was cited as having identified a bodyguard who roughed her up and prevented her from using a telephone. NBC then linked the man to the GOP campaign organization. The very next NBC story concerned the arrest of a former GOP security officer in the Watergate burglary. The same story also described a Democratic party suit concerning invasion of privacy in the Watergate burglary.

CBS carried three adjacent news stories about Vietnam in one evening news show. Each dealt with military affairs in the war-ravaged land. The first described testimony before the Senate Armed Services Committee by General Abrams, then being reviewed to be chief of staff, about unauthorized bombing in Vietnam. The second reported that six anti-war activists who had negotiated the release of three American P.O.W.'s and several relatives departed on a trip to Hanoi to accompany the released P.O.W.'s out of North Vietnam.

The third story described an interview that one of the P.O.W.'s, Edward Elias, had given to Swedish television while in prison. He stated that he was not aware of damage done to the North Vietnamese civilian population by U.S. bombing.

The NBC and the CBS stories about related topics were originally broadcast as described on 12 September and 13 September. The problem arises in distinguishing between the stories on each day. Both NBC stories are about leading Republicans. The break between the two stories is coded when emphasis shifts from Martha Mitchell to the Watergate case, even though no dramatic shift in topics occurred and the transition is very smooth. The NBC anchorman read both stories with little pause between them.

Each of the CBS stories concerns Vietnam. The first concerns a Congressional hearing, involving bombing policy in Vietnam, and is clearly distinguished from the next two stories. Defining the dividing line between the next two CBS stories was more difficult. The second story that coders distinguished was about six Americans who left for Hanoi to escort three P.O.W.'s back to the United States. The third story was about one of the six Americans, Edward Elias, and his views on the war (presented in truncated form). All three CBS stories dealt with Vietnam as a general topic. Yet, each story stressed a different aspect or was developed and presented in a different way. The last two CBS stories stressed different aspects of the same general topic.

Very short, one-sentence stories were sometimes presented in rapid succession. Each was given the status of a story whenever it was judged to comprise a self-contained set of meanings about a subject. In general, juxtaposed sentences about one candidate and then the other "on the campaign trail" were counted as several different stories. This decision increased the extent to which candidate, party, and campaign stories could be reliably coded because it is less difficult to make simpler than more complex judgments.

Regular network interruptions for commercials were treated as divisions between stories in most instances. Material that occurred before and after a commercial was rarely included in the same story. Information about the same subject separated by other stories was always coded as belonging to separate stories. It was assumed that a break in the flow of information, whether because of commercials or for other reasons, was a disruption in the way a story was perceived by viewers.

Stories were assumed to be seen as organized wholes and to occur in contiguous units of information. Thus the impact of several short, disjointed stories about the McGovern campaign, for example, was assumed to be different from the impact of a single, long, continuous story about McGovern. Decisions of this kind were necessary, moreover, to provide criteria that allowed different news stories to be distinguished by coders in a reliable fashion. If rules for coding information from the news stories were unclear, ambiguous, and not well understood by different coders, then the coders would not usually come to the same decision in their work. More "commonsensical" but ambiguous rules, for instance, led to a great amount of disagreement concerning the substance of different stories. This investigation required a set of rules to identify stories in a reliable way so that two or more coders who understood the rules would arrive at the same set of judgments when classifying stories. This included classifying where one story stopped and another story started.

### Classifying Stories by Major Political Dimensions

Some additional rules should further illustrate basic political dimensions or categories that were used to classify news stories. An attempt was made to classify stories parallel to the perceptions that Americans use to conceptualize and evaluate the world of political affairs. Each story was classified according to its major orientation or thrust. The classes included candidate, political issue, party and campaign stories, and combinations of these categories. Stories were assigned appropriate classifications on the basis of their main emphasis.

To be considered a candidate story, for instance, an item had to more than mention Nixon or McGovern, or one of the host of candidates for lesser offices. A three-minute story about Watergate that included the statement "Mr. Nixon has so far made no comment about the incident" as the only reference to the candidate was not coded as a candidate story.

Stories were occasionally about two or more candidates. This was particularly likely to occur when an issue theme, such as a position on amnesty or the draft, was being developed in a candidate story. Reporters frequently discussed opposing views on the same issue in an interlocking fashion in order to emphasize the differences between the candidates or to highlight the conflicting extremes common to the issue. If the major emphasis of the story concerned both candidates' positions on an issue, then the story was coded as a candidate story (and, perhaps, as an issue story as well).

The candidate given the most coverage was also coded. In situations where each of the candidates received about the same amount of attention as the other, the candidate discussed first was considered to be the one emphasized by the news story. If one of the candidates in a story was running for a higher office, then he was assigned the emphasis in the story. In coding by these rules, the first-mentioned candidate was assumed to have a somewhat greater impact in creating a "set" in one's mind, and candidates for more prestigious offices were assumed to have a greater impact on peoples' views than candidates for less prestigious ones. National offices were assumed to be more prestigious than state offices. Reports based on professionally conducted independent polls—e.g., the Gallup or Harris polls—were considered to have specific candidate emphasis in accord with the amount of attention given to each of the candidates.

Issue emphasis was coded when the story concerned something explicitly or implicitly associated with national issues. These linkages could occur, of course, in a variety of ways. For instance all issues mentioned in either major party platform were included, as were issues that were attributed national significance by a reporter. These criteria included domestic concerns that we would normally think of as issues. Stories about foreign countries were also included as issues when they were about international conflict or tension, or when they concerned the relationship between a foreign country and the United States. News stories about domestic issues in foreign countries that omitted mention of American involvement in any way (for instance, a report of an earthquake in Iran) were classified as "other" in this study, since the United States did not have extensive involvements in this country at the time of the initial reports and no direct linkages between Iran and the United States were created by the story.

The specific issues in stories were coded in a way similar to candidate stories. Issues mentioned first in the story were judged to be of greater significance than issues mentioned later in the story when the length of coverage was the same. In coding, issues with national or international significance usually were given priority over issues of local significance. Issues were coded by a variety of classifications, allowing for considerable variation in the relative specificity of codes used. The more detailed codes are discussed in later sections of this book.

Party or campaign emphasis was coded for all stories that explicitly mention political party activities in general, or more specific political campaign activities in particular. A simple mention of party sufficed for the story to be assigned a party classification. The party

31

category was made more inclusive than the other general categories because relatively few stories explicitly referred to campaign organizations, and political parties were not frequently discussed apart from candidates and election issues.

Priorities for classifying more specific party designations were established as above. In cases where about the same amount of attention was given to parties, mention of a party or campaign organization in the first part of a story was assigned greater emphasis than mentions appearing later in the story. Similarly, national campaigns or parties were assigned higher priority than local political groups on the assumption that the public was relatively more interested in, and concerned with, national campaigns and parties—especially the race for the presidency—than any specific local campaign or party. Interest and concern, moreover, were assumed to influence viewer impact as far as specific content of news stories was concerned.

Coding of emphasis was based on the amount of attention given to pictures in stories. A party, issue, or candidate associated with a picture was attributed greater emphasis than a party, issue, or candidate in the same story not associated with a picture. Similarly, action film—film of ongoing scenes—was attributed greater emphasis than location film—film of a reporter portrayed against a background scene where action may have occurred at another time. Film of any kind was attributed greater emphasis than the still pictures that are sometimes included in stories. Beyond this, all these decisions were based on the assumption that an item of information presented first tends to have a greater impact in creating impressions than an item of information presented later in a story. In general, stories about politics, just like other subjects, were defined in simple subject terms and then given a dramatic form by the networks.[23]

### Contextual Information and the Problem of Structural Bias

Network and the day of broadcast were two basic characteristics used for comparison in this study. Network and day of broadcast, contextual variables, were more inclusive coding categories than a single story and provided background information, or information about the context in which the story was broadcast. Campaigns begin, grow, and end in ways that are largely independent of specific network news coverage. Yet campaigns are fought out within the context of network television, and great concern was given to the way that the networks reported the candidacies, issues, and party and campaign efforts involved.

Networks carry stories about American politics and images that are part and parcel of an incentive system. Networks also operate within a set of constraints independent of specific campaign, candidate, or issue stories. Comparisons between the networks' treatment of candidates, issues, and parties provide one basis for discriminating between biases that may be caused by factors associated with the medium itself. These factors include: the need to maintain an audience by dramatization of stories; the excessively brief time period that even the most important story can be given; and biases that may be caused by political views held by individual news personnel or executives. The first type of bias will be called "structural bias" and the second type "political bias."

The "residual" definition of political bias is far from completely satisfactory. Structurally biased material may, for one thing, have unfavorable consequences for one side in a political dispute. But even of more import is the argument that some people make, that the networks are all biased in the same way. Thus when similar coverage is interpreted as evidence that structural rather than political bias is present, critics are free to assert that this meaning of political bias is overly restrictive.

The critics may be correct. Several observations can be made to bolster the view of political bias that is used in this study. First, it is unlikely that news coverage by three independent networks would be similar *in detail* if political rather than structural bias were present. The analysis shows great similarity in detailed political coverage. The common experiences, values, and beliefs of news people that are asserted by some to underlie political bias in TV news would seem to account for parallels in broad network coverage to a much greater extent than in detailed coverage. Second, news organizations are large, complex institutions that reward regularized coverage and penalize politically tinged idiosyncracies. Finally, much of the evaluative coverage turned out, in fact, to be neutral rather than favorable or unfavorable in nature. But these arguments are not completely satisfactory, and the viability of the definitions must be left to the reader's evaluation.

Structural bias was assumed to have occurred to the extent that all three networks reported stories about the same topic in a similar way. This may not always be true, because people in all three networks may have similar political prejudices. But in the absence of interviews into the motives and beliefs of news personnel, similarities among the networks provide evidence that structural biases may exist. Political biases, on the other hand, were assumed to be more likely whenever differences appeared among the ways in which the networks reported stories. Again, such differences do not necessarily mean news people are giving vent to their political biases in any explicit sense, but it is possible that differences among the networks could arise in this way. If networks are not compared, then there is little basis for complaining about political partiality and unfairness, except, of course, when we personally observe events and are confident that our prejudices have not distorted our observations.

Structural biases in television news reporting occur when some things are selected to be reported rather than other things *because* of the character of the medium or because of the incentives that apply to commercial news programming instead of partisan prejudices held by newsmen. This study indicates that network news tended to be no less subject to the structural biases during the 1972 presidential election campaign than at other times. Each network devoted about the same proportion of stories and of time to the same subjects. Each network presented political material in a similar way. About the same attention was given to stories about candidates, political issues, and parties on each network. This was also true of briefer time periods during the campaign. Each of the presidential candidates was given about the same proportion of stories on each network; the same was true of each of the vice-presidential candidates and of opponents for other offices. Networks were similar, moreover, in their practice of failing to give much coverage to minor parties and to minor-party contenders for public office.

The proclivity of each network to dramatize politics and make politics exciting and interesting to the general public—the most important ramification of structural biases as far as network news is concerned—is, perhaps, most clearly found in the use of film and action settings in news stories. Political stories received much more film and action coverage than nonpolitical stories. Similarly, partisan and institutional sources appeared in the bulk of stories about politics, although network reporters were the only source portrayed in many news stories. But, once again, each network's coverage was very similar to the coverage of the other networks.

The specific context of news reporting may also be of considerable significance in assessing the notion of structural bias. The precise ways in which constraints on the networks affect news coverage may vary sharply according to the situation. Candidates for office, for instance, usually try to obtain as much free coverage as possible in the media. Free coverage on television usually, but not always, involves news coverage. Candidate A makes a speech in Peoria declaring that consumers will have to pay more for food if his opponent is elected. In a speech to labor leaders in Detroit, candidate B asserts that the economy will continue to deteriorate if his opponent remains in office. News coverage benefits both A and B, and each tries to see that his speech is carried in the media.

Candidates nearly always benefit from television exposure. This is especially true for candidates who are underdogs, whose campaigns are relatively poorly funded, or who have somehow not run an effective media campaign. Voters come to identify a name and associate images with the name from news programs no less than from other candidate exposure. Candidates may not always be successful, of course, in presenting a favorable image through television news stories. They are not in control of what is said in the same ways that they are in control of other kinds of televised exposure, such as paid commercials. But nearly any kind of exposure is likely to be more helpful than harmful when a candidate is less well known than his opponent.

Imagine a situation in which candidate A, an incumbent whose name is a household word, holds a large lead in national polls over candidate B, who is less well known. Indeed, imagine that B is a decided underdog in the polls and is viewed by many as being too radical. The polls also reveal that large numbers of B's partisan compatriots are defecting to A, and that the situation appears hopeless for B.

In this situation candidate A might conduct a campaign involving relatively few personal appearances, but candidate B would have to be far more aggressive in stumping the country. Candidate B would need to organize his campaigning to maximize his exposure in the media as well. He would especially need to maximize the amount of free coverage on television news, since funding would probably be in relatively short supply and the amount of overall exposure he received would be important. Candidate A would be far less harried by campaigning. He could remain relatively aloof from the personal aspects of campaigning, and devote his time to political affairs of state, thus enhancing an image of "president of all the people."

Candidate B would be expected to receive more coverage than A under these conditions because B's situation favors more extensive coverage. Candidate B also might take pains to be more available to newsmen than A because B wants to receive more campaign coverage. Candidate B also plans his campaign around the needs of television news: he is careful to publicize schedules in advance, to appear in locations that are favorable for television cameras, to make large numbers of personal appearances, and to be particularly friendly with news people. Candidate A might be less available to the press and less likely to plan his campaign around the news needs. Under these conditions one would not assume that candidates A and B would receive the same amount of coverage.

More detailed analyses of partisan biases—characteristics of news programming that tend to favor one side or the other—are presented later in this book. Greater attention was given to the Democrats in general, and to the McGovern candidacy in particular, than to the Republicans and the Nixon candidacy. This finding was true both in terms of the proportion of stories and the amount of time devoted to stories about the respective sides. Democratic sources, moreover, were consulted somewhat more frequently in stories about Democrats than Republican sources were in stories about Republicans. These discrepancies, however, were reduced once institutional sources were included along with partisan sources. In part this was due to the use of "surrogates" by the Republicans, and, in part, to the fact that they were incumbents. Several cabinet officials, for example, were given important roles in publicizing the GOP candidate's positions and, in effect, standing in for him on numerous occasions.

### A Mapping Operation

The preceding points may be illustrated by looking at how much was said about the candidates, issues, parties, and campaign efforts in the course of weekday evening news programs during the 1972 presidential campaign. We are interested in tracing the general outlines of network evening weekday news treatment of politics during the campaign, that is, mapping out the terrain covered by the evening news. We are also concerned with several additional features of news broadcasting that are reported later in this study.

Stories in this study were classified according to their predominant emphasis concerning candidates, issues, parties and campaigns, or combinations of these subjects. Candidates, issues, and parties are among the most basic dimensions by which American citizens conceptualize and evaluate the political world and public affairs.

Table 1 presents the relative frequencies and lengths of news stories in minutes in each subject category. Story subjects were also classified by network in order to enable comparisons among the types of stories that CBS, NBC, and ABC broadcast during the period.

Stories about social issues dominated news programming during the 1972 presidential election campaign period. These issue stories were not, however, necessarily political; they were not focused on candidates or parties explicitly involved in the campaign. Indeed, about 9.5 hours were dedicated to nonpolitical issue coverage on each network, and about 8.5 hours were dedicated to issue coverage that was essentially political in nature. About two of every five stories (excluding stories about sports and features with no social or political implications) concerned nonpolitical issues, and about one story in five concerned issues associated with candidates or parties and campaigns. When one considers that each network broadcast between twenty-six (ABC) and thirty (CBS) hours of news stories that were included in the analysis, the large proportion of total time dedicated to "the issues" becomes clear. But even at the height of the political campaign, a large proportion of the news failed to touch on issues related to American domestic politics.

TABLE 1

RELATIVE FREQUENCY AND LENGTH OF STORIES BY TYPE AND NETWORK

| TYPE OF STORY | CBS | | NBC | | ABC | |
|---|---|---|---|---|---|---|
| | % of Stories | Length | % of Stories | Length | % of Stories | Length |
| Candidate | 2.0 | 24.8 | 2.2 | 25.3 | 1.9 | 20.7 |
| Issue | 39.4 | 616.4 | 42.8 | 659.9 | 40.9 | 569.5 |
| Party | 2.4 | 33.6 | 2.9 | 65.0 | 2.6 | 40.2 |
| Candidate and issue | 9.6 | 118.1 | 5.0 | 110.0 | 6.7 | 113.3 |
| Candidate and party | 5.2 | 235.5 | 7.8 | 178.4 | 11.8 | 254.1 |
| Issue and party | 5.2 | 144.2 | 4.7 | 100.8 | 5.8 | 111.3 |
| Candidate, issue, party | 13.4 | 366.5 | 10.8 | 322.2 | 13.1 | 302.9 |
| Other, ambiguous | 21.1 | 246.6 | 23.9 | 288.3 | 17.2 | 205.4 |
| Total | 100.0 (1,420) | 1,785.7 | 100.0 (1,576) | 1,749.9 | 99.9 (1,351) | 1,617.4 |

NOTE: Relative frequency is expressed as the percentage of the respective network's total number of stories included in the study; length of story is expressed in total number of minutes.

In sharp contrast, only about 2 percent of the stories were exclusively about the candidates, and only 3 percent were exclusively about the parties and campaign efforts. Less than thirty minutes were devoted exclusively to coverage of candidates, and between thirty and seventy minutes were devoted exclusively to coverage of parties. NBC devoted more coverage exclusively to parties than did the other networks (65 minutes, in contrast to 33.6 minutes on CBS and 40.2 minutes on ABC), and about the same amount of time was devoted exclusively to candidates on each network. These figures should not be too surprising, since they show simply that news stories are rarely restricted to discussions of candidates or political parties in a way that is exclusive of other issue and group content. News stories usually were more complex and multifaceted.

The assumption that politically relevant news stories concern more than a single focus was borne out by inspecting the frequency and time devoted to combinations of candidate, issue, and party stories in table 1. Indeed, combinations of candidate, issue, and party were included in more than 25 percent of all stories and eleven hours of time on each network during the campaign period that was analyzed. As expected, news stories about several topics were longer than stories about a single topic, according to the data in table 1.

Stories about both candidates and issues made up about 6 percent of the total number of stories; stories about both candidates and parties (including campaign organizations, strategies, and so on) made up nearly 10 percent of the total; and stories about both issues and parties made up about 6 percent of the total. When we compare the three networks, it is evident that CBS devoted the most time to candidate and issue stories and to issue and party stories (118.1 and 144.2 minutes), and ABC devoted the most time to candidates and party stories (254.1 minutes). NBC devoted the least time to each combination of stories. The sharpest difference in the amount of attention occurred in stories about candidates and parties. NBC devoted nearly an hour less to candidate and party stories than the other networks did. It is important to note, however, that the differences in time spent on each type of story loomed considerably larger than the differences in the relative frequency with which types of stories were broadcast. The similarity in overall network profiles was striking in this latter regard.

Stories that explicitly concerned all three categories—candidates, issues, and parties—might be considered to be general campaign stories. In this sense such stories made up about 12 percent of the total number of stories broadcast during the campaign on each network. Somewhat more than five hours was devoted to these stories during the campaign, with little variation in either relative frequency or total time devoted to stories about candidates, issues, and parties particularly apparent among the networks. CBS broadcast 366.5 minutes and 13.4 percent. ABC devoted the least time and NBC the least frequent coverage to these stories, 302.9 minutes and 10.8 percent, respectively. Thus about one news story in eight could be considered a general campaign story.

About one story in five failed to meet criteria for classification under any of the preceding rules or was judged to be ambiguous in emphasis. The emphasis of stories in this analysis had to be clear and explicit in order for the story to be classified. Otherwise, as in most other coding of story content in this study, coders used "other" and "ambiguous" categories whenever the appropriate classification of a story was in doubt. This practice had the effect of "purifying" the analysis in the sense that findings were based on the clearest and most straightforward classification of content. It is important to note that most of the stories in the "other" and "ambiguous" classes were short, averaging less than one minute in length. They were "one-liners," which are common in televised reporting.

Several other observations should be noted from the information in table 1. First, the absolute number of stories broadcast during the 10 July to 6 November study period varied appreciably by network. There was also some variation in the total time devoted to news stories: NBC broadcast 1,576 stories (during 29.2 hours), ABC, 1,351 stories (during 27.0 hours), and CBS, 1,420 stories (during 29.8 hours). ABC produced the fewest stories and spent the least time on public affairs, and NBC appeared to have produced more —but shorter—stories than CBS.

The *patterns* of what evening news stories emphasized were nearly identical for the three networks, despite differences in the absolute number of, and total time devoted to, the stories. Little variation existed in the *proportion* of political story subjects or in the average length of these stories. However, the proportion of time devoted to political subjects did differ slightly more than the frequency.

### A Longitudinal Look at Candidate, Issue, and Party Stories

Changes in news content and emphasis might be expected to coincide with the growth and climax of the presidential campaign. One might expect coverage to increase in both frequency and length as the campaign moved through the national conventions. As the momentum developed, from the traditional beginning of the campaign on Labor Day to election eve, even further increases in coverage might be expected. In this sense, reporting of news stories about politics might be expected to parallel campaign activity levels in both the substance and the amount of attention devoted to electoral news. This view is referred to as a "campaign politics" model of news coverage.

An alternative view of news reporting is suggested by the kinds of incentives that network news people face. These incentives lead to different assumptions about the substance and amount of coverage of political news during the campaign period. News is what is new, different, and esoteric; but most of all, news is what news editors think captures the interest of the public. Thus it might be expected that campaign coverage would be most extensive during the period of peak public excitement in the campaign. Clearly, the most public and exciting periods during many campaigns surround the national conventions and the final days of the election. Thus we would expect coverage to increase during the Democratic and Republican national conventions, then to drop off, and finally to increase as election eve approaches. This view is called an "incentive" model of news coverage.

Before we observe patterns of network campaign coverage, it is necessary to deal with several problems. First, we must compare different time periods during the campaign in assessing campaign coverage. It is possible that the analysis results will vary according to how these comparisons are made. All information in this study was initially coded according to day of broadcast and network to ensure that the most precise daily comparisons of news content could be made.

But daily comparisons would not be very meaningful in establishing patterns of campaign coverage. Very few stories about a specific subject are reported on any given day. Thus an unusual or abnormal event, such as the capture and destruction of an American aircraft by Arab terrorists, for instance, would be expected to capture the bulk of news attention whenever such an event occurred. A broadcast emphasizing such an unusual event would have less time available for other news stories, including those about presidential campaigns. This would not be because of regularities in network news coverage about presidential politics, but because the unusual event appeared to have greater news value than whatever occurred on the campaign trail that day.

The very next day an unusual event of apparently high news value might occur on the campaign trail, and then a larger than average amount of time might be devoted to campaign coverage. Thus comparisons based on the daily patterns of news reporting are likely to be extremely irregular and unrepresentative of broader trends in political coverage. To remedy this problem, one could group days together into larger periods of time so that any unusual event occurring within the period would have a diminished impact on the outcome of an analysis.

But there are problems caused by grouping large numbers of days together. The longer the time period in which stories are grouped together, the greater the likelihood that important trends in news coverage will be obscured and masked by the grouping.

Consider the pre– and post–Labor Day periods. If all news stories were grouped into these two periods and comparisons concerning stories in each of these two groups made, it is likely that at least some distortion would result. Stories emphasizing candidates might be reported extensively during the convention weeks of 10 July and 20 August, and stories emphasizing parties and political organizations might be reported in the interim between the conventions. If the same total number of stories was reported, then one might conclude that little variation in reporting candidate and party stories occurred during the period; but this conclusion could be in error. The way stories were grouped would be far too general to be sensitive to analysis. Certainly an audience would receive different impressions by watching the news stories and reading the analysis.

A trade-off is necessary, therefore, between sensitivity to specific changes in news content and instability caused by abnormal events. One is likely to draw erroneous conclusions if story groupings are too great, but it may be impossible to form any conclusions about overall reporting trends if story groupings are not large enough.

Two different grouping bases have been employed in this study, although, in most instances, only one of them is reported in tabular information. Stories are most often grouped into monthly intervals when detailed tabulations are reported. The monthly period is assumed to be long enough so that irregularities caused by highly transient events are minimal, and yet short enough to reflect important changes in news reporting coinciding with important political events. Stories are also grouped into intervals of two weeks each when less-detailed tabulations are presented. The second grouping allows more precise statements to be made about trends. In most instances, however, more observations were needed than are present in the shorter two-week period to conduct detailed analyses. This was particularly true when studying those kinds of stories that were infrequently broadcast.

Some stories, such as those about McGovern's difficulties with organized labor or Nixon's difficulties with Watergate, were reported throughout the campaign period. But these stories did not occur frequently enough in any two-week period for conclusive analysis. In order to analyze and discuss such stories, it is necessary to make larger story groupings.

### Expectations and Realities

The incentive model of campaign coverage is given strong support by the data concerning coverage of candidates, issues, and parties. Candidate emphasis in news coverage reached a low point in Sep-

41

tember, after having been high in July and August. The first month (September) of the traditional campaign period emphasized candidate coverage less than at other times during the campaign (except on ABC). Only about one story in five concerned candidates. Less than thirty minutes a week was devoted to stories about candidates during September (again, except on ABC), according to information summarized in table 2. Similar patterns were repeated on each of the networks. Predictably, the frequency of stories and amount of time committed to candidates increased on each network as the election drew nearer in October and early November.

TABLE 2

RELATIVE FREQUENCY AND LENGTH OF STORIES ABOUT CANDIDATES
BY NETWORK AND TIME

| TIME PERIOD | CBS | | | NBC | | | ABC | | |
|---|---|---|---|---|---|---|---|---|---|
| | % of Total | Length | N | % of Total | Length | N | % of Total | Length | N |
| 10 July–21 July | 37.3 | 103.0 | 161 | 34.6 | 92.5 | 156 | 43.0 | 106.8 | 151 |
| 24 July–4 Aug. | 29.4 | 89.3 | 163 | 20.4 | 74.2 | 181 | 39.1 | 103.4 | 151 |
| 7 Aug.–18 Aug. | 33.5 | 91.4 | 161 | 28.0 | 74.4 | 168 | 28.7 | 65.7 | 157 |
| 21 Aug.–1 Sept. | 35.1 | 108.6 | 168 | 26.7 | 82.2 | 176 | 29.8 | 66.5 | 161 |
| 4 Sept.–15 Sept. | 20.0 | 54.8 | 185 | 20.0 | 57.2 | 200 | 20.6 | 52.8 | 155 |
| 18 Sept.–29 Sept. | 21.2 | 53.3 | 170 | 20.2 | 59.6 | 208 | 34.3 | 83.3 | 166 |
| 2 Oct.–13 Oct. | 33.3 | 71.9 | 171 | 27.0 | 75.4 | 204 | 33.7 | 72.9 | 166 |
| 16 Oct.–27 Oct. | 34.8 | 99.4 | 141 | 26.1 | 67.6 | 188 | 32.7 | 82.7 | 153 |
| 30 Oct.–7 Nov.[a] | 44.4 | 68.8 | 108 | 35.0 | 52.9 | 103 | 40.4 | 57.0 | 99 |
| Total | 31.4 | 740.5 | 1,428 | 25.7 | 636.0 | 1,584 | 33.3 | 691.1 | 1,359 |

NOTE: Candidate, issue, and party classifications are not necessarily mutually exclusive, since a story may explicitly concern more than one of these classes. The reader should recall that the Democratic National Convention convened 10-14 July, and the Republican National Convention convened 21-23 August. Percentages are of all stories broadcast during the period by the respective networks. Length is expressed as the average (mean) number of seconds that the candidate stories consume.

[a] It may seem surprising that the amount of time devoted to stories about candidates is less for each of the networks in this period than in the period immediately preceding, even though the percentage of stories given to candidates is greater. This seeming contradiction, however, is explained by the fact that the final analysis period includes only 9 days of newscasts as compared with 12 days in each of the earlier periods.

It is important to note that CBS and NBC gave the most time to candidates during the national conventions. ABC allotted 106.8 minutes to candidate coverage during the Democratic National Convention but only 66.5 minutes to candidate coverage during the Republican National Convention A rough correspondence between amount of time and frequency of stories about candidates also occurred, so that a greater proportion of stories during the conventions coincided with more total time committed to the candidates during this period. This correspondence was also true for stories broadcast late in the campaign period.

Thus the more traditional incentive view of news coverage was supported by stories that emphasized news about the candidates. Stories were both more frequent and somewhat longer during periods when dramatic and spectacular events—the national conventions and the election—occurred. Coverage did not run parallel to the amount of energy and activity expended on campaign affairs by the parties, which is more incremental and cumulative in nature.

News stories about parties and campaign efforts assumed a similar pattern. The relative frequency of news stories about parties and campaigns reached a low point during September, following a time of considerable emphasis in July and August. Then the frequency with which parties and campaigns were emphasized in news stories increased as the traditional campaign machinery built momentum during October and approached the final resolution early in November. Similar patterns emerged whether one considers relative frequency of party stories or the total length of party stories. More coverage occurred on all three networks during the conventions and at the time of the election than at other points during the campaign.

News reporting emphasizing political parties, campaigns, and issues assumed the same general pattern as news reporting emphasizing candidates and parties. The relative frequency of news stories about these topics generally was high in late August, declined into September, and then began to increase as the election approached. The same can be said for the total amount of time devoted to these concerns.

Thus the basic patterns of coverage about political candidates, issues, and parties appear to follow an incentive model. Coverage is greatest when excitement is greatest. This tendency clearly emphasizes the view of American presidential politics as a spectator sport, with the national news networks entertaining as well as informing the general public each evening. Political coverage is most extensive during the national conventions and near the election. It tends to be less important during the regular campaign period.

CONCLUSION

This chapter has outlined some of the more general considerations that should be taken into account when conducting a study of political bias. Selected characteristics of news stories broadcast during the 1972 presidential election campaign were included to illustrate prominent features of network news programming and characteristics needed for a systematic analysis of news content.

Tendencies to play up stories about major-party contenders for the presidency at the expense of minor-party candidates and candidates for other offices, and to emphasize periods of greater excitement and drama and to deemphasize periods of lesser excitement and drama, were noted in these examples. Marked similarities among networks in the proportion of stories and in the amount of time devoted to stories with these characteristics suggests that short-term, more partisan types of bias were not pervasive in programming.

Structural biases most likely explain several of the campaign coverage characteristics that appear. The situation, or context, of the 1972 presidential campaign was significant in this regard. McGovern and the Democrats received more coverage than Nixon and the Republicans, according to this study's data. Slight variations among the networks, moreover, appeared in this coverage, with the difference in attention given to Democrats and Republicans being greatest on ABC. Yet the 1972 campaign pitted an underdog challenger who scrambled for coverage against an incumbent who personally avoided coverage. We should have been surprised if McGovern and the Democrats had failed to receive more coverage than Nixon and the Republicans, since this situation existed. Campaign organizations typically distribute information to the press, stage "news events," and give news reporters special access to encourage greater coverage. But coverage can also be discouraged by reversing these tactics. Newscasters, especially television newscasters with bulky and expensive equipment and stringent deadlines, can only be expected to gravitate toward "easier pickings."

Yet a modicum of caution suggests that further analysis of the qualitative characteristics of news coverage about candidates, political issues, and parties be undertaken before strong claims about partisan bias can be made. Indeed, it is likely that the images associated with the candidates, issues, and parties are of much greater significance than the raw amount of coverage that each candidate, issue, and party receives. More qualitative aspects of news coverage are discussed in the remainder of this book.

---

1. Selection of what to include in a story is not necessarily as simple and straightforward as some may infer from this statement. Many values may impinge on choices of material. See, for instance, George A. Bailey and Lawrence W. Lichty, "Rough Justice on a Saigon Street: A Gatekeeper Study of NBC's TET Execution film," *Journalism Quarterly* 50 (Summer 1972): 221-29, 238.

2. Robert M. Liebert, "Television and Social Learning: Some Relationships between Viewing Violence and Behaving," in John P. Murray et al., eds., *Television and Social Learning*, vol. 2, *Television and Social Behavior* (Washington: Government Printing Office, 1969); Neal E. Miller and John Dollard, *Social Learning and Imitation* (New Haven, Conn.: Yale University Press, 1941); John Dollard and Neal E. Miller, *Personality and Psychotherapy: An Analysis in Terms of Learning, Thinking, and Culture* (New York: McGraw-Hill, 1950), pp. 25-124.

3. Albert Bandura and R. H. Walters, *Social Learning and Personality Development* (New York: Holt, Rinehart, and Winston, 1963).

4. Herbert E. Krugman, "The Impact of Television Advertising: Learning without Involvement," *Public Opinion Quarterly* 29 (Fall 1965): 485-94; Herbert E. Krugman and Eugene L. Hartley, "Passive Learning from Television," *Public Opinion Quarterly* 34 (Summer 1970).

5. Kurt Lang and Gladys Lang, *Politics and Television* (Chicago: Quadrangle Books, 1968), pp. 305-6; Walter Weiss, "Effects of the Mass Media of Communication," in Gardner Lindzey and Elliot Aronson, eds., *Applied Social Psychology*, vol. 5, *The Handbook of Social Psychology*, 2d ed. (Reading, Mass.: Addison-Wesley, 1969), p. 89.

6. Maxwell E. McCombs and Donald L. Shaw, "The Agenda-Setting Function of Mass Media," *Public Opinion Quarterly* 36 (Summer 1972): 177; Doris Graber, "The Press as Opinion Resource during the 1968 Presidential Campaign," *Public Opinion Quarterly* 35 (Summer 1971): 168.

7. Phillip E. Converse, "Information Flow and the Stability of Partisan Attitudes," *Public Opinion Quarterly* 26 (1962): 578-99.

8. Serena Wade and Wilbur Schramm, "The Mass Media as Sources of Public Affairs, Science, and Health Knowledge," *Public Opinion Quarterly* 33 (Summer 1969): 209.

9. Robert T. Bower, *Television and the Public* (New York: Holt, Rinehart, and Winston, 1973).

10. The most widely known are reported in Bernard R. Berelson et al., *Voting* (Chicago: University of Chicago Press, 1954); Angus Campbell et al., *The American Voter* (New York: Wiley, 1960); V. O. Key, *The Responsible Electorate: Rationality in Presidential Voting, 1936-1960* (Cambridge, Mass.: Harvard University Press, Belknap Press, 1966); Angus Campbell et al., *Elections and the Political Order* (New York: Wiley, 1966).

11. Donald E. Stokes. "Some Dynamic Elements of Contests for the Presidency," *American Political Science Review* 60 (March 1966).

12. John H. Kessel, "Comment: The Issues in Issue Voting," *American Political Science Review* 66 (1972).

13. Ithiel de Sola Pool, *Candidates, Issues, and Strategies: A Computer Simulation of the 1960 Presidential Election* (Cambridge, Mass.: MIT Press, 1964); Key, *Responsible Electorate*; David E. RePass, "Issue Salience and Party Choice," *American Political Science Review* 65 (June 1971); John C. Pierce, "Party Identification and the Changing Role of Ideology in American Politics," *Midwest Journal of Political Science* 14 (February 1970): and Richard W. Boyd, "Popular Control of Public Policy: A Normal Vote Analysis of the 1968 Election," *American Political Science Review* 66 (June 1972).

14. Kessel, "Issues in Issue Voting."

15. Berelson et al., *Voting*; Lang and Lang, *Politics and Television*; Harold Mendelsohn and Irving Crespi, *Polls, Television, and the New Politics* (Scranton: Chandler Publishing Co., 1970); Barbara Hinckley et al., "Information and the Vote: A Comparative Election Study," *American Politics Quarterly* 2 (April 1974): 131-58.

16. Special acknowledgment is due to James P. Pilkington, administrator of the archive, for his aid in the acquisition of the videotapes. The Television News Archive, of course, does not bear responsibility for errors of commission or omission that may appear in this study. The study would not have been feasible without the materials that have been available in the Television News Archive.

17. Edith Efron, *The News Twisters* (Los Angeles: Nash Publishing, 1971); also see Charles Winick, "Critique of the Methodology of Edith Efron's *The News Twisters*," mimeographed (7 October 1971); and Edith Efron, *How CBS Tried to Kill a Book* (Los Angeles: Nash Publishing, 1972).

18. Mary Jane Judge and C. Richard Hofstetter, *Content Analysis of Taped Television News Stories: Coding Manual, Working Paper Number 2 in the Television Election News Coverage Project (TENCP)* (Columbus: Ohio State University, Polimetrics Laboratory Report No. 15, 1974); and Deborah

45

Rock Evans, C. Richard Hofstetter, and William Oiler, *Thematic Analysis of Network News Story Content during the 1972 Campaign: Working Paper Number 3 in the Television Election News Coverage Project (TENCP)* (Columbus: Ohio State University, Polimetrics Laboratory Report No. 16, 1974).

19.  C. Richard Hofstetter and Mary Jane Judge, *Reliability of Television Election News Coverage Content Coding: Working Paper Number 4 in the Television Election News Coverage Project (TENCP)* (Columbus: Ohio State University, Polimetrics Laboratory Report No. 17, 1974); C. Richard Hofstetter and Mary Jane Judge, *An Analysis of Learning from Television News: Working Paper Number 5 in the Television Election News Coverage Project (TENCP)* (Columbus: Ohio State University, Polimetrics Laboratory Report No. 19, 1974).

20.  An excellent discussion of reliability and techniques for measuring it are presented in J. P. Guilford, *Psychometric Methods* (New York: McGraw-Hill, 1954), pp. 373-98. Also see George W. Bohrnstedt, "Reliability and Validity Assessment in *Attitude Measurement* (Chicago: Rand McNally, 1970), pp. 80-99; and Ole R. Holsti, *Content Analysis for the Social Sciences and Humanities* (Reading, Mass.: Addison-Wesley, 1969), pp. 135-42.

21.  See sources cited in note 20 above.

22.  Edward Jay Epstein, *News from Nowhere: Television and the News* (New York: Random House, 1973).

23.  Ibid.

# 3. How the Candidates Fared during the Campaign

INTRODUCTION

At the heart of the controversy over political bias in network news is a discussion of the nature and amount of attention given to public officials and their critics. Some officeholders say their critics received an unwarranted amount of favorable network attention considering the value of the criticism made. Of course, many critics argue that the networks are impervious and insensitive to their particular points of view, and that networks refuse to allow them to adequately develop criticisms in a public forum[1] Officials further view television as having gone out of its way to stress failures, inadequacies in governmental performance, and other "bad" things at the expense of news coverage of success, high levels of performance, and other "good" things.

These sentiments are echoed by candidates for office, who are rarely satisfied with the coverage they receive from the media and often feel that they have been treated unjustly. This criticism tends to focus on network television news programming because broadcast news is the most popular and, therefore, most important medium of communication during a campaign, and because reporters are sometimes perceived as being hostile or suspicious in their responses toward candidates.[2]

To some extent, reporters *are* hostile and suspicious of politicians in general and candidates for public office in particular.[3] Weaver develops a reasonable and plausible model of professional journalists' perceptions of politicians in which the model assumes that politics is a game with such stakes as personal gain and power for politicians. The game is competitive, and the electorate bestows victory or defeat through elections. According to this view, basic social and political values may be involved in the game, but their expression is directed at manipulating the electorate for purposes of personal gain by candidates. Political behavior by officials is viewed as being directed at manipulative goals to further personal careers.

According to Weaver, the news reporter's job is to bear the truth to the public so citizens can act intelligently and wisely in elections. The job involves publicizing candidates and their stands on issues in a critical way. It means that the journalist should continuously work to expose the "hypocrisy" involved in attempts to manipulate popular sentiments. This implies that the wrath of the media focuses on elected officials between elections. Thus an iconoclastic spirit would be expected to undergird most public affairs reporting. The model, however, does not suggest that partisan bias should necessarily be found in material bearing this "anti-political bias." That is, one would expect to find news reporters assuming a stance of "a plague on all your houses," rather than a plague on particular houses.

This chapter concerns television news reporting about Republican and Democratic candidates for office and focuses on the way that Nixon and McGovern stories were handled during the 1972 campaign. Did one candidate receive better coverage than the other? Were news stories systematically prejudiced in a way derogatory to one candidate and beneficial to his opponent? Most significantly, did Nixon receive worse, better, or about the same treatment as was afforded McGovern by network news? Is there reason to believe that biases in network coverage lead to one candidate's advantage in terms of an electoral victory?

COVERAGE OF REPUBLICAN AND DEMOCRATIC CANDIDATES

McGovern received more exposure by television news programming than Nixon, a pattern apparent on each network. The Democratic candidate was emphasized in 316.0 minutes coverage on CBS, 275.2 on NBC, and 314.6 on ABC, and Nixon was emphasized in 269.9 minutes coverage on CBS, 221.6 on NBC, and 201.2 minutes on ABC. Thus Nixon received slightly more coverage on CBS than on the other networks relative to the amount of coverage McGovern received, but he received less coverage on ABC relative to the coverage devoted to McGovern. In terms of the percentage of stories, Nixon received nearly as much coverage on NBC as McGovern (48.6 percent for Nixon, and 51.4 percent for McGovern), but considerably less coverage than McGovern on ABC (42.8 percent for Nixon and 57.2 percent for McGovern). Nixon received 47.0 percent of the major-party candidate stories on CBS.* But these are crude, purely quantitative indicators of gross coverage. We now turn to a more qualitative analysis of the character of this exposure.

Agnew received slightly greater attention from two of the three networks than did Shriver (36.5 minutes in comparison with 24.7 minutes on CBS, 38.6 minutes in comparison with 30.0 minutes on NBC, and 34.2 minutes in comparison with 36.1 minutes on ABC). Agnew's greater exposure did not decrease very much compared with Shriver's exposure during the last several months of the campaign despite the fact that Shriver received no coverage prior to his replacement of Eagleton. The frequency of stories concerning the vice-presidential candidates, moreover, paralleled the relative amount of time networks devoted to them.*

Stories about major Republican and Democratic candidates were classified as favorable, neutral, or unfavorable. A story was considered favorable to the respective parties if good things—for instance, success, honesty, peace, and such—were associated with the party or its representatives. A story was considered unfavorable to the respective parties if bad things, including failure, corruption or impropriety, war, and so on, were associated with a party or its representatives.

Stories that conveyed about the same amount of each type of information in relation to the parties were coded neutral, regardless of the extensiveness of the information included. These conventions assume that general evaluations of partisan representatives in stories about candidates for public office will be associated with the respective candidates. Stories reflecting favorably on Republican partisans should, therefore, be favorable to Republican candidates, and stories reflecting unfavorably on Republican partisans should have unfavorable implications for Republican candidates. The same association would be expected to hold for Democratic partisans and candidates.

One news story on ABC was coded as favorable to the Republican candidate. This particular story noted both favorable and unfavorable aspects of both candidates. It asserted that citizens would have a difficult time choosing between Nixon and McGovern since the virtues and faults of each were alleged to be complementary. The story asserted that Nixon's strength was in foreign affairs, especially in relations with China and Russia, but that he was not interested in domestic affairs. The story also asserted that McGovern "feels deeply" for domestic needs, but that he was tinged with radicalism.

If only the text were included, the story would have been coded neutral. When video content was included among coding considerations, however, coders judged the story to be favorable to the GOP candidate: Nixon's successes and strengths were judged to outweigh his weakness in the presentation.

Another news story, broadcast on CBS, was coded as unfavorable to the Democratic candidate. McGovern had been meeting with workers at a plant. The story reported an argument between candidate McGovern and several members of a crowd. A disagreement about policy in Vietnam—especially concerning amnesty—occurred. The eye of the camera reported the numerous exchanges between McGovern and several workers in the crowd. The sharp, often bitter, dialogue was assumed to undermine the force of the Democrat's

49

statements. The story was assumed to imply that popular disagreement with several McGovern positions was widespread among voters and that McGovern was not able to control dissent in a crowd in a masterful way.

About 12 percent of the stories were judged to contain information that was predominantly favorable to Republican partisans, and 8 percent were judged favorable to Democratic partisans. Just over 11 percent were unfavorable to the Republicans, and 14 percent unfavorable to the Democrats. By far the largest proportion of candidate stories, however, 77 percent for the Republicans and 78 percent for the Democrats, were neutral or ambiguous with regard to partisans.

These findings illustrate one of the most strongly supported conclusions of this study: most news stories cannot be coded as favorable or unfavorable to a candidate, political issue, or party. Coders could not classify stories in an unambiguous and reliable way when forced to judge all stories as being favorable or unfavorable. Reliable classification could be achieved only when a neutral category was added to the other categories. When this category was added, more stories fit under that head than under "favorable" and "unfavorable" combined. This finding for the 1972 campaign makes suspect other accounts of campaign coverage without reference to a "neutral," "ambiguous," or "other" classification. Even more importantly, the finding certainly challenges studies that assert strong biases in favor of, or in opposition to, a candidate are present in news coverage.

It is also important to note that misconceptions may be created by the method of calculating percentages favorable and unfavorable to candidates. If the total of favorable and unfavorable stories is the base, 52 percent of the stories are favorable to the Republicans and 36 percent are favorable to the Democrats. But if the base is all stories, including the neutral category, these percentages drop to 12 and 8, respectively. Obviously, the differences are matters of proportionality to the trained eye, but they do give very different impressions to the lay reader than he receives from the original statistics.

This candidate evaluation pattern reflected in network coverage suggests that the networks were less favorable and more unfavorable to the Democratic candidates than to Republican candidates. This is true both in the proportion of favorable, neutral, and unfavorable stories about candidates in each party and the total amount of time devoted to stories about these candidates. Differences were not very great in either the percentages or time devoted to stories in these categories. Table 3 indicates, moreover, that NBC gave about twenty-two minutes more time to stories that were unfavorable to Republican candidates than to Democratic candidates, but this was not a large amount of time in terms of the total candidate coverage by NBC. In terms of air time, CBS programming was most neutral to the Republicans, and ABC was both most favorable and most unfavorable to the Republicans. CBS was most unfavorable and ABC most favorable to Democratic candidates, although differences in time involved but a few minutes in each case.

Favorable and unfavorable stories about Republican candidates were broadcast later in the campaigns while the proportion of stories and the amount of time devoted to stories on each of the major networks increased as the campaign reached its climax in late October. Both Republican and Democratic candidates received more favorable coverage as election time drew near, although the number of stories and the time committed to them unfavorable to Democratic candidates diminished. Unfavorable stories about Republicans, in contrast, increased as the election approached. The trend was less evident on ABC than on the other networks, but it was nonetheless present for all three.

Thus Democratic candidates received a slight boost in the sense that the amount of unfavorable coverage about them decreased as the election progressed. Meanwhile, the amount of favorable and neutral coverage increased for candidates in both the parties. ABC was perhaps the most evenhanded, in a statistical sense, in its treatment of partisan candidates. Differences were, however, very slight, and one should not overinterpret them to reach conclusions about partisan bias.

### Nixon and McGovern Stories

The coverage of Nixon and McGovern on the campaign trail was considerably different from the coverage of the men as individuals. By and large, Nixon appeared to receive the better treatment of the two candidates, and gained more favorable and less unfavorable coverage than McGovern in terms of both the proportion of stories broadcast and the total time devoted to these stories on each network.

The findings hold true despite the fact that each network devoted much more time to McGovern than to Nixon. ABC was particularly unfavorable to McGovern: he received sixty-three minutes of unfavorable coverage to fifty-four minutes of favorable coverage, whereas

## TABLE 3

### Percentages of Stories and Time Devoted to Favorable, Neutral, and Unfavorable Coverage of Candidates by Party, Network, and Period in Campaign

| PERIOD IN CAMPAIGN | Republican Candidates | | | | | | | Democratic Candidates | | | | | | |
|---|---|---|---|---|---|---|---|---|---|---|---|---|---|---|
| | Favorable % | Time | Neutral % | Time | Unfavorable % | Time | N | Favorable % | Time | Neutral % | Time | Unfavorable % | Time | N |
| **CBS** | | | | | | | | | | | | | | |
| July | 7.4 | 8.1 | 87.0 | 171.7 | 5.6 | 12.5 | 108 | 7.4 | 24.9 | 73.1 | 118.2 | 19.4 | 49.1 | 108 |
| August | 8.9 | 18.9 | 78.6 | 155.5 | 12.5 | 22.6 | 112 | 4.5 | 6.9 | 78.4 | 153.9 | 17.1 | 33.5 | 111 |
| September | 13.9 | 11.4 | 76.4 | 80.6 | 9.7 | 15.6 | 72 | 6.9 | 13.7 | 70.8 | 72.9 | 22.2 | 21.0 | 72 |
| October | 14.6 | 33.2 | 74.1 | 173.1 | 11.7 | 32.4 | 158 | 10.1 | 22.0 | 82.5 | 203.7 | 7.6 | 15.9 | 158 |
| Total | 11.3 | 71.6 | 78.7 | 581.0 | 10.0 | 83.2 | 450 | 7.6 | 67.5 | 77.3 | 551.8 | 15.1 | 119.6 | 449 |
| **NBC** | | | | | | | | | | | | | | |
| July | 5.5 | 6.7 | 89.0 | 142.8 | 5.5 | 17.1 | 91 | 5.5 | 16.9 | 83.5 | 136.6 | 11.0 | 13.1 | 91 |
| August | 12.6 | 27.3 | 77.9 | 119.6 | 9.5 | 13.2 | 95 | 7.4 | 9.5 | 80.0 | 124.4 | 12.6 | 24.7 | 95 |
| September | 12.3 | 12.8 | 71.6 | 78.5 | 16.0 | 25.2 | 81 | 8.6 | 11.1 | 76.5 | 90.0 | 14.8 | 15.4 | 81 |
| October | 17.1 | 37.3 | 70.0 | 126.8 | 12.9 | 31.7 | 140 | 10.0 | 26.9 | 79.3 | 157.4 | 10.7 | 11.5 | 140 |
| Total | 12.5 | 84.1 | 76.4 | 467.8 | 11.1 | 87.3 | 407 | 8.1 | 64.5 | 79.9 | 508.4 | 12.0 | 64.8 | 407 |
| **ABC** | | | | | | | | | | | | | | |
| July | 7.3 | 13.9 | 86.3 | 173.2 | 6.5 | 23.1 | 124 | 7.3 | 20.0 | 77.2 | 157.7 | 15.4 | 30.6 | 123 |
| August | 11.8 | 15.8 | 75.3 | 98.0 | 12.9 | 18.3 | 93 | 7.5 | 12.6 | 65.6 | 86.4 | 26.9 | 33.1 | 93 |
| September | 15.7 | 23.5 | 67.4 | 93.0 | 16.9 | 19.6 | 89 | 9.1 | 12.1 | 77.3 | 101.8 | 13.6 | 20.5 | 88 |
| October | 15.1 | 32.2 | 70.5 | 148.6 | 14.4 | 30.2 | 146 | 7.5 | 24.9 | 81.6 | 165.9 | 10.9 | 23.1 | 147 |
| Total | 12.4 | 85.4 | 75.2 | 512.8 | 12.4 | 91.2 | 452 | 7.8 | 69.7 | 76.3 | 510.9 | 16.0 | 107.3 | 451 |

Nixon received sixteen minutes of unfavorable coverage to fifty-six minutes of favorable coverage. CBS was most evenhanded in regard to time spent on favorable and unfavorable stories about McGovern: he received forty-eight minutes of unfavorable coverage and fifty-four minutes of favorable coverage. NBC coverage of McGovern fairly closely paralleled that of CBS in both the amount and character of coverage.

Nixon received the largest amount of time devoted to unfavorable coverage on CBS and the largest amount of time devoted to favorable coverage on NBC and ABC. He gained the greatest proportion of favorable to unfavorable stories from ABC. Thus it appears that McGovern received his most favorable treatment from NBC and Nixon received his most favorable treatment from ABC.

The proportion of stories about McGovern judged to be favorable to his candidacy increased and the proportion of stories unfavorable to him decreased as election day approached. The amount of time given to favorable and unfavorable McGovern stories followed roughly similar patterns. A great amount of time was devoted to favorable and unfavorable McGovern stories during July (and the Democratic National Convention), but this coverage never quite attained the same level at any point later in the campaign.

McGovern's coverage contrasted sharply with that given Nixon. Coverage of Nixon was sparse during July, but increased in frequency and duration during the campaign. The proportion of stories unfavorable to Nixon, the amount of time devoted to unfavorable stories, and the total amount of time committed to these stories was low throughout the campaign period.

Stories about Nixon that coders judged to be favorable followed a different pattern. A sharp decrease in favorable coverage of Nixon occurred during September, and was consequently followed by an equally sharp increase in favorable coverage during October. If the July and August Nixon stories were combined and compared with the September and October Nixon stories, it appears that little difference in favorable coverage of Nixon was present during the study period, although ABC gave more total time but fewer stories to favorable Nixon coverage later in the campaign. (Little time was devoted to favorable coverage of Nixon in either July or September, but more was afforded him in August and October.)

One should also scrutinize the information in table 4 in terms of the coverage given favorable stories relative to the coverage given unfavorable stories about each candidate. In most instances the balance of favorable to unfavorable stories weighed in favor of Nixon

## TABLE 4

### Percentages of Stories and Time Devoted to Favorable, Neutral, and Unfavorable Nixon and McGovern Coverage by Network and Period in Campaign

| PERIOD IN CAMPAIGN | NIXON Favorable % | Time | Neutral % | Time | Unfavorable % | Time | N | McGOVERN Favorable % | Time | Neutral % | Time | Unfavorable % | Time | N |
|---|---|---|---|---|---|---|---|---|---|---|---|---|---|---|
| **CBS** | | | | | | | | | | | | | | |
| July | 21.4 | 6.1 | 71.4 | 20.1 | 7.1 | 4.2 | 28 | 9.3 | 19.6 | 68.5 | 60.1 | 22.2 | 20.3 | 54 |
| August | 13.0 | 12.3 | 79.6 | 81.6 | 7.4 | 3.8 | 54 | 9.5 | 5.2 | 71.4 | 50.6 | 19.0 | 11.3 | 42 |
| September | 14.8 | 3.3 | 81.5 | 36.2 | 3.7 | 2.2 | 27 | 12.8 | 13.7 | 61.5 | 33.5 | 25.6 | 13.9 | 39 |
| October | 16.9 | 13.1 | 73.8 | 67.8 | 9.2 | 12.3 | 65 | 21.0 | 15.2 | 74.2 | 70.2 | 4.8 | 1.9 | 62 |
| Total | 16.1 | 34.8 | 76.4 | 205.8 | 7.5 | 22.6 | 174 | 13.7 | 53.7 | 69.5 | 214.5 | 16.8 | 47.5 | 197 |
| **NBC** | | | | | | | | | | | | | | |
| July | 27.8 | 6.7 | 66.7 | 21.0 | 5.6 | 1.9 | 18 | 8.5 | 15.7 | 85.1 | 66.7 | 6.4 | 6.1 | 47 |
| August | 23.1 | 21.1 | 76.9 | 47.1 | 0.0 | 0.0 | 39 | 15.8 | 7.3 | 63.2 | 33.6 | 21.1 | 19.8 | 38 |
| September | 17.9 | 4.4 | 75.0 | 22.6 | 7.1 | 5.2 | 28 | 13.9 | 9.1 | 72.2 | 43.4 | 13.9 | 8.6 | 36 |
| October | 23.5 | 24.1 | 69.1 | 57.2 | 7.4 | 9.6 | 68 | 26.8 | 20.9 | 63.4 | 40.0 | 9.8 | 1.7 | 41 |
| Total | 22.9 | 56.4 | 71.9 | 147.9 | 5.2 | 16.7 | 153 | 16.0 | 53.1 | 71.6 | 183.8 | 12.3 | 36.2 | 162 |
| **ABC** | | | | | | | | | | | | | | |
| July | 26.3 | 8.9 | 68.4 | 19.0 | 5.3 | 2.2 | 19 | 12.3 | 18.0 | 64.6 | 66.2 | 23.1 | 22.9 | 65 |
| August | 27.0 | 13.4 | 70.3 | 26.7 | 2.7 | 2.5 | 37 | 14.3 | 10.9 | 54.8 | 42.3 | 31.0 | 18.4 | 42 |
| September | 29.6 | 12.1 | 63.0 | 26.4 | 7.4 | 5.3 | 27 | 17.0 | 12.1 | 66.0 | 39.5 | 17.0 | 14.8 | 47 |
| October | 21.5 | 21.2 | 72.3 | 57.6 | 6.2 | 5.6 | 65 | 16.3 | 13.2 | 74.4 | 47.8 | 9.3 | 6.5 | 43 |
| Total | 25.0 | 55.6 | 69.6 | 129.8 | 5.4 | 15.7 | 148 | 14.7 | 54.2 | 65.0 | 195.9 | 20.3 | 62.6 | 197 |

at the expense of McGovern. Both the proportion of stories that are favorable to Nixon and the amount of time devoted to them were from 1.5 to 3 times as great as were the comparable numbers of unfavorable stories about Nixon. In contrast, McGovern received more unfavorable than favorable coverage on ABC, and the ratio of favorable to unfavorable coverage he received on CBS was slightly tipped to the favorable side in terms of time but to the unfavorable side in terms of proportion of stories. The balance of favorable to unfavorable McGovern stories shifted in McGovern's favor as time passed during the campaign, whereas little change occurred in the ratio of favorable to unfavorable Nixon stories. However, there were many more unfavorable McGovern stories for each favorable one than there were unfavorable Nixon stories for each favorable one. It would appear that McGovern might have benefited from a bandwagon effect that involved broadcasting favorable news stories were it not for the fact that Nixon received about the same number (or more) of favorable stories as McGovern.

Viewers may also have received impressions about the "other party" or "other candidates" from stories about the candidates. In order to discern these effects, coders were instructed to judge stories about Nixon in terms of their favorable, neutral, or unfavorable implications about Democratic partisans and to judge stories about McGovern in terms of similar implications for Republican partisans. The data are not presented here, but parallel what one might expect from the preceding trends.

Stories about McGovern had slightly more polarized ramifications for Republican partisans than stories about Nixon had for Democratic partisans. This was true on each network, with not much difference between networks in regard to time or proportion of stories broadcast that were favorable, neutral, or unfavorable. Approximately 5 percent of the stories about McGovern were judged to relate to the GOP in a positive way and about 15 percent in a negative way. In contrast, about 12 percent of the Nixon stories were judged to relate to Democratic partisans in an unfavorable way, but nearly none of these stories related to Democratic partisans in a favorable manner. This is what one would be lead to expect, given the relatively unfavorable treatment of McGovern and the relatively favorable treatment afforded Nixon.

It is difficult to disentangle what we have called structural and political forms of bias in this mass of information. The complexities of trends and exceptions to generalizations are many. But it would appear that a viewer who tuned in on all of the network stories about the candidates would leave with a more positive impression of Nixon than of McGovern. The relative constancy of favorable to unfavorable stories on each network suggests that: there may have been more unfavorable stories to report about McGovern than about Nixon; Nixon was more difficult to cover than McGovern; unfavorable stories were more difficult to discern in Nixon's case; or internal conflicts and not so muted disputes within the Democratic party and the McGovern-Shriver committee were all too easy to unearth.

It may be, for instance, that news value associated with conflict in the Democratic ranks prejudiced the McGovern crusade. Few large open conflicts marked the Republican contest for the nomination or later campaign activities, and the Watergate episode was not given enough coverage relative to other stories about the Republicans to compensate for difficulties the Democrats faced. Nor did the few Watergate stories appearing relate to Nixon as much as to individuals associated with the Committee to Re-Elect the President. It may also be that the symbolic character of the office shields an incumbent candidate from the unfavorable glare of all but the most harsh and sensational stories. These interpretations suggest that structural biases would outweigh possible political biases in determining the overall pattern of candidate coverage. Nixon received less total coverage than McGovern, but what he received was more favorable. Structural, rather than political, biases appear to have been responsible for these differentials. The predominant neutrality of stories about each candidate further diminishes the extent to which either side would seem justified in complaining about news bias.

## MODES OF PRESENTING CANDIDATES

Given the preceding very general judgments concerning candidate stories, it is worthwhile to probe more deeply into the ways that stories were presented by news reporters. The ways in which stories were presented contribute to evaluations of the favorable or unfavorable character of stories. Sarcasm or enthusiasm exhibited by reporters, the use of quotations or visuals, the placement of stories in a broadcast, all may lead to differing emphases within the same story. They may, therefore, result in different shades of interpretation.

The ways in which stories are presented may have a great deal to do with the impressions that build up in the viewers' minds. Methods of presenting stories may, therefore, be an important component of partisan bias in news reporting. A great deal of enthusiasm, action, drama, pictures, quotation, and program emphasis may lead to greater viewer receptivity of a candidate, party, or issue. Alternative characteristics in news stories may jaundice the image of a candidate, party, or issue in viewers' eyes.

Several characteristics associated with the ways in which news stories about candidates are presented have been selected for analysis. These include the positional emphasis of a story (whether the story appears early or later in a broadcast); the appearance of quotations, enthusiasm, and sarcasm in news reporting; and the use of various visual techniques (including pictures, film, action settings, flashbacks, and closeups). Other modes of story presentation could have been studied, but we singled out those for study that we assumed to be the most important. We will scrutinize positional emphasis closely by way of illustration, and then briefly summarize the other characteristics of news presentation.

### Positional Emphasis

Generally speaking, stories that appeared early in a broadcast were assumed to be attributed greater significance than stories that appeared later. The most important stories were assumed to be presented first, followed by stories of less importance, in a way that resembles the layout of a newspaper. The usual rule is that the most attention-provoking stories are arranged so that they will capture the reader's or the viewer's attention. Were stories about Nixon or stories about McGovern given greater positional emphasis?

It was noted whether or not news stories emphasizing Nixon and McGovern appeared in the first five stories in each broadcast. The first five stories were chosen because about 30 percent of all stories were included in that figure. Thus the first five were moderately exclusive, but not so exclusive that extremely few stories had an opportunity to appear. Although the figure five is arbitrary, there was no reason to believe that the following conclusions would be appreciably altered if four or six or seven, rather than five, had been chosen.

Stories about McGovern were emphasized more than stories about Nixon on each of the networks. About 160 minutes of McGovern stories received positional prominence in comparison with 117 minutes of Nixon stories on CBS; comparable coverage on NBC and ABC was 133 to 107 and 164 to 90 minutes respectively. Some of this differential was due to the greater overall coverage that McGovern received. Thus McGovern would be expected to receive greater prominence simply because there were more stories about him.

This possibility was not, however, borne out by the evidence in table 5. Not only did McGovern receive more time during the first five stories of news programs but a greater proportion of his stories were among the first five in newscasts on each network. Almost half of the McGovern stories, in comparison with 44 percent of the Nixon stories, for instance, were among the first five stories on CBS. About 44 percent of the McGovern stories on NBC and 49 percent on ABC received similar prominence, and 42 percent of the Nixon stories on NBC and 37 percent of the Nixon stories on ABC had comparable status. Even when McGovern's greater coverage was taken into account, it appears that his stories tended to get greater positional prominence than did Nixon's stories.

Closer scrutiny of table 5, however, reveals that these conclusions may be incorrect. Although McGovern received greater overall prominence, this advantage was nearly entirely due to early coverage of the Democratic standard-bearer. Indeed, prominence given McGovern stories declined precipitously as the campaign progressed, and prominence given Nixon stories rose just as precipitously. During October, for instance, half the stories about Nixon, in comparison with 32 percent of the stories about McGovern, were given prominence on CBS. About 47 percent of the Nixon stories on NBC and 43 percent on ABC were given prominence, in comparison with about 29 percent of the McGovern stories on NBC and 40 percent of the McGovern stories on ABC. Although each candidate received less attention during September compared with earlier or later in the campaign, the overall trend present in McGovern coverage was one of decreasing prominence as the election approached, and the trend in Nixon coverage was one of increasing prominence.

### Quotation, Sarcasm, and Enthusiasm

McGovern was more frequently quoted directly than Nixon on each network. This was also true in terms of time devoted to stories including direct quotations. Stories about Nixon, moreover, were far less likely in terms of time to include any type of quotation—direct or indirect—than were stories about McGovern. Thus a viewer was less likely to see Nixon "stating his case" than he was to see McGovern doing so during the 1972 campaign.

Very little sarcasm, of either a favorable or unfavorable kind, was discerned in stories about Nixon or McGovern. Differences between the candidates as objects of sarcasm were negligible, although sarcastic comments were more likely to be unflattering than flattering to a candidate when they occurred.

Enthusiasm, in contrast, was present in most news stories about Nixon and McGovern. Slightly less enthusiasm was present in Nixon

## TABLE 5

### Percentages of Stories and Time Presented among the First Five and Remaining Stories in Nixon and McGovern Coverage by Network and Period in Campaign

| PERIOD IN CAMPAIGN | CBS | | | | | NBC | | | | | ABC | | | | |
|---|---|---|---|---|---|---|---|---|---|---|---|---|---|---|---|
| | First | | Last | | N | First | | Last | | N | First | | Last | | N |
| | % | Time | % | Time | | % | Time | % | Time | | % | Time | % | Time | |
| **Nixon** | | | | | | | | | | | | | | | |
| July | 32.1 | 12.1 | 67.9 | 18.4 | 28 | 16.7 | 5.7 | 83.3 | 24.0 | 18 | 21.1 | 9.1 | 78.9 | 21.0 | 19 |
| August | 48.1 | 41.9 | 51.9 | 55.8 | 54 | 55.0 | 45.3 | 45.0 | 23.6 | 40 | 48.6 | 24.3 | 51.4 | 18.4 | 37 |
| September | 35.7 | 12.0 | 64.3 | 30.2 | 28 | 25.0 | 10.2 | 75.0 | 22.0 | 28 | 18.5 | 13.3 | 81.5 | 30.6 | 27 |
| October | 50.0 | 50.6 | 50.0 | 48.9 | 66 | 47.1 | 46.1 | 52.9 | 44.8 | 68 | 43.1 | 43.1 | 56.9 | 41.3 | 65 |
| Total | 44.3 | 116.6 | 55.7 | 153.3 | 176 | 41.6 | 107.2 | 58.4 | 114.4 | 154 | 37.2 | 89.8 | 62.8 | 111.3 | 148 |
| **McGovern** | | | | | | | | | | | | | | | |
| July | 68.5 | 70.2 | 31.5 | 29.9 | 54 | 72.3 | 64.2 | 27.7 | 24.3 | 47 | 63.6 | 71.8 | 36.4 | 37.2 | 66 |
| August | 50.0 | 33.8 | 50.0 | 33.3 | 42 | 38.5 | 28.5 | 61.5 | 34.4 | 39 | 57.1 | 47.9 | 42.9 | 23.6 | 42 |
| September | 48.7 | 31.9 | 51.3 | 29.2 | 39 | 30.6 | 19.5 | 69.4 | 41.6 | 36 | 29.8 | 19.3 | 70.2 | 47.3 | 47 |
| October | 31.7 | 24.3 | 68.3 | 63.4 | 63 | 29.3 | 20.4 | 70.7 | 42.3 | 41 | 39.5 | 25.3 | 60.5 | 42.2 | 43 |
| Total | 49.0 | 160.3 | 51.0 | 155.8 | 198 | 44.2 | 132.6 | 55.8 | 142.6 | 163 | 49.0 | 164.3 | 51.0 | 150.2 | 198 |

stories; but enthusiasm decreased in McGovern stories during the campaign. Enthusiasm in McGovern coverage decreased most rapidly on CBS, while enthusiasm in Nixon coverage increased most dramatically on NBC.

*Thus little difference appeared in the way that CBS, NBC, and ABC reported stories about the major candidates, at least in terms of quotations, sarcasm, and enthusiasm.** McGovern probably benefited because he was quoted more frequently, and reporter enthusiasm was slightly greater in McGovern stories. Still, it is impossible to make a case for the presence of an anti-Nixon bias on the basis of these observations.

### The Candidates in Visuals

Visual material provides an added dimension to a news story. Television news uniquely allows viewers to see what is going on while the visual material is being interpreted by a reporter. Thus the sense of reality created by this combination of oral and pictorial communication should be particularly significant in influencing viewers' perceptions of candidates. Other things equal, we would assume that the greater use of visual material in stories about a candidate benefits that candidate. Candidate stories were classified according to whether or not pictures were used at all; whether or not film was included and action settings employed; and whether or not flashbacks or closeups of the candidates appeared during stories.

*McGovern received somewhat more coverage in stories that included pictures than Nixon did.* This is not because a larger proportion of McGovern stories included pictures, since both candidates received pictorial coverage in nearly identical proportions, but because he received more overall coverage.

Each candidate received about the same proportion of stories including pictures, but McGovern received more coverage that included film, action settings, flashbacks, and close-ups.* It appeared that differences in candidate coverage were more closely associated with differences in the opportunity to obtain visual material in a lengthy, overt barnstorming campaign than in a quiet, more serene and withdrawn campaign rather than with matters of political bias, because network patterns ran fairly parallel to each other in the qualities of coverage. Yet, differences among networks did arise. ABC appeared to broadcast more favorable coverage of Nixon relative to coverage of McGovern than the other networks.

#### CANDIDATE LINKAGES

Candidates become tied to various groups, individuals, social causes, and practices by being associated with them in news stories.

For instance, if labor union members are frequently pictured in the presence of the Democratic party nominee and members of the business community are frequently pictured in the presence of the Republican party nominee, then impetus is provided for the public to view these two groups as being positively associated with the respective parties. The "principle of contiguity" is involved in the idea that viewers tend to associate people and things frequently seen with partisans as being associated with the partisans.

### Republican and Democratic Party Associations

The respective parties are the two most important political reference groups in the United States. "Good Democrats" should be associated positively with the Democratic party and negatively with the Republican party. Similarly, "good Republicans" should be associated positively with the Republican party and negatively with the Democratic party. Television news coverage of campaigns can enhance or mute these relationships by emphasizing or deemphasizing their coverage. To the extent that polarized, explicit battlelines fail to be drawn, the partisan character of an election is muted. The traditional support of the candidates is undermined to the extent that the appropriate partisan associations and dissociations fail to be reinforced by popular imagery.

Stories about Nixon and McGovern were classified according to whether pictures or words drew a candidate toward, or associated him with, his own party or the other party; whether pictures or words impelled a candidate away from or dissociated him from, his own or the other party; or whether no clear associations or dissociations appeared in the story. Candidates saying complimentary things about a party, or representatives of the party saying complimentary things about the candidate, associated the candidate with the party. Similarly, the candidate saying uncomplimentary things about a party, or representatives of the party saying uncomplimentary things about the candidate, dissociated the candidate from the party.

The bulk of the stories about Nixon and McGovern carried during the campaign failed to associate or dissociate the candidates with the major political parties in any clearcut way.* Fewer than 20 percent of the stories about Nixon associated him in any way with the Republican party, and approximately 30 percent of the stories about Nixon made some connection with the Democratic party. Similarly, fewer than 20 percent of the McGovern stories associated him in any way with the Democratic party, and slightly less than 30 percent made a connection with the opposing party. Patterns among the networks were remarkably similar in the extent to which they failed to emphasize partisan polarities in this regard.

The aggregate linkages of Nixon and McGovern to the Republican and Democratic parties were nearly mirror reflections of each other. The same did not appear to be true of the pattern of linkages at different times during the campaign. Nixon stories associated him with the Republican party about 10 percent of the time and dissociated him (or associated him in a negative way) from the GOP 4 to 6 percent of the time. Party leaders, for instance, were more prone to actively identify with Nixon than to condemn him. Nixon, in contrast, was associated with the Democratic party about 1 percent of the time, and dissociated from the Democrats about 30 percent of the time. Democrats, quite naturally, were more critical than laudatory of Nixon. McGovern was rarely if ever associated with the GOP, but was associated with the Democratic party 8 to 12 percent of the time. He was dissociated from the Democrats between 5 and 7 percent of the time and from the Republicans about 27 percent of the time.

In terms of time allocated to stories that associated or dissociated Nixon and McGovern and the parties, CBS gave the most coverage to polarized stories concerning Nixon (thirty-two minutes associating him with the GOP and 127 minutes dissociating him from the Democrats) and McGovern (fifty minutes associating him with the Democrats and twenty-seven minutes dissociating him from the Republicans). ABC presented the least polarized view of Nixon, and NBC the least polarized view of McGovern. NBC spent the greatest time on stories showing Nixon associated with the Democrats (about six minutes). NBC carried the only broadcast showing an affinity between McGovern and the Republicans (one story about six seconds long).

The partisan implications of polarization trends among candidate associations during the campaign is even more significant. Nixon was increasingly associated with the Republicans and dissociated from the Democrats. This was generally true when both time and the proportion of stories were considered. McGovern, in stark contrast, was decreasingly associated with, and dissociated from, the Democratic party. Apparently, the Democratic standard-bearer was decreasingly associated with either of the parties in network coverage. Some exceptions did occur, of course. But by and large, the viewer would conclude that McGovern's campaign was disintegrating right up to the election. This might have mitigated any last-minute reactivation of partisan sympathies stirring in Democratic holdouts.

*Coalitional Associations*

A variety of groups have been classified as belonging to "coalitions" comprising the basic constituencies of the Democratic and Republican parties. Continuous association with appropriate groups in the coalitions would be expected to reinforce that group's loyalty to the party. Association with the other party's coalition would suggest that a fissure had occurred in the opposition's forces. Racial or religious minorities, urban dwellers, labor union members, and the poor have traditionally been identified as belonging to the Democratic coalition. The more affluent, rural dwellers, and white Protestants who are particularly cultured have been identified as belonging to the Republican coalition. It must be noted that the coalitions exist in only a very loose sense, because they are composed of continually shifting masses of people. Few major social groups are the exclusive captives of either party.

Note was taken whenever racial or religious minorities, common people (the average person who is not distinguished in any sociological way), cultured persons (members of elite social groups), experts (people who are distinguished because of their knowledge or capabilities), social deviants (those who do not follow the prevailing beliefs and behavior patterns), wealthy persons (individuals who, because of their dress or setting, are obviously wealthy), and military persons appeared in Nixon and McGovern stories. References by the broadcaster to the candidate's family, other politicians, foreign officials, and famous persons were also coded for each candidate story on the assumption that highly valued associations would lead to positive candidate images being formed by viewers. In these instances prestigious associations and those in accord with traditional values were assumed to be beneficial to candidates. Each story about Nixon and McGovern was then classified according to whether a positive, neutral, or negative association existed between the candidate and the group (see table 6). Unfortunately, in most cases very few associations were present because it was difficult to discern clearly identified individuals or groups in news stories.

Stories linking the candidates to common people, experts, and other politicians appeared most frequently. McGovern was more often linked to famous people and minorities; Nixon was more frequently linked to foreign officials and military people. Thus elements in the party coalitions became visible in news reporting.

Nixon was predominantly (more than 50 percent of the time) associated with family, famous, common, and wealthy persons in a positive way, and McGovern was predominantly associated with

## TABLE 6

### Percentages of Stories and Time Devoted to Positive, Neutral, and Negative Group Linkages to McGovern and Nixon by Network

| | Nixon | | | | | | | McGovern | | | | | | |
| | Positive | | Neutral | | Negative | | | Positive | | Neutral | | Negative | | |
| Network | % | Time | % | Time | % | Time | N | % | Time | % | Time | % | Time | N |
|---|---|---|---|---|---|---|---|---|---|---|---|---|---|---|
| *Famous People* | | | | | | | | | | | | | | |
| CBS | 80.0 | 11.1 | 20.0 | 1.9 | 0.0 | 0.0 | 5 | 25.0 | 0.7 | 0.0 | 0.0 | 75.0 | 8.5 | 4 |
| NBC | 75.0 | 5.8 | 25.0 | 0.2 | 0.0 | 0.0 | 4 | 0.0 | 0.0 | 50.0 | 0.7 | 50.0 | 2.6 | 2 |
| ABC | 50.0 | 2.0 | 50.0 | 0.5 | 0.0 | 0.0 | 2 | 0.0 | 0.0 | 0.0 | 0.0 | 0.0 | 0.0 | 0 |
| *Minorities* | | | | | | | | | | | | | | |
| CBS | 25.0 | 15.2 | 75.0 | 10.7 | 0.0 | 0.0 | 8 | 30.8 | 15.2 | 30.8 | 10.8 | 38.5 | 15.0 | 13 |
| NBC | 40.0 | 4.3 | 60.0 | 7.1 | 0.0 | 0.0 | 5 | 36.4 | 4.2 | 54.5 | 10.8 | 9.1 | 1.7 | 11 |
| ABC | 50.0 | 6.0 | 25.0 | 6.4 | 25.0 | 5.3 | 8 | 53.3 | 15.7 | 33.3 | 14.4 | 13.3 | 4.8 | 15 |
| *Common People* | | | | | | | | | | | | | | |
| CBS | 57.7 | 22.3 | 42.3 | 19.5 | 0.0 | 0.0 | 26 | 61.8 | 87.5 | 27.9 | 33.3 | 10.3 | 14.8 | 68 |
| NBC | 68.0 | 32.5 | 28.0 | 12.0 | 4.0 | 2.2 | 25 | 60.5 | 51.8 | 30.2 | 30.9 | 9.3 | 6.4 | 43 |
| ABC | 62.1 | 37.1 | 34.5 | 24.9 | 3.4 | 3.4 | 29 | 64.2 | 69.2 | 24.5 | 34.6 | 11.3 | 9.1 | 53 |
| *Cultured People* | | | | | | | | | | | | | | |
| CBS | 0.0 | 0.0 | 0.0 | 0.0 | 0.0 | 0.0 | 0 | 0.0 | 0.0 | 0.0 | 0.0 | 100.0 | 4.5 | 1 |
| NBC | 100.0 | 0.6 | 0.0 | 0.0 | 0.0 | 0.0 | 1 | 50.0 | 2.7 | 50.0 | 3.6 | 0.0 | 0.0 | 2 |
| ABC | 100.0 | 2.0 | 0.0 | 0.0 | 0.0 | 0.0 | 1 | 50.0 | 0.4 | 50.0 | 0.4 | 0.0 | 0.0 | 2 |
| *Experts* | | | | | | | | | | | | | | |
| CBS | 51.6 | 47.2 | 45.2 | 18.3 | 3.2 | 0.5 | 31 | 17.6 | 6.3 | 70.6 | 37.3 | 11.8 | 11.5 | 34 |
| NBC | 37.5 | 20.9 | 54.2 | 9.1 | 8.3 | 6.4 | 24 | 5.0 | 3.6 | 80.0 | 25.5 | 15.0 | 5.6 | 20 |
| ABC | 36.7 | 23.1 | 60.0 | 23.2 | 3.3 | 2.5 | 30 | 14.7 | 7.9 | 64.7 | 36.6 | 20.6 | 13.8 | 34 |

TABLE 6 (continued)

| NETWORK | NIXON Positive % | Time | Neutral % | Time | Negative % | Time | N | McGOVERN Positive % | Time | Neutral % | Time | Negative % | Time | N |
|---|---|---|---|---|---|---|---|---|---|---|---|---|---|---|
| *Social Deviants* | | | | | | | | | | | | | | |
| CBS | 0.0 | 0.0 | 0.0 | 0.0 | 100.0 | 2.7 | 2 | 50.0 | 0.8 | 0.0 | 0.0 | 50.0 | 4.5 | 2 |
| NBC | 0.0 | 0.0 | 0.0 | 0.0 | 100.0 | 4.5 | 3 | 0.0 | 0.0 | 25.0 | 2.0 | 75.0 | 6.4 | 4 |
| ABC | 0.0 | 0.0 | 0.0 | 0.0 | 100.0 | 5.4 | 5 | 0.0 | 0.0 | 25.0 | 2.9 | 75.0 | 5.7 | 4 |
| *Wealthy* | | | | | | | | | | | | | | |
| CBS | 100.0 | 5.1 | 0.0 | 0.0 | 0.0 | 0.0 | 2 | 20.0 | 0.7 | 20.0 | 2.5 | 60.0 | 8.7 | 5 |
| NBC | 100.0 | 1.0 | 0.0 | 0.0 | 0.0 | 0.0 | 2 | 0.0 | 0.0 | 0.0 | 0.0 | 100.0 | 2.6 | 1 |
| ABC | 100.0 | 3.7 | 0.0 | 0.0 | 0.0 | 0.0 | 2 | 0.0 | 0.0 | 0.0 | 0.0 | 100.0 | 7.8 | 4 |
| *Foreign Officials* | | | | | | | | | | | | | | |
| CBS | 31.8 | 11.4 | 59.1 | 17.4 | 9.1 | 3.8 | 22 | 0.0 | 0.0 | 20.0 | 1.8 | 80.0 | 7.0 | 5 |
| NBC | 42.9 | 12.1 | 52.4 | 20.9 | 4.8 | 1.9 | 21 | 20.0 | 2.3 | 60.0 | 4.4 | 20.0 | 10.4 | 5 |
| ABC | 35.0 | 12.4 | 40.0 | 16.4 | 25.0 | 6.0 | 20 | 0.0 | 0.0 | 75.0 | 5.4 | 25.0 | 0.6 | 4 |
| *Military* | | | | | | | | | | | | | | |
| CBS | 31.8 | 11.4 | 59.1 | 17.4 | 9.1 | 3.8 | 22 | 0.0 | 0.0 | 20.0 | 1.8 | 80.0 | 7.0 | 5 |
| NBC | 42.9 | 12.1 | 52.4 | 20.9 | 4.8 | 1.9 | 21 | 20.0 | 2.3 | 60.0 | 4.4 | 20.0 | 10.4 | 5 |
| ABC | 35.0 | 12.4 | 40.0 | 16.4 | 25.0 | 6.0 | 20 | 0.0 | 0.0 | 75.0 | 5.4 | 25.0 | 0.6 | 4 |
| *Other Politicians* | | | | | | | | | | | | | | |
| CBS | 43.9 | 58.1 | 26.3 | 19.5 | 29.8 | 19.4 | 57 | 36.8 | 69.8 | 35.6 | 63.1 | 27.6 | 44.1 | 87 |
| NBC | 42.0 | 38.6 | 38.0 | 23.8 | 20.0 | 19.3 | 50 | 51.2 | 78.4 | 29.3 | 52.0 | 19.5 | 27.0 | 82 |
| ABC | 48.9 | 33.8 | 40.0 | 25.0 | 11.1 | 3.8 | 45 | 31.1 | 53.1 | 40.0 | 66.3 | 28.9 | 40.1 | 90 |
| *Family* | | | | | | | | | | | | | | |
| CBS | 100.0 | 36.3 | 0.0 | 0.0 | 0.0 | 0.0 | 13 | 100.0 | 11.8 | 0.0 | 0.0 | 0.0 | 0.0 | 5 |
| NBC | 100.0 | 27.9 | 0.0 | 0.0 | 0.0 | 0.0 | 13 | 100.0 | 18.5 | 0.0 | 0.0 | 0.0 | 0.0 | 8 |
| ABC | 90.0 | 17.9 | 10.0 | 2.7 | 0.0 | 0.0 | 10 | 90.0 | 23.5 | 10.0 | 2.6 | 0.0 | 0.0 | 10 |

common people and family in a positive way. McGovern was more likely than Nixon to be associated in a negative way with minorities, experts, foreign officials, the military, and famous, common, cultured, and wealthy persons.

Some variations in groups associated favorably and unfavorably with Nixon and McGovern did appear among the networks. However, the amount of time and percentage of stories that included specific groups was so small as to preclude strong conclusions. One might speculate that Nixon was somewhat more favorably linked to many groups than McGovern. This is true of not only traditional, more pro-Republican groups but also of several traditional, more pro-Democratic groups, such as minorities. A fair amount of attention was devoted to unfavorable ties between groups and McGovern. More similarities than differences in network profiles, however, appeared in these data.

### Candidate Supporters

Candidates derive support from a variety of groups in a more formal sense. Nixon and McGovern stories were coded according to whether or not candidate support was present from an unorganized crowd, political rally, testimonial, or campaign contributions. It was assumed that displays of positive sentiment, or other kinds of support, were beneficial to the candidates. The candidate who appeared to have the greatest support was assumed to hold an advantage in comparison with the underdog, in most instances. Each of the groups included in this study was one of the more important bases of support for Nixon or McGovern.

Support from unorganized crowds occurred in stories about McGovern more frequently than in stories about Nixon.* A similar pattern arose in coverage of political rallies. McGovern rallies were about four times as likely to appear on CBS and NBC as Nixon rallies, and about half again as likely on ABC. About four times as much time was consumed by McGovern rally stories as by Nixon rally stories on each network, in comparison with about the same amount of time for other stories. NBC and CBS covered political rallies most extensively, whereas ABC dedicated less time to these events. Finally, McGovern rallies were more frequently reported as the campaign approached the election, and there was very little change in the propensity of CBS, NBC, and ABC to cover Nixon rallies.

Very little time was devoted to testimonials for either candidate. About 1 to 2 percent of the stories on CBS and less than 1 percent on NBC and ABC concerned candidate testimonials, and very few stories of this kind were related to Nixon. Most of the coverage of testimonials for candidates occurred quite early in the campaign. No testimonials were covered during the last month of the campaign.

Campaigns cost extraordinarily large sums of money, and contributions are sometimes viewed as expressions of support. This is particularly true of smaller contributions when it is unlikely that anything will ever be asked in return. The small contribution is viewed as virtuous, and the large contribution as suspect. But very few Nixon and McGovern stories related to campaign contributions of any kind.

Thus McGovern benefited from network coverage of several traditional political activities. As portrayed on network news, McGovern captured more support from unorganized crowds, rallies, testimonials, and campaign contributors than Nixon. Not a great deal of the total campaign coverage was devoted to any of these topics; however, the viewer would gain the impression that more traditional political support was going to McGovern than to Nixon by watching the few stories that reported such activities.

SOURCES OF CANDIDATE STORIES

Credibility, to a certain extent, is dependent on the particular source used in reporting. Some sources, especially the well-known network anchormen, may be highly trusted and esteemed. Other sources may be unfamiliar or even distrusted. If an unfamiliar or distrusted source asserts an unpopular opinion, the viewer might write off the disagreement by attacking the source's credibility. It is also true that finding relevant sources, especially partisan sources, may be an important indicator of a reporter's thoroughness in his job. Only the minority of political news stories, for example, explicitly showed that reporters cross-checked information by including other people with knowledge and interest in the story. And reporters cross-checked stories only some of the time by including coverage of a source in disagreement with the initial story source.

### Sources of Candidate Stories

The predominant source of each story was coded with second-source status given to reporters whenever any other source was included in a story. This rule resulted in the discovery of many sources other than reporters, but a very large proportion of stories turned out to have the network reporters as their only obvious source. Whenever

67

two or more sources (other than network reporters) appeared in a story, the source given the greatest air time or the first mention in the story (if about equal amount of time were allotted to several sources) was coded.

Reporters were the sole source of about the same proportion of Nixon and McGovern stories. Not surprisingly, the Republicans were sources of many more Nixon than McGovern stories, and the Democrats played a similar role with respect to their standard-bearer. Stories from institutional sources were primarily about Nixon rather than McGovern. More stories on CBS that originated with interest groups were about Nixon. Those on NBC were evenly split between Nixon and McGovern, and most of those on ABC were about McGovern. Very few candidate stories had foreign sources, but those that did were predominantly about Nixon. The few stories originating with citizens were distributed in a similarly erratic way. The two citizen CBS stories were both about McGovern, six citizen stories on NBC were predominantly about Nixon, and the 10 citizen stories on ABC were split evenly. (The data are shown in table 7.)

Considerably more time was devoted to McGovern stories with Democratic sources than to Nixon stories with Republican sources on each network. But these differences were reduced when institutional sources were included in the totals. The Nixon campaign relied to a greater extent on the "surrogate" campaigner, sometimes a cabinet official or other institutional employee, when announcements of a programmatic *and* partisan nature were made. McGovern's lack of access to such sources was apparent; no more than sixteen minutes of McGovern stories throughout the entire campaign originated with institutional sources, as compared with thirty to fifty-one minutes of Nixon stories. The remaining discrepancies in partisan sources, moreover, are proportional to the overall advantage in coverage that McGovern enjoyed throughout the campaign. Each candidate therefore appeared to have received "his share" of coverage from his own party group.

Foreigners, usually appearing as formal representatives of their governments, were sources of several stories. Just as would be expected, these stories were mostly about Nixon. The president conducted foreign policy regardless of campaign activities. Indeed, Nixon purposely avoided campaigning, some argue, in order to further American foreign policy. Experts were associated with the candidates partially because of the roles candidates and experts might play in a campaign and partially because of roles they might assume in the campaign organization itself.

## TABLE 7

### PERCENTAGES OF STORIES AND TIME DEVOTED TO NIXON AND MCGOVERN COVERAGE BY MOST IMPORTANT SOURCE, SECOND MOST IMPORTANT SOURCE, AND NETWORK

#### Most Important Source

| SOURCE | CBS Nixon % | Nixon Time | McGovern % | McGovern Time | N | NBC Nixon % | Nixon Time | McGovern % | McGovern Time | N | ABC Nixon % | Nixon Time | McGovern % | McGovern Time | N |
|---|---|---|---|---|---|---|---|---|---|---|---|---|---|---|---|
| Reporters | 48.1 | 24.7 | 51.9 | 30.1 | 52 | 54.5 | 19.9 | 45.5 | 28.8 | 66 | 50.0 | 23.6 | 50.0 | 23.8 | 56 |
| Republicans | 82.6 | 128.1 | 17.4 | 22.6 | 92 | 83.6 | 94.1 | 16.4 | 22.8 | 61 | 80.6 | 75.7 | 19.4 | 26.1 | 72 |
| Democrats | 5.5 | 12.4 | 94.5 | 209.1 | 128 | 5.6 | 7.9 | 94.4 | 189.5 | 108 | 6.6 | 16.0 | 93.4 | 193.3 | 122 |
| Other party | 0.0 | 0.0 | 0.0 | 0.0 | 0 | 0.0 | 0.0 | 0.0 | 0.0 | 0 | 0.0 | 0.0 | 0.0 | 0.0 | 0 |
| Institutions | 80.0 | 50.9 | 20.0 | 14.2 | 45 | 84.4 | 41.0 | 15.6 | 8.0 | 32 | 73.5 | 30.8 | 26.5 | 13.9 | 34 |
| Interest groups | 60.0 | 32.6 | 40.0 | 16.3 | 25 | 50.0 | 18.4 | 50.0 | 17.6 | 18 | 19.0 | 12.0 | 81.0 | 32.8 | 21 |
| Foreign | 85.7 | 8.6 | 14.3 | 0.1 | 7 | 100.0 | 6.3 | 0.0 | 0.0 | 3 | 100.0 | 14.8 | 0.0 | 0.0 | 8 |
| Citizens | 0.0 | 0.0 | 100.0 | 5.9 | 2 | 66.7 | 12.3 | 33.3 | 4.8 | 6 | 50.0 | 15.6 | 50.0 | 15.2 | 10 |
| Experts | 47.8 | 12.6 | 52.2 | 17.7 | 23 | 78.3 | 21.7 | 21.7 | 3.8 | 23 | 54.5 | 12.7 | 45.5 | 6.4 | 22 |
| Total | 47.1 | 269.9 | 52.9 | 316.0 | 374 | 48.6 | 221.6 | 51.4 | 275.2 | 317 | 42.9 | 201.1 | 57.1 | 311.5 | 345 |

#### Second Most Important Source

| SOURCE | CBS Nixon % | Nixon Time | McGovern % | McGovern Time | N | NBC Nixon % | Nixon Time | McGovern % | McGovern Time | N | ABC Nixon % | Nixon Time | McGovern % | McGovern Time | N |
|---|---|---|---|---|---|---|---|---|---|---|---|---|---|---|---|
| Reporters | 42.1 | 70.3 | 57.9 | 119.5 | 121 | 47.4 | 62.6 | 52.6 | 74.1 | 78 | 36.5 | 54.8 | 63.5 | 117.0 | 104 |
| Republicans | 58.3 | 21.6 | 41.7 | 11.8 | 12 | 50.0 | 15.6 | 50.0 | 14.2 | 12 | 66.7 | 10.0 | 33.3 | 6.5 | 9 |
| Democrats | 18.9 | 15.7 | 81.1 | 74.1 | 37 | 22.2 | 7.5 | 77.8 | 59.5 | 27 | 7.7 | 5.2 | 92.3 | 51.3 | 26 |
| Other party | 0.0 | 0.0 | 0.0 | 0.0 | 0 | 0.0 | 0.0 | 0.0 | 0.0 | 0 | 0.0 | 0.0 | 0.0 | 0.0 | 0 |
| Institutions | 80.0 | 33.4 | 20.0 | 5.5 | 15 | 58.8 | 26.3 | 41.2 | 11.5 | 17 | 57.1 | 18.3 | 42.9 | 24.0 | 21 |
| Interest groups | 50.0 | 16.6 | 50.0 | 9.4 | 10 | 20.0 | 2.1 | 80.0 | 8.3 | 5 | 50.0 | 11.4 | 50.0 | 8.8 | 8 |
| Foreign | 100.0 | 13.4 | 0.0 | 0.0 | 5 | 100.0 | 9.1 | 0.0 | 0.0 | 3 | 100.0 | 7.8 | 0.0 | 0.0 | 4 |
| Citizens | 0.0 | 0.0 | 0.0 | 0.0 | 0 | 66.7 | 7.1 | 33.3 | 2.7 | 3 | 66.7 | 14.5 | 33.3 | 5.9 | 6 |
| Experts | 70.0 | 11.6 | 30.0 | 5.2 | 10 | 37.5 | 4.2 | 62.5 | 9.6 | 8 | 80.0 | 5.4 | 20.0 | 0.6 | 5 |
| Total | 44.5 | 182.6 | 55.5 | 225.1 | 211 | 44.4 | 134.5 | 55.6 | 179.9 | 153 | 40.4 | 127.6 | 59.6 | 214.0 | 183 |

Nixon and McGovern stories retained the same general pattern when the second-most-important sources were scrutinized in the candidate stories. Trends are muted somewhat since between one-third and one-half of the stories used only one source. Reporters were more likely to be secondary sources for McGovern than for Nixon stories on each of the networks, and the parties tended to be sources for their respective candidates less often. Indeed, on NBC the Republicans were just as likely to be a source of information about McGovern as about Nixon, and 42 percent of the stories with Republican sources on CBS and 33 percent on ABC were about McGovern. Democrats were much less likely to be secondary sources for Nixon stories. This occurred with greatest frequency on CBS, but only about one story in five from Democratic sources was about Nixon. Institutionally originated stories continued to be about Nixon more frequently than about McGovern. This was true in the proportion of stories from this source and the amount of time devoted to these stories (except for ABC coverage in this particular instance).

### Favorable and Unfavorable Sources of Nixon and McGovern Stories

Favorable, neutral, and unfavorable Nixon and McGovern stories were cross-classified by the most important story source in order to discover if certain sources were more unfavorable to one candidate or the other (see table 8). It may be that political biases in news reporting are inherent in only some story sources. Partisan sources used in the evening news, for instance, would be assumed to reflect partisan attitudes.

Nixon stories were more frequently favorable when news reporters, Republicans, institutions, interest groups, foreign representatives, and experts were sources. And even Democratic party sources provided relatively more stories favorable to Nixon than to McGovern on CBS and ABC. McGovern received favorable reporting more frequently than Nixon only in stories with Democratic sources on NBC.

The amount of time spent reporting favorable stories altered this sad picture for the Democratic standard-bearer only a small bit. McGovern received favorable coverage in stories consuming substantially more time than those about Nixon only when story sources were Democratic partisans. Reporters on NBC and interest groups on ABC originated stories giving the Democratic candidate only a very slight margin in favorable stories.

Nixon received more unfavorable stories than McGovern received from Democratic sources, although reporters on CBS originated a few more stories that were unfavorable to Nixon than were unfavorable to McGovern. Just the converse was true of interest groups on ABC. Except for partisan Democrats, these sources were so sparse as to be inconsequential in overall campaign reporting. In terms of time allocated to stories, none of the networks consistently showed that one source was more unfavorable to Nixon than to McGovern, although many of the sources were consistently more unfavorable to the Democratic contender. CBS reporters spent more time reporting unfavorable Nixon stories than unfavorable McGovern stories (but only by 2.9 minutes), as did Democratic sources on CBS (but not on NBC or ABC), institutions on CBS and NBC, experts on NBC, and foreign representatives on ABC. It must be noted that very few minutes of reporting were involved in any of these classes of stories, as is clear in table 8.

Thus it appears that no particular source of stories provided consistent unfavorable or favorable types of support for a candidate as we might suppose. Not even the antagonists of the election, the Democratic and Republican parties, were as consistently favorable to their own candidates and consistently unfavorable to their opponents as one might suspect. The very small number of stories classified as favorable and unfavorable is troubling when it is necessary to generalize on the basis of candidate stories. It is wise to conclude that the case for political bias remains to be established.

### Juxtaposition of Sources

One source is juxtaposed with a second source whenever more than one source is consulted about the same problem. Network reporters as sources for purposes of analysis were eliminated, and judgments were made concerning the extent to which juxtapositions tended to support or undermine what an initial source had asserted. If a second source was reported in a way that substantially confirmed or corroborated what an initial source had maintained, then the story was classified as having a supporting juxtaposition. If a second source refuted or cast doubt on what an initial source had claimed to be true, then the story was coded as having an opposing juxtaposition.

When juxtaposition occurred in either Nixon or McGovern stories, it was far more likely to be supporting than opposing in nature. Information sources beyond an initial informant appeared to reassert overwhelmingly whatever had been said by the prior source. It is interesting to note that reporters on all three networks apparently used sources to close questions rather than to raise questions in candidate stories. Except on ABC, there was more supporting juxtaposi-

TABLE 8

Percentages of Stories and Time Devoted to Favorable, Neutral, and Unfavorable Nixon and McGovern Coverage by Source and Network

**CBS**

| Most Important Source | Nixon | | | | | | | McGovern | | | | | | |
|---|---|---|---|---|---|---|---|---|---|---|---|---|---|---|
| | Favorable % | Favorable Time | Neutral % | Neutral Time | Unfavorable % | Unfavorable Time | N | Favorable % | Favorable Time | Neutral % | Neutral Time | Unfavorable % | Unfavorable Time | N |
| Reporter | 20.0 | 6.3 | 76.0 | 15.5 | 4.0 | 2.9 | 25 | 7.7 | 1.9 | 92.3 | 27.9 | 0.0 | 0.0 | 26 |
| Republican | 11.8 | 16.7 | 80.3 | 100.6 | 7.9 | 10.8 | 76 | 6.3 | 2.2 | 50.0 | 12.0 | 43.8 | 8.3 | 16 |
| Democratic | 28.6 | 2.0 | 57.1 | 10.1 | 14.3 | 0.3 | 7 | 17.4 | 41.5 | 70.2 | 144.4 | 12.4 | 23.3 | 121 |
| Other Party | 0.0 | 0.0 | 0.0 | 0.0 | 0.0 | 0.0 | 0 | 0.0 | 0.0 | 0.0 | 0.0 | 0.0 | 0.0 | 0 |
| Institution | 2.9 | 1.8 | 85.3 | 34.1 | 11.8 | 8.3 | 34 | 0.0 | 0.0 | 55.6 | 10.6 | 44.4 | 3.6 | 9 |
| Interest Groups | 20.0 | 3.0 | 73.3 | 29.3 | 6.7 | 0.3 | 15 | 0.0 | 0.0 | 80.0 | 11.8 | 20.0 | 4.5 | 10 |
| Foreign | 16.7 | 0.2 | 83.3 | 8.4 | 0.0 | 0.0 | 6 | 0.0 | 0.0 | 100.0 | 0.1 | 0.0 | 0.0 | 1 |
| Citizens | 0.0 | 0.0 | 0.0 | 0.0 | 0.0 | 0.0 | 0 | 50.0 | 3.5 | 0.0 | 0.0 | 50.0 | 2.4 | 2 |
| Experts | 63.6 | 4.8 | 36.4 | 7.8 | 0.0 | 0.0 | 11 | 16.7 | 4.7 | 50.0 | 7.7 | 33.3 | 5.3 | 12 |
| Total | 16.1 | 34.8 | 76.4 | 205.8 | 7.5 | 22.6 | 174 | 13.7 | 53.7 | 69.5 | 214.5 | 16.8 | 47.5 | 197 |

**NBC**

| Most Important Source | Nixon | | | | | | | McGovern | | | | | | |
|---|---|---|---|---|---|---|---|---|---|---|---|---|---|---|
| | Favorable % | Favorable Time | Neutral % | Neutral Time | Unfavorable % | Unfavorable Time | N | Favorable % | Favorable Time | Neutral % | Neutral Time | Unfavorable % | Unfavorable Time | N |
| Reporter | 13.9 | 4.2 | 86.1 | 15.8 | 0.0 | 0.0 | 36 | 10.0 | 4.7 | 76.7 | 19.1 | 13.3 | 5.0 | 30 |
| Republican | 33.3 | 39.6 | 60.8 | 48.0 | 5.9 | 6.4 | 51 | 0.0 | 0.0 | 70.0 | 14.9 | 30.0 | 7.9 | 10 |
| Democratic | 16.7 | 0.2 | 50.0 | 5.9 | 33.3 | 1.7 | 6 | 20.8 | 45.6 | 73.3 | 128.6 | 5.9 | 13.1 | 101 |
| Other Party | 0.0 | 0.0 | 0.0 | 0.0 | 0.0 | 0.0 | 0 | 0.0 | 0.0 | 0.0 | 0.0 | 0.0 | 0.0 | 0 |
| Institution | 3.7 | 1.8 | 88.9 | 35.1 | 7.4 | 4.1 | 27 | 0.0 | 0.0 | 80.0 | 6.3 | 20.0 | 1.7 | 5 |
| Interest Groups | 37.5 | 5.2 | 62.5 | 12.5 | 0.0 | 0.0 | 8 | 11.1 | 2.2 | 77.8 | 12.8 | 11.1 | 2.6 | 9 |
| Foreign | 0.0 | 0.0 | 100.0 | 6.3 | 0.0 | 0.0 | 3 | 0.0 | 0.0 | 0.0 | 0.0 | 0.0 | 0.0 | 0 |
| Citizens | 25.0 | 2.1 | 75.0 | 10.2 | 0.0 | 0.0 | 4 | 0.0 | 0.0 | 0.0 | 0.0 | 100.0 | 4.8 | 2 |
| Experts | 38.9 | 3.2 | 55.6 | 14.0 | 5.6 | 4.5 | 18 | 20.0 | 0.6 | 20.0 | 2.2 | 60.0 | 1.0 | 5 |
| Total | 22.9 | 56.4 | 71.9 | 147.9 | 5.2 | 16.7 | 153 | 16.0 | 53.1 | 71.6 | 183.8 | 12.3 | 36.2 | 162 |

TABLE 8 (continued)

ABC

| Most Important Source | Nixon | | | | | | | McGovern | | | | | | |
|---|---|---|---|---|---|---|---|---|---|---|---|---|---|---|
| | Favorable | | Neutral | | Unfavorable | | | Favorable | | Neutral | | Unfavorable | | |
| | % | Time | % | Time | % | Time | N | % | Time | % | Time | % | Time | N |
| Reporter | 10.7 | 2.1 | 85.7 | 21.3 | 3.6 | 0.2 | 28 | 3.7 | 1.9 | 55.6 | 8.3 | 40.7 | 11.7 | 27 |
| Republican | 32.8 | 30.3 | 63.8 | 40.9 | 3.4 | 4.5 | 58 | 0.0 | 0.0 | 64.3 | 15.8 | 35.7 | 10.4 | 14 |
| Democratic | 25.0 | 4.9 | 62.5 | 10.3 | 12.5 | 0.7 | 8 | 20.2 | 48.1 | 71.1 | 129.8 | 8.8 | 15.3 | 114 |
| Other Party | 0.0 | 0.0 | 0.0 | 0.0 | 0.0 | 0.0 | 0 | 0.0 | 0.0 | 0.0 | 0.0 | 0.0 | 0.0 | 0 |
| Institution | 20.0 | 10.1 | 76.0 | 18.4 | 4.0 | 2.2 | 25 | 0.0 | 0.0 | 66.7 | 9.0 | 33.3 | 4.9 | 9 |
| Interest Groups | 25.0 | 1.8 | 50.0 | 6.8 | 25.0 | 3.4 | 4 | 17.6 | 3.6 | 52.9 | 18.1 | 29.4 | 11.0 | 17 |
| Foreign | 12.5 | 2.4 | 62.5 | 7.6 | 25.0 | 4.7 | 8 | 0.0 | 0.0 | 0.0 | 0.0 | 0.0 | 0.0 | 0 |
| Citizens | 20.0 | 2.4 | 80.0 | 13.3 | 0.0 | 0.0 | 5 | 0.0 | 0.0 | 60.0 | 8.5 | 40.0 | 6.7 | 5 |
| Experts | 41.7 | 1.5 | 58.3 | 11.1 | 0.0 | 0.0 | 12 | 20.0 | 0.5 | 40.0 | 3.5 | 40.0 | 2.5 | 10 |
| Total | 25.0 | 55.6 | 69.6 | 129.8 | 5.4 | 15.7 | 148 | 14.8 | 54.2 | 64.8 | 192.9 | 20.4 | 62.6 | 196 |

[a] One ABC story unfavorable to McGovern was attributed to another source, so that analysis was based on 196 stories rather than on 197 stories

tion in McGovern stories than in Nixon stories. Indeed, there is a differential of over 20 percent and nearly thirty minutes in ABC coverage and coverage by NBC and CBS in this regard. In contrast, each of the networks reported about the same proportion of McGovern stories with both supporting and opposing juxtaposition. CBS and NBC stories about Nixon contained more opposing juxtaposition than ABC stories.

Supporting juxtaposition tended to diminish slightly or remain about the same in Nixon stories as the campaign progressed. CBS and NBC used supporting juxtaposition in a greater proportion of McGovern stories and ABC in a decreasing proportion of McGovern stories as the campaign moved toward the election. Opposing juxtaposition increased in Nixon stories during the campaign, while it remained about the same or very slightly decreased in McGovern stories on CBS and NBC. Opposing juxtaposition in McGovern stories increased on ABC. The data are presented in table 9.

CONCLUSION

This chapter evaluated coverage about candidates Nixon and McGovern. Two questions arose in this discussion. Who benefited most from television coverage? Who benefited most from coverage that was due to political biases in television news reporting? Complex as the campaign coverage was of the 1972 election, the first question is much easier to answer than the second.

*Both* Nixon and McGovern *benefited* from *different aspects* of campaign coverage. McGovern received by far the most coverage on each network, perhaps because he campaigned in a more active, television-conscious, and appealing way than Nixon. Yet McGovern did not receive as many favorable or supportive stories as Nixon despite his greater coverage. And many acknowledged that McGovern was by far the weaker of the candidates, running a campaign fraught with internal divisiveness, conflict, and at least some indecision and bad luck.

Our analysis presented little to support outraged cries that either side had been unduly injured by evening television news. Neutrality was the hallmark of TV news coverage of Nixon and McGovern. Any injury was probably inherent in the style and character of the candidates' campaigns and the ideas they carried into the campaigns. Yet, the issue of political bias remains sharply drawn, and the following chapters scrutinize the extent to which political bias may have crept into coverage of political issues, political parties, and campaign efforts during 1972.

TABLE 9

Percentages of Stories and Time Devoted to Nixon and McGovern Coverage That Included Multiple Sources That Supported, Opposed, or Were Neutral to Each Other by Network and Time

| Time | Nixon | | | | | | | McGovern | | | | | | |
|---|---|---|---|---|---|---|---|---|---|---|---|---|---|---|
| | Supporting | | Neutral | | Opposing | | N | Supporting | | Neutral | | Opposing | | N |
| | % | Time | % | Time | % | Time | | % | Time | % | Time | % | Time | |
| **CBS** | | | | | | | | | | | | | | |
| July | 57.1 | 13.3 | 35.7 | 7.4 | 7.1 | 2.1 | 14 | 58.6 | 36.3 | 10.3 | 6.4 | 31.0 | 26.0 | 29 |
| August | 39.4 | 23.9 | 33.3 | 20.1 | 27.3 | 20.5 | 33 | 42.9 | 19.6 | 25.0 | 12.6 | 32.1 | 19.3 | 28 |
| September | 9.1 | 0.4 | 27.3 | 1.4 | 63.6 | 20.1 | 11 | 45.0 | 14.8 | 5.0 | 1.4 | 50.0 | 22.8 | 20 |
| October | 51.4 | 24.8 | 5.4 | 2.8 | 43.2 | 46.3 | 37 | 77.5 | 41.9 | 5.0 | 6.6 | 17.5 | 19.1 | 40 |
| Total | 43.2 | 62.4 | 22.1 | 31.7 | 34.7 | 89.0 | 95 | 59.0 | 112.6 | 11.1 | 27.0 | 29.9 | 87.2 | 117 |
| **NBC** | | | | | | | | | | | | | | |
| July | 57.1 | 8.2 | 14.3 | 3.1 | 28.6 | 8.6 | 7 | 47.8 | 31.0 | 17.4 | 8.3 | 34.8 | 18.3 | 23 |
| August | 42.1 | 16.9 | 31.6 | 12.2 | 26.3 | 13.5 | 19 | 50.0 | 21.3 | 20.0 | 6.3 | 30.0 | 13.6 | 20 |
| September | 30.0 | 5.8 | 30.0 | 6.1 | 40.0 | 2.9 | 10 | 52.4 | 21.2 | 9.5 | 3.8 | 38.1 | 16.3 | 21 |
| October | 50.0 | 29.9 | 6.3 | 0.6 | 43.8 | 26.7 | 32 | 66.7 | 24.9 | 4.8 | 1.8 | 28.6 | 13.1 | 21 |
| Total | 45.6 | 60.8 | 17.6 | 22.0 | 36.8 | 51.6 | 68 | 54.1 | 98.3 | 12.9 | 20.3 | 32.9 | 61.3 | 85 |
| **ABC** | | | | | | | | | | | | | | |
| July | 72.7 | 13.0 | 9.1 | 2.1 | 18.2 | 5.1 | 11 | 61.1 | 38.2 | 13.9 | 13.3 | 25.0 | 16.9 | 36 |
| August | 62.5 | 15.0 | 12.5 | 2.3 | 25.0 | 2.8 | 16 | 69.2 | 41.1 | 19.2 | 10.2 | 11.5 | 9.0 | 26 |
| September | 64.3 | 21.0 | 14.3 | 2.7 | 21.4 | 6.4 | 14 | 46.4 | 26.9 | 10.7 | 2.8 | 42.9 | 18.1 | 28 |
| October | 72.7 | 37.9 | 0.0 | 0.0 | 27.3 | 19.1 | 33 | 55.0 | 17.7 | 10.0 | 1.5 | 35.0 | 18.8 | 20 |
| Total | 68.9 | 87.0 | 6.8 | 7.2 | 24.3 | 33.4 | 74 | 58.2 | 123.9 | 13.6 | 27.8 | 28.2 | 62.8 | 110 |

* Detailed statistical tabulations are available from the author upon request.

1.   In this regard, for instance, see Efron, *How CBS Tried to Kill a Book;* or James Keogh, *President Nixon and the Press* (New York: Funk and Wagnalls, 1972); or Timothy Crouse, *The Boys on the Bus* (New York: Random House, 1972).

2.   Theodore H. White, *The Making of the President, 1972* (New York: Atheneum, 1973), especially pp. 245-68.

3.   Paul H. Weaver, "Is Television News Biased?", *Public Interest* 26 (Winter 1972): 69-73. See also Epstein, *News from Nowhere,* and Crouse, *The Boys on the Bus.*

# 4. Issue Coverage during the Campaign

INTRODUCTION

Campaign coverage analysis must discuss the *kinds* of issues and the *ways* in which they are reported. There are two reasons for this. (1) Issue preferences are key elements in the preferences of most, if not all, voters. Images relating to issues were assumed to be substantially influenced by public affairs programming, including television news.[1] (2) The style and character of issue coverage have been at the very center of much controversy about the way in which television networks report the news.[2] The stakes of politically biased or possibly misleading coverage are seen as very great by those who argue that news reporting has considerable impact on the way the public perceives events.

Much public information about national and international affairs is obtained from television, either directly by watching programs or indirectly by listening to someone who has been watching. Although many persons also obtain this information from other news media, commercial television boasts larger audiences and higher credibility than its competitors.[3]

The news broadcast is, perhaps, the most important source of public affairs information. Some critics assert that the news presents issues in a "liberal, left-wing" fashion, and others argue that it presents issues in a "conservative, corporate establishment way." These arguments are based on claims about *what is reported* about *which events* (or "non-events," as the case may be) in *which ways* or styles.[4]

Does the campaign-period news coverage systematically contain stories highly unfavorable to conservative views? Or, alternatively, do reports systematically stress stories unfavorable to liberal views? Are stories presented in ways consistently sympathetic or antagonistic to the stories' subjects? Or, is criticism consistently directed to one side and sympathy to the other?

WHAT IS REPORTED

### Issue Stories

Issue emphasis was coded whenever the main theme of a story concerned a topic explicitly linked to national problems, when questions of national policy were involved, or when the theme of a story involved general citizen concerns.[5] These criteria usually overlapped, so that most stories were classified as issue stories for more than one reason. The criteria were broadly defined, and, therefore, most stories were coded as having issue relevance. The following illustrations of coding rules will perhaps clarify this point.

Mention of major-party platform problems or explicit association with the execution of policies by the national government qualified a story for this category. For instance, a story about Alabama school busing contained policy relevance as far as the national government was concerned and also was noted in a party platform. Terrorism at the Munich Olympic Games was attributed issue status because it was linked to Arab-Israeli-American relations, which in turn were explicitly related to American foreign policy. Stories about strip mining, furthermore, were coded as issue stories because strip mining is generally recognized as a national concern that goes beyond the local interest of a given area and because it also involves national policies about natural resource preservation.

Stories about domestic events in Israel, Vietnam, or other countries were excluded from the issue classification if they had no explicit relevance for American foreign policy. Narrow political questions reported entirely within the context of party or candidate activities were coded as party or candidate stories without issue content, although most candidate and party stories also contained considerable material considered relevant to the coding scheme.

Two NBC stories about racial matters (which were classified as being unfavorable with regard to the issues in question) provide examples of issues that were included in the analysis. The first story, a commentary by Brinkley, described a bill to eliminate busing to attain racial balance in public schools that was being filibustered by northern liberals. Integration comprised a plank in each party's platform, and the specific issue of busing was widely discussed during the campaigns.

The story asserted that Senate liberals had successfully beaten back a move to choke off their filibuster. It also stated that the House had passed similar legislation to the original bill, where liberals were not as successful in stopping the measure. The story then asserted that popular opposition to busing was strong in both the North and South, and that pressures for legislation to end busing were strong enough so that a roll call vote on the legislation would probably pass the Senate.

The commentary then went on to report that busing was an issue in Michigan, long-range prospects for busing were doubtful, that the schools could not solve social problems anyway (according to a book that had just been published), and that school experiences might not be as great a determinant of later life chances as had been argued by proponents of busing. The story concluded that research has not shown that busing could be justified on grounds of benefit to children, although moral reasons for busing might be present.

The second story described a takeover of the Bureau of Indian Affairs by a group of Indians. The story asserted that the group of Indians was from a yet larger group that had traveled to Washington to urge reforms in federal Indian policies. Classification of each story was unfavorable, since the first story emphasized the lack of success of a policy and the second focused on illegal activity that was alleged to have originated in policy that required reform. Reform had not yet occurred. Neither story was classified as related to either candidates or parties, since neither was mentioned nor was any association made in the video portions of the stories.

### Issue Predominance

The main issue emphasis was considered to be the topic receiving the greatest amount of attention in each story. Although many news stories concerned only a single predominant issue and only mentioned others, some stories paid considerable attention to several issues. In these cases the issue with the broadest context was attributed predominance so that it was considered the first issue in coding. If two issues arose within the same story and each received about the same amount of attention as the other, the issue presented first was classified as the more important issue and the other was regarded as secondary. Thus, with other things equal, the issue presentation order corresponded to classification of issue predominance.

Campaign reports, for example, frequently concerned more than one issue. McGovern may have made a speech in which he criticized Nixon's war policy, but in the same story he may have made some recommendations for welfare reform. If both welfare and the war were allotted the same degree of coverage during the story and no other issue received as much emphasis, then the following coding conventions would apply. The issue coded as having greatest emphasis would be the war because it was presented first in the story. The story would, of course, be coded as emphasizing issues as well as candidates, and possibly also coded for emphasis on the Democratic party and the campaign effort.

In some instances stories were coded for *aspects* of issue content, even when the stories did not predominantly emphasize a substantive issue, or when the issue *was* a party or candidate's activity rather than an issue as previously defined. This story classification method allowed nearly all material to be classified according to issue criteria. The more inclusive set of issue codes was used whenever possible in the analysis so that issue coverage could be described in general terms.

In some cases the more restricted issue set was used for analysis. Quite obviously, only news stories with issue emphasis, as defined previously, could be included in analyses that focused on judgments about the way in which issues were covered in a story. For instance, if a judgment was required about whether a story was favorable, neutral, or unfavorable with respect to Vietnam, then only stories emphasizing Vietnam could be included. Stories that touched on Vietnam only in passing, or stories that did not deal very extensively with the topic, were too limited to make reliable judgments about favorable, neutral, or unfavorable issue coverage. At the extreme, such stories might have been considered neutral with regard to Vietnam.

### Problem Area Codes

In this analysis a very broad coding scheme was used to classify the partisan and issue content of news stories. The coding scheme was initially designed to classify popularly perceived policy areas during election campaigns.[6] The coding scheme was chosen in order to utilize the same categories to classify both story content and the perceptions of individuals exposed to television news and other mass media. The problem area code has been used repeatedly during the last twenty years to classify individuals' political cognitions. If effects of media news coverage on citizens' views of political and social problems are of interest—as is the case in the larger study of which this is a part—then it is necessary to use known categories that provide reliable means of classifying popular perceptions.[7]

When the problem area code was applied to classification of news content, over 110 different issues were revealed. Classifications were then simplified by combining specific issues into more general categories, although the initial classifications could, of course, be recategorized for purposes of reanalysis. The general categories coincide with those used by citizens to conceptualize the political world. They included: social welfare; racial and civil liberties; law and order; agriculture and natural resources; labor and labor-management relations; general economic, consumer, and business topics; Vietnam; other foreign affairs; national defense; the functioning of government; specifically partisan matters; and miscellaneous topics.

Vietnam was distinguished from other foreign affairs because of the large numbers of stories broadcast about the war (over 500 during the campaign period). Similarly, matters of civil liberties and race were distinguished from law and order (categories usually combined in analyses of citizen perceptions). It was assumed that very different kinds of issues were raised in news stories by these categories, and fair numbers of stories about each distinct area were carried on each network. The reader could, in most instances, combine such categories in order to discern the effects of these specific decisions on news content analysis and conclusions. Finally, partisan concerns were distinguished from other government concerns because of the large number of candidate and campaign stories that could be clearly distinguished. McGovern and Nixon campaign stories, for instance, were distinguished from stories about how the Justice Department was run.

### Basic Dimensions of Story Content

Party politics—stories about the candidates, campaigns, and party organizations—received most attention when stories were classified by the problem area code. About 27 percent of the stories on NBC and 35 percent of the stories on ABC concerned party politics. More than twice as much time, moreover, was devoted to discussions of party politics than to any other problem area (except on NBC, where not quite twice as much time was devoted to party politics as to stories emphasizing Vietnam). Vietnam was the next-most-emphasized story area in terms of both percentage of stories and time devoted to it.

Stories about the economy and business also received considerable attention on network news programs, as did issues associated with law and order. ABC stressed law and order less than the other two networks. CBS devoted more time and a larger proportion of its stories to issues relating to the general management of government, for example, and to stories about Watergate than either NBC or ABC. Even less time was devoted to stories that concerned social welfare, labor-management, civil rights, racial problems, national defense, and other problem areas not clearly covered by policy areas in table 10.

### Favorable and Unfavorable Issue Implications

Each story was classified in terms of its favorable, neutral, or unfavorable implications for the issue covered (or the issue given greatest prominence in coverage, if more than one issue was covered); the

81

Republican and Democratic campaigns and parties; the Nixon and McGovern candidacies; and the Nixon administration. These classifications were based on judgments about the way in which issues were handled in relation to the preceding substantive policy areas. In the following discussion, emphasis is placed on the amount of time spent on issues rather than the frequency of coverage because some individual policy areas were rarely covered in the news.

TABLE 10

PERCENTAGES OF STORIES AND TIME DEVOTED TO SUBSTANTIVE POLICY ISSUES
IN NEWS STORIES BY NETWORK

| GENERAL POLICY AREAS | CBS | | NBC | | ABC | |
|---|---|---|---|---|---|---|
| | % | Time | % | Time | % | Time |
| Social Welfare | 2.6 | 49.5 | 2.3 | 27.5 | 2.8 | 37.9 |
| Agriculture, Natural Resources | 2.9 | 48.9 | 2.4 | 38.4 | 1.8 | 39.6 |
| Labor-Management | 1.0 | 13.0 | 1.2 | 20.4 | 1.2 | 11.4 |
| Race, Civil Liberties | 3.9 | 48.3 | 3.3 | 44.4 | 2.7 | 44.8 |
| Law and Order, Crime | 7.9 | 138.7 | 7.8 | 127.2 | 6.5 | 96.6 |
| Economic, Business | 12.6 | 107.8 | 11.6 | 123.6 | 9.0 | 87.3 |
| Vietnam | 16.9 | 305.1 | 19.4 | 336.1 | 18.4 | 255.8 |
| Foreign Affairs | 11.5 | 165.5 | 15.5 | 223.0 | 13.6 | 195.1 |
| National Defense | 3.4 | 39.1 | 3.3 | 41.4 | 2.8 | 30.9 |
| Government Operation | 5.6 | 106.3 | 3.9 | 64.3 | 4.7 | 75.5 |
| Republican Party | 13.7 | 316.7 | 12.3 | 281.2 | 13.9 | 260.0 |
| Democratic Party | 16.1 | 387.6 | 14.3 | 365.6 | 20.8 | 438.3 |
| Other | 2.1 | 29.6 | 2.7 | 37.0 | 1.8 | 18.9 |
| Total | 100.0 (1,399) | 1,756.1 | 100.0 (1,564) | 1,730.1 | 100.0 (1,329) | 1,592.1 |

If coverage of an issue, campaign or party, candidate, or the administration was associated with success, desirable means or ends, optimism, or other positive values, the story was classified as favorable. If issue coverage was associated with failure, undesirable means or ends, pessimism, or other negative values, the story was classified as unfavorable.[8] Neutral (or ambiguous) classifications were used in cases of uncertainty. If a story contained about the same amount of favorable and unfavorable coverage, or the coder felt he could not make a clear judgment, then a neutral classification was used. Finally, a "not-linked" (or unassociated) classification was employed when the predominant issue of a story was irrelevant to campaigns, parties, candidates, or the administration.

Two NBC stories serve as examples of stories that were classified as relating to the social welfare cluster of issues. The first story reported that President Nixon had signed anti-poverty legislation that increased social welfare expenditures. It also reported the signing of a bill to increase expenditures for research and treatment of heart, circulatory, and lung diseases. Finally, the story reported that the Senate Finance Committee had approved new Social Security benefits. A second story reported that President Nixon had lost a fight to veto a bill increasing railroad retirement benefits.

Both stories were brief in content, but contained a fair amount of information. The first story was classified as favorable to social welfare since it described a series of successful actions that had been taken. The item concerning anti-poverty policy was also considered to be favorable to the administration because the president was reported to have signed the bill into law, a favorable act that associated success with his programs in the social area. He also signed another medical bill that had been sponsored by Senator Kennedy.

The second news story was coded as unfavorable to the administration in terms of adminstrative action on social welfare because it reported that the administration's position on a measure (a Nixon veto of a bill) had been overridden in Congress. The story was, at the same time, favorable to the social welfare issue, since successful action was taken on a bill (the veto override).

In general, two classification rules were followed. First, coders classified content as neutral (or ambiguous) whenever clear and explicit reasons were not evident to enable favorable or unfavorable classification. Second, these categories were grouped together with the "not linked" category for purposes of analysis. This decision reduced the magnitude of percentages slightly, but in no other way did grouping these classes together into an overall neutral class affect the analysis outcomes.

### Implications of Coverage for Issues

Criticism of network issue coverage is a common basis for the complaint that the networks maintain political biases. If one set of issue positions was viewed as being propounded by conservatives, then treatment systematically favorable to one set of issue positions or treatment systematically unfavorable to the other set might well be taken as evidence that political bias was at work.[9]

Again, severe problems of selectivity have affected some better-known studies of televised issue coverage. Efron has been criticized, for instance, because she selected a fairly limited (if nonetheless important) set of issues to study.[10] In most instances this study tries to circumvent the problem of selectivity by generally focusing on broad classes of issues rather than on specific issues. A variety of issues, for example, was encompassed under the problem area rubric "social welfare." In other instances, such as Vietnam, all stories emphasizing the topic were classified under the rubric "Vietnam," regardless of the particular aspect of coverage emphasized. Thus some degree of specificity was sacrificed in order to increase the scope of issue reporting included in the study. It should be noted that the problem of classification is always present in any scientific study.

Two NBC stories about Vietnam illustrate favorable and unfavorable coverage of the issue. One story about peace talks to end the war was judged to be favorable about the Vietnam issue. Despite coverage of problems involved in the peace talks that were being conducted at the time in France, the story concluded that action that was being taken by Washington was designed to accomplish policy objectives. The strategy that was reported to have been formulated by the president was interpreted in the optimistic vein.

The second story about Vietnam was coded as unfavorable. It portrayed the effects of U.S. bombing on civilians in Hanoi. The story was coded as unfavorable because personal dimensions of the bombing were shown. Few sane people could react to such content with anything except repulsion. The story, for example, included film that had been shot by a Swedish news team in Haiphong. This film included pictures of a destroyed market area and a number of residences that had also been destroyed. Finally, pictures of dazed civilians sifting through rubble in the area were included.

Yet another NBC story that was broadcast on the same day was even more clearly unfavorable in content. It recounted loss of military equipment by the South Vietnamese, the ostensible American allies. The story reported that an "unaccidental" series of explosions at Bien Hoa Airbase was probably the worst loss of war materials during the entire war. The story asserted that as much as 20 percent of the South Vietnamese air capacity had been wiped out.

Although issue stories were mostly neutral, about three times as many stories were unfavorable as were favorable, and more time was devoted to unfavorable than to favorable stories about issues. CBS was the least favorable and most unfavorable, by far, in terms of the amount of time devoted to issue coverage: only twenty minutes of favorable coverage in comparison with 210 minutes of unfavorable coverage. In contrast, NBC devoted fifty-one minutes to favorable and 187 minutes to unfavorable coverage of issues, and ABC devoted forty-eight minutes to favorable and 177 minutes to unfavorable coverage of issue stories. Thus CBS appeared to be the most acerbic network in its coverage of the issue stories.

Issue coverage, as noted, was predominantly neutral on all three networks. Between 84 percent (ABC) and 86 percent (CBS) of the issue stories during the period studied fell within the neutral class of coverage. Between thirteen and seventeen hours of issue coverage fell within the neutral category, or about 75 percent of the time allotted to issues on each of the networks. CBS devoted the largest proportion of time to neutral coverage; about four times as much time was spent in reporting neutral stories as was spent reporting favorable or unfavorable stories. ABC devoted the smallest proportion of its time to neutral coverage; about 3.5 times as much time was devoted to reporting neutral stories as was spent reporting other favorable or unfavorable stories. These differences in proportions were not large, and most likely not very significant. It should be noted, however, that at least part of the difference among networks was based on the differing amounts of time that CBS, NBC, and ABC devoted to issue coverage.

Table 11 shows considerable variation in favorable and unfavorable story reporting across the problem areas. In terms of the relative number of stories, CBS reported stories about the economy and labor-management problems more favorably than other stories, and stories about the functioning of government (heavily laced with stories about Watergate), partisan affairs, Vietnam, social welfare, agriculture, and natural resources in a relatively unfavorable way. Time was spent, however, reporting very few of these problem areas in an unfavorable way. More than twenty minutes of unfavorable coverage, for instance, was used on CBS only for stories about Vietnam, government functioning, and partisan affairs.

The most favorable coverage on NBC was given to foreign affairs, the economy, and agriculture and natural resources, and the least favorable coverage to stories about government functioning, partisan affairs, labor-management problems, law and order, and Vietnam. In terms of time, NBC provided more than ten minutes of favorable coverage only to stories about Vietnam and other foreign affairs. More than twenty minutes of unfavorable NBC coverage was given to stories about government functioning, partisan affairs, and Vietnam.

ABC carried relatively favorable coverage in stories about agriculture and natural resources, labor-management problems, and the economy, and relatively unfavorable coverage in stories about agriculture and natural resources, racial problems and civil liberties, Vietnam, government functioning, and Democratic party problems. ABC, however, devoted more than ten minutes of favorable coverage only to stories about Vietnam. It is evident from table 11 that the proportion of stories reported favorably by ABC were based on very small frequencies (only twenty-two stories about agriculture and natural resources were reported during the entire period on ABC). More than twenty minutes of unfavorable coverage was devoted to stories about Vietnam and partisan affairs, but *not* to stories

TABLE 11

PERCENTAGES OF STORIES AND TIME DEVOTED TO FAVORABLE, NEUTRAL, AND
UNFAVORABLE ISSUE COVERAGE BY ISSUE AND NETWORK

| PROBLEM AREA | Favorable | | Neutral | | Unfavorable | | N |
|---|---|---|---|---|---|---|---|
| | % | Time | % | Time | % | Time | |
| | CBS | | | | | | |
| Social welfare | 3.7 | 2.2 | 85.2 | 30.7 | 11.1 | 8.3 | 27 |
| Agriculture, natural resources | 3.0 | 0.5 | 84.8 | 37.5 | 12.1 | 12.8 | 33 |
| Labor-management | 9.1 | 0.5 | 81.8 | 9.0 | 9.1 | 2.3 | 11 |
| Race, civil liberties | 2.0 | 0.5 | 88.2 | 30.6 | 9.8 | 12.8 | 51 |
| Law and order | 0.0 | 0.0 | 92.1 | 77.2 | 7.9 | 14.8 | 76 |
| Economic, business | 13.1 | 4.7 | 79.8 | 49.5 | 7.1 | 8.1 | 84 |
| Vietnam | 2.3 | 5.4 | 87.2 | 233.2 | 10.5 | 42.1 | 219 |
| Foreign affairs | 3.2 | 3.7 | 91.9 | 56.4 | 4.8 | 4.4 | 62 |
| National defense | 2.6 | 0.4 | 92.1 | 22.6 | 5.3 | 6.2 | 38 |
| Government functioning | 0.0 | 0.0 | 80.0 | 57.6 | 20.0 | 31.7 | 55 |
| Republican party affairs | 0.8 | 1.8 | 87.8 | 182.7 | 11.4 | 35.0 | 123 |
| Democratic party affairs | 0.9 | 0.4 | 83.0 | 178.6 | 16.1 | 28.5 | 112 |
| Other | 0.0 | 0.0 | 85.7 | 4.7 | 14.3 | 2.8 | 7 |
| Total | 2.8 | 20.3 | 86.4 | 970.4 | 10.8 | 209.8 | 898 |
| | NBC | | | | | | |
| Social welfare | 4.2 | 0.5 | 87.5 | 11.0 | 8.3 | 4.5 | 24 |
| Agriculture, natural resources | 6.5 | 2.2 | 83.9 | 29.3 | 9.7 | 3.4 | 31 |
| Labor-management | 5.9 | 0.2 | 82.4 | 16.2 | 11.8 | 3.7 | 17 |
| Race, civil liberties | 2.0 | 3.8 | 88.2 | 27.9 | 9.8 | 10.6 | 51 |
| Law and order | 2.5 | 0.5 | 84.8 | 75.0 | 12.7 | 13.4 | 79 |
| Economic, business | 7.8 | 1.7 | 81.8 | 58.6 | 10.4 | 17.8 | 77 |
| Vietnam | 1.7 | 13.8 | 86.3 | 263.3 | 11.9 | 54.7 | 293 |
| Foreign affairs | 8.0 | 12.8 | 89.3 | 56.2 | 2.1 | 2.2 | 75 |
| National defense | 4.4 | 2.7 | 88.9 | 29.1 | 6.7 | 5.6 | 45 |
| Government functioning | 0.0 | 0.0 | 73.2 | 26.2 | 26.8 | 20.3 | 41 |
| Republican party affairs | 3.7 | 7.9 | 85.3 | 142.0 | 11.0 | 21.8 | 109 |
| Democratic party affairs | 3.4 | 4.8 | 84.0 | 181.2 | 12.6 | 28.7 | 119 |
| Other | 0.0 | 0.0 | 100.0 | 3.3 | 0.0 | 0.0 | 5 |
| Total | 3.5 | 50.9 | 85.3 | 919.4 | 11.2 | 186.7 | 966 |
| | ABC | | | | | | |
| Social welfare | 6.9 | 2.2 | 86.2 | 23.5 | 6.9 | 5.8 | 29 |
| Agriculture, natural resources | 13.6 | 6.5 | 59.1 | 20.9 | 27.3 | 9.6 | 22 |
| Labor-management | 8.3 | 0.3 | 91.7 | 7.1 | 0.0 | 0.0 | 12 |
| Race, civil liberties | 2.9 | 2.3 | 80.0 | 28.5 | 17.1 | 12.4 | 35 |
| Law and order | 1.7 | 1.7 | 89.7 | 50.2 | 8.6 | 8.0 | 58 |
| Economic, business | 9.8 | 4.4 | 82.0 | 45.7 | 8.2 | 9.4 | 61 |
| Vietnam | 2.1 | 10.8 | 82.1 | 188.9 | 15.8 | 50.8 | 234 |
| Foreign affairs | 6.1 | 7.4 | 84.8 | 54.7 | 9.1 | 8.1 | 66 |
| National defense | 0.0 | 0.0 | 91.7 | 17.0 | 8.3 | 1.9 | 24 |
| Government functioning | 0.0 | 0.0 | 85.7 | 41.0 | 14.3 | 11.8 | 42 |
| Republican party affairs | 4.8 | 7.0 | 85.7 | 120.0 | 9.5 | 21.9 | 105 |
| Democratic party affairs | 2.0 | 5.0 | 83.4 | 202.2 | 14.6 | 37.3 | 151 |
| Other | 0.0 | 0.0 | 100.0 | 0.6 | 0.0 | 0.0 | 2 |
| Total | 3.7 | 47.6 | 83.6 | 800.4 | 12.7 | 177.1 | 841 |

about government functioning (which would include some coverage of Watergate).

Several contrasts should be noted in issue coverage by the networks during the campaign. CBS devoted considerably more time to reporting stories about government functioning than did either of the other two networks. Many of these stories were about aspects of Watergate, an issue that had decidedly unfavorable partisan implications for Republicans and particularly the Nixon administration. CBS devoted about thirty-two minutes to unfavorable coverage of stories about government functioning, in comparison with twenty minutes of NBC coverage and twelve minutes of ABC coverage. No favorable stories were reported about government functioning on any of the networks, but CBS reported about fifty-eight minutes of neutral stories about the topic in comparison to twenty-six minutes on NBC and forty-one minutes on ABC.

Differences among the networks in partisan coverage linked to issues also appeared. ABC and NBC reported issue stories about Republicans more favorably and less unfavorably than about Democrats, and CBS reported issue stories about Republicans more unfavorably than about Democrats. Thus it would appear that CBS linked issues relatively unfavorably to the GOP during campaign coverage in contrast to reporting on the other two networks. But it must be noted that differences in time were fairly small, given that seventeen weeks of coverage were being considered. The ratio of time devoted to neutral stories compared with that devoted to favorable stories in the area of government functioning was about the same for all three networks.

### Implications of Issue Coverage for the Administration

Each issue story was also coded according to its favorable, neutral, or unfavorable implications for the Nixon administration. Political bias may be inherent in the way in which issues that were covered were related to the government, in this case the incumbent administration. CBS and NBC devoted relatively less time and fewer stories to issue coverage that had favorable ramifications for the administration than did ABC. At the same time, CBS devoted more time to issue coverage that had unfavorable implications for the administration, and ABC devoted the least time to stories of this kind. In general, CBS issue coverage could be regarded as somewhat more unfavorable with regard to the Nixon administration than was comparable coverage by the other two networks. (This is the type of finding that supports assertions that political bias is present in issue reporting.)

It was necessary to scrutinize which problem areas led to favorable or unfavorable implications for the Nixon administration in order to better understand the grosser overall relationships noted above. Very few issue areas had favorable linkages to the Nixon administration on any of the networks. (see table 12). More than ten minutes of

TABLE 12

Percentages of Stories and Time Devoted to Favorable, Neutral, and Unfavorable Issue Coverage in Relation to the Nixon Administration by Problem Area and Network

| Problem Area | Favorable | | Neutral | | Unfavorable | | N |
|---|---|---|---|---|---|---|---|
| | % | Time | % | Time | % | Time | |
| **CBS** | | | | | | | |
| Social welfare | 0.0 | 0.0 | 88.5 | 22.1 | 11.5 | 16.7 | 26 |
| Agriculture, natural resources | 6.3 | 1.4 | 90.6 | 37.3 | 3.1 | 0.9 | 32 |
| Labor-management | 0.0 | 0.0 | 72.7 | 8.8 | 27.3 | 3.0 | 11 |
| Race, civil liberties | 0.0 | 0.0 | 98.0 | 43.8 | 2.0 | 0.6 | 50 |
| Law and order | 0.0 | 0.0 | 98.7 | 95.1 | 1.3 | 11.1 | 79 |
| Economic, business | 10.7 | 8.0 | 82.1 | 44.5 | 7.1 | 14.1 | 84 |
| Vietnam | 0.4 | 1.2 | 95.6 | 274.7 | 3.9 | 17.9 | 229 |
| Foreign affairs | 3.4 | 1.6 | 94.9 | 56.1 | 1.7 | 2.0 | 59 |
| National defense | 5.0 | 1.9 | 95.0 | 31.7 | 0.0 | 0.0 | 40 |
| Government functioning | 1.8 | 0.3 | 78.6 | 63.7 | 19.6 | 23.4 | 56 |
| Republican party affairs | 12.5 | 17.0 | 70.8 | 132.8 | 16.7 | 55.4 | 120 |
| Democratic party affairs | 1.7 | 3.8 | 69.8 | 149.5 | 28.4 | 54.2 | 116 |
| Other | 0.0 | 0.0 | 100.0 | 7.5 | 0.0 | 0.0 | 8 |
| Total | 3.7 | 35.3 | 86.5 | 984.9 | 9.8 | 199.3 | 910 |
| **NBC** | | | | | | | |
| Social welfare | 4.2 | 0.5 | 91.7 | 15.3 | 4.2 | 0.3 | 24 |
| Agriculture, natural resources | 0.0 | 0.0 | 93.5 | 31.8 | 6.3 | 3.3 | 32 |
| Labor-management | 0.0 | 0.0 | 100.0 | 20.1 | 0.0 | 0.0 | 17 |
| Race, civil liberties | 0.0 | 0.0 | 100.0 | 44.4 | 0.0 | 0.0 | 52 |
| Law and order | 0.0 | 0.0 | 100.0 | 91.7 | 0.0 | 0.0 | 82 |
| Economic, business | 9.1 | 5.7 | 80.5 | 61.0 | 10.4 | 14.2 | 77 |
| Vietnam | 0.7 | 4.1 | 97.3 | 318.1 | 2.0 | 11.3 | 298 |
| Foreign affairs | 5.1 | 8.9 | 92.4 | 62.2 | 2.5 | 3.7 | 79 |
| National defense | 4.3 | 1.1 | 95.7 | 39.1 | 0.0 | 0.0 | 47 |
| Government functioning | 0.0 | 0.0 | 90.5 | 41.5 | 9.5 | 5.7 | 42 |
| Republican party affairs | 7.4 | 15.4 | 76.9 | 113.8 | 15.7 | 36.4 | 108 |
| Democratic party affairs | 0.8 | 2.5 | 74.8 | 165.3 | 24.4 | 53.0 | 123 |
| Other | 16.7 | 0.6 | 83.3 | 2.8 | 0.0 | 0.0 | 6 |
| Total | 2.6 | 38.8 | 90.3 | 1,007.2 | 7.1 | 127.9 | 987 |
| **ABC** | | | | | | | |
| Social welfare | 3.2 | 0.3 | 93.5 | 29.3 | 3.2 | 3.3 | 31 |
| Agriculture, natural resources | 0.0 | 0.0 | 95.0 | 34.6 | 5.0 | 0.7 | 20 |
| Labor-management | 7.7 | 0.3 | 92.3 | 9.2 | 0.0 | 0.0 | 13 |
| Race, civil liberties | 0.0 | 0.0 | 100.0 | 44.8 | 0.0 | 0.0 | 36 |
| Law and order | 0.0 | 0.0 | 98.4 | 64.9 | 1.6 | 1.8 | 62 |
| Economic, business | 11.8 | 6.6 | 82.4 | 51.6 | 5.9 | 9.0 | 68 |
| Vietnam | 2.1 | 12.0 | 95.9 | 229.9 | 2.1 | 8.9 | 241 |
| Foreign affairs | 4.1 | 5.1 | 95.9 | 75.8 | 0.0 | 0.0 | 73 |
| National defense | 3.2 | 0.0 | 96.8 | 24.2 | 0.0 | 0.0 | 31 |
| Government functioning | 4.4 | 2.9 | 82.2 | 45.5 | 13.3 | 10.8 | 45 |
| Republican party affairs | 11.4 | 17.6 | 79.0 | 113.4 | 9.5 | 18.9 | 105 |
| Democratic party affairs | 3.2 | 8.5 | 75.3 | 178.5 | 21.5 | 61.2 | 158 |
| Other | 0.0 | 0.0 | 100.0 | 1.0 | 0.0 | 0.0 | 3 |
| Total | 4.3 | 55.8 | 88.7 | 902.8 | 7.0 | 114.7 | 886 |

favorable issue coverage was linked to the administration in stories about Republican party affairs on each network and in stories about Vietnam on ABC. Coverage of other issues had very little positive to say about the Nixon administration on any of the networks.

Not unexpectedly, stories about Democratic party affairs received nearly an hour of coverage that was unfavorable to the administration during the campaign. This was clearly no surprise, since much of the campaign of a party challenging an incumbent administration leader would be expected to focus on attacking the administration's record. It would, therefore, be classified under the issue rubric. But fifty-five minutes of CBS coverage of even Republican party affairs was unfavorable to the administration. The same was true of almost twenty-five minutes' coverage of issues involved in the functioning of government. No doubt much of this coverage concerned Watergate. But neither NBC nor ABC spent as much time on stories with unfavorable implications for the administration in either of these areas, although differences among the networks' favorable and unfavorable coverage of other problem areas was not very great.

Thus it appeared that CBS reported considerably more stories that were unfavorable to the administration than either NBC or ABC. A large part of the differential involved stories about party affairs and the functioning of government; and much of this appeared to be due to coverage of Watergate. It was also clear that both NBC and ABC were more likely than CBS to link stories to the administration in a neutral way when the object of evaluation was the issue itself (compare the figures in tables 11 and 12 on this point). CBS, in contrast, was slightly more likely to report stories about the Nixon administration in a neutral way than it was to report the issues themselves in a neutral way.

### Implications of Issue Coverage for the Republican and Democratic Parties

Issue coverage was linked to the Republican and Democratic parties in a predominantly neutral way or not linked to the parties at all.* Less than one hour of issue coverage contained favorable or unfavorable implications for either of the major parties. This was true on each of the three networks.

Issue coverage associated with either of the major parties was nearly always unfavorably associated with that party. For instance, CBS devoted fifty-two minutes of coverage to issues unfavorable to the Republican party, but only six minutes of coverage to issues favorable to the GOP. NBC devoted forty-six minutes to unfavorable issue coverage as opposed to four minutes favorable to the Republicans, and ABC devoted thirty minutes to unfavorable issue coverage as opposed to one minute of favorable.

The Democratic party fared considerably better in a comparative sense than the Republicans in terms of the total amount of unfavorable issue coverage. But this occurred only because more stories were linked in a neutral way, or not linked at all, to the Democratic party, and not because the Democrats received more favorable issue coverage. About nineteen minutes of unfavorable and six minutes of favorable time were broadcast on CBS, twenty minutes of unfavorable and seven minutes of favorable time on NBC, and fifteen minutes of unfavorable and six minutes of favorable time on ABC.

Nearly all the issues reflecting favorably or unfavorably on the Republican party concerned Democratic or Republican party affairs and the functioning of government. No other issue area related to the GOP received as much as five minutes coverage during the entire campaign. Similarly, most of the issues associated with the Democratic party, either favorably or unfavorably, were about strictly partisan issues that concerned either the Republican or the Democratic party. Again, no other problem area received as much as five minutes' coverage during the seventeen weeks under study.

### Implications of Issue Coverage for the Republican and Democratic Campaigns

When we turned to inspect the way that issue stories were related to the Nixon and McGovern presidential campaigns, the picture was somewhat different. Although issue coverage was predominantly neutral or not linked to the presidential campaigns on network television, a fair amount of association remained between issues and the campaigns.* Sufficient variation existed in that association, moreover, to allow some meaningful statistical comparisons to be made by issue or problem area.

ABC devoted more time to issue coverage favorable to the Republican presidential campaign, and NBC devoted the least time to issue coverage unfavorable to the GOP campaign. Although ABC also devoted more time to issue coverage favorable to the Democratic campaign than the other networks, CBS rather than NBC devoted the least time to issue coverage unfavorable to the McGovern efforts. ABC carried about sixty-seven minutes of issue coverage favorable to the Republican campaign, and 106 minutes of unfavorable issue coverage. NBC devoted about fifty minutes to favorable issue coverage and ninety-three minutes to unfavorable GOP coverage; and CBS spent about fifty-six minutes on favorable issue coverage and 139 minutes on unfavorable Republican coverage.

Much less time was spent relating issues to the McGovern campaign in either a favorable or an unfavorable way. ABC, for instance, devoted thirty-six minutes of favorable issue coverage and eighty-four minutes of unfavorable McGovern coverage. NBC spent twenty-five minutes on favorable issue coverage and seventy-seven minutes on unfavorable McGovern issue coverage. CBS devoted twenty-two minutes to issue coverage that was favorable and sixty-eight minutes to issue coverage that was unfavorable to the Democratic presidential campaign.

Most of the stories favorable or unfavorable to the major party campaign efforts were partisan ones in the sense that the issues directly concerned the major parties. In the case of the Republicans, as noted in previous findings, stories about the functioning of government were fairly frequently related to the parties in a favorable or unfavorable way. The networks did, however, treat the campaigns somewhat differently in this regard. ABC, for instance, devoted about twenty-five minutes to issue coverage about the Democratic party and about eighteen minutes to issue coverage about the Republican party favorable to the Republican campaign. Both CBS and NBC devoted about thirty minutes to issue coverage about the Republican party favorable to the GOP presidential campaign, but nearly no time at all to issue coverage about the Democratic party favorable to the GOP.

CBS, moreover, devoted about twenty-four minutes to issue coverage about the functioning of government (mainly Watergate stories) that was unfavorable to the Republican presidential campaign, whereas NBC spent only about ten minutes and ABC about sixteen minutes on comparable stories. CBS also devoted considerably more time to stories about the Republican party that were unfavorable to the GOP campaign (sixty-two minutes) than either NBC (thirty-four minutes) or ABC (twenty-eight minutes). ABC devoted a bit more time (fifty minutes) to issue coverage about the Democratic party that was unfavorable to the Republican campaign than NBC (forty-four minutes) or CBS (forty-three minutes).

Except for stories concerning the functioning of government, McGovern campaign coverage followed a similar pattern. About the only issue coverage favorable to the Democratic presidential campaign appeared in stories about the Democratic party. ABC devoted thirty-two minutes to such coverage, NBC twenty minutes, and CBS about nineteen minutes. ABC also devoted more time than the other networks to issue coverage about the Democratic party unfavorable to the McGovern presidential campaign (fifty-two minutes in comparison with forty-four minutes on NBC and twenty-eight minutes on CBS), and each network devoted roughly twenty minutes to issue coverage about the Republican party that was unfavorable to the Democratic presidential campaign. Except for issue coverage regarding Vietnam (which included eight minutes of unfavorable coverage on ABC), no other issue area constituted as much as five minutes of coverage favorable or unfavorable to the McGovern campaign on any network. By and large, issue coverage on the networks, except for the traditional coverage of the major parties, was not tied in favorable or unfavorable ways to the Democratic campaign. With the exception of one story (about Vietnam) absolutely no non-party issue coverage was related to McGovern's campaign in a favorable way.

The Republican presidential campaign did, however, receive some favorable association with issues, however small the association may have been. Most of the non-party issue coverage that was favorably related to the Republican presidential campaign concerned Vietnam. ABC devoted about fourteen minutes to Vietnam coverage favorable to the GOP campaign, and CBS spent about ten minutes and NBC about four minutes on comparable stories. But only economic issues on NBC were given as much as five minutes' coverage favorable to the Republican presidential campaign. ABC devoted six minutes to issue coverage about the economy unfavorable to the Republican presidential campaign, but no other issue area (except the partisan ones and government functioning noted above) received as much coverage unfavorable to the GOP presidential efforts.

### Crowds and Visuals in Issue Coverage

Patterns of crowd coverage in issue stories generally corresponded to the amount of time devoted to coverage of specific policy areas. Large crowds were somewhat more likely to appear in CBS stories about social welfare, race and civil liberties, foreign affairs, law and order, Vietnam, and partisan affairs. NBC, in contrast, devoted more time to stories that included large crowds concerning race and civil liberties, the economy, partisan affairs, Vietnam, and foreign affairs; and ABC included crowds in stories about Republican party affairs more often than CBS or NBC.*

ABC was much more likely than NBC or CBS to include pictures in its issue coverage (about 98 percent of all stories about issues).

CBS was more likely to include pictures in coverage of social welfare and race and civil liberties than NBC, and NBC was more likely to include pictures in coverage of government functioning, partisan affairs, and law and order. Although ABC included pictures in a larger proportion of issue stories than CBS and NBC, only in the areas of race and civil liberties and Democratic party affairs did ABC devote more total time to issue stories that included pictures.

Patterns of issue coverage characterized by the use of film and action settings tended to follow the patterns established by networks in the use of pictures. Still, some discrepancies occurred. CBS, for instance, was more likely than ABC and NBC to include action settings in issue coverage. Coverage of issues that somehow related to parties was most likely to contain action settings (as was true of issue coverage that included pictures). Tendencies to use closeups and flashbacks also followed the trends established for the use of pictures in issue stories, although overall differences were not very great among networks for specific issue areas.

### Positional Emphasis of Issue Stories

Issue stories received about the same overall positional emphasis. They appeared in the first five stories reported during broadcasts, excluding headlines and commercials, on each of the networks, although a fair amount of variation existed in the types of issues emphasized. This was true both in terms of the proportion of issue stories that received early placement and in terms of the time devoted to issue stories emphasized on the broadcasts (see table 13).

Stories about Democratic party issues were emphasized more than stories about Republican party issues on each of the networks, although the discrepancies in the treatment of the parties were greatest for ABC and CBS and least for NBC. About 52 percent of the ABC and CBS issue stories, and about 40 percent of the NBC issue stories, that related to the Democratic party occurred within the first five stories broadcast during news programs on the networks. This contrasted to 34 percent, 40 percent, and 36 percent of the issue stories that concerned Republican party affairs receiving positional emphasis that were broadcast on ABC, CBS and NBC, respectively. Similar discrepancies occurred when the amount of time devoted to partisan issue coverage was inspected on each network. The ratio of time devoted to Republican stories with positional emphasis to comparable Democratic stories in ABC coverage was nearly 3:1, whereas the same ratio in CBS coverage was about

## TABLE 13

### Percentages of Stories and Time Devoted to Stories That Appeared among the First Five and Other Stories about Issues by Problem Area and Network

| Problem Area | CBS | | | | | NBC | | | | | ABC | | | | |
|---|---|---|---|---|---|---|---|---|---|---|---|---|---|---|---|
| | First % | First Time | Not First % | Not First Time | (N) | First % | First Time | Not First % | Not First Time | (N) | First % | First Time | Not First % | Not First Time | (N) |
| Social welfare | 10.8 | 3.1 | 89.2 | 46.4 | 37 | 8.3 | 4.3 | 91.7 | 23.2 | 36 | 13.5 | 4.4 | 86.5 | 33.5 | 37 |
| Agriculture, natural resources | 15.0 | 11.8 | 85.0 | 37.0 | 42 | 5.3 | 3.2 | 94.7 | 35.2 | 37 | 8.3 | 3.5 | 91.7 | 36.0 | 24 |
| Labor-management | 21.4 | 3.6 | 78.6 | 9.3 | 15 | 5.6 | 2.4 | 94.4 | 18.0 | 18 | 6.3 | 0.4 | 93.8 | 11.1 | 16 |
| Race, civil liberties | 1.9 | 0.4 | 98.1 | 47.9 | 54 | 11.5 | 8.3 | 88.5 | 36.2 | 52 | 8.3 | 3.5 | 91.7 | 41.3 | 36 |
| Law and order | 9.1 | 21.4 | 90.9 | 117.3 | 107 | 9.8 | 26.4 | 90.2 | 100.8 | 118 | 10.5 | 18.3 | 89.5 | 78.4 | 86 |
| Economic, business | 10.2 | 18.1 | 89.8 | 89.7 | 177 | 5.5 | 14.1 | 94.5 | 106.3 | 181 | 16.0 | 24.8 | 84.0 | 62.5 | 119 |
| Vietnam | 43.2 | 146.4 | 56.8 | 158.7 | 229 | 47.5 | 194.7 | 52.5 | 141.4 | 298 | 46.9 | 151.4 | 53.1 | 104.3 | 245 |
| Foreign affairs | 23.6 | 50.1 | 76.4 | 115.4 | 160 | 17.8 | 61.3 | 82.2 | 171.7 | 232 | 17.7 | 48.3 | 82.3 | 146.7 | 181 |
| National defense | 14.9 | 5.1 | 85.1 | 34.1 | 46 | 25.5 | 14.1 | 74.5 | 27.3 | 49 | 21.6 | 9.9 | 78.4 | 21.0 | 37 |
| Government functioning | 40.5 | 45.0 | 59.5 | 61.4 | 79 | 31.1 | 25.6 | 68.9 | 88.7 | 61 | 24.2 | 19.0 | 75.8 | 56.5 | 62 |
| Republican party affairs | 40.3 | 108.7 | 59.7 | 208.1 | 191 | 35.8 | 117.3 | 63.6 | 163.9 | 187 | 33.5 | 88.4 | 66.5 | 171.6 | 185 |
| Democratic party affairs | 50.7 | 204.9 | 49.3 | 182.7 | 221 | 39.9 | 179.9 | 59.6 | 185.7 | 218 | 51.3 | 239.3 | 48.7 | 199.0 | 277 |
| Total | 29.7 | 618.6 | 70.3 | 1108.0 | 1399 | 26.5 | 651.6 | 73.5 | 1098.4 | 1564 | 31.5 | 611.2 | 68.5 | 961.9 | 1329 |

Stories were classified according to whether or not they are reported as one of the first five stories in a broadcast. Although somewhat arbitrary in delineation of what is first, it is assumed in this analysis that stories that are broadcast first are attributed greater importance than stories that are broadcast later.

2:1. A discrepancy existed in NBC coverage, but the difference in time devoted to issue stories about Democratic and Republican affairs was considerably less marked on NBC than on either of the other two networks.

Issue stories about Vietnam received slightly greater positional emphasis than partisan issue stories about Democratic affairs on NBC and nearly as much emphasis on CBS and ABC: each network attributed positional emphasis to Vietnam coverage in between 43 (CBS) and 47 percent (NBC and ABC) of the stories. NBC devoted the most time to these stories; ABC and CBS each devoted about forty-five minutes less coverage to Vietnam. CBS attributed considerably greater positional emphasis to issue stories about labor-management and government functioning than NBC or ABC in terms of both the proportion of stories and time devoted to them. CBS devoted less attention to stories about national defense than the other two networks. ABC devoted somewhat more attention to stories about the economy than the other networks in terms of the relative frequency with which stories received positional emphasis and the time devoted to stories that were emphasized, although differences were not particularly large.

NBC emphasized stories about social welfare, agriculture and natural resources, and the economy less than the other networks, although once again differences were fairly small with regard to either time or the proportions of stories that were discussed.

To summarize, when one inspected the relative emphasis attributed to issue stories by the networks, very similar rankings of emphasis among issues appeared among the networks. Thus it appears that stories about issues relevant to the major parties, Vietnam, government functioning, foreign affairs, and national defense were emphasized more frequently than stories about agriculture and natural resources, social welfare, the economy, law and order, race and civil liberties, and labor-management concerns. Only NBC emphasized Vietnam more than issues related to either major party, although CBS and ABC gave greater emphasis to Vietnam stories than to issue stories relating to the Republican party. Finally, ABC attributed greater positional emphasis to stories about the economy and social welfare than the other two networks in a relative sense.

### Positional Emphasis in Stories about Nixon and McGovern

One way of assessing candidate coverage is to investigate the way in which issues were linked to Nixon and McGovern. This type of analysis has, in part, been reported in chapter 3. But it is also possible to investigate the kinds of issues that were emphasized in association with each candidate. If Vietnam, for instance, failed to be emphasized in stories about McGovern, then associations between McGovern and his positions on the problems concerning Vietnam would be less likely to be perceived clearly in the public's mind. It is useful, therefore, to inspect the kinds of issues that appeared in stories about the candidates among the first five stories on newscasts.

Most of the general issue categories discussed in this chapter were emphasized in stories about Nixon.* The stories receiving greatest positional emphasis concerned government functioning, Vietnam, and foreign affairs on CBS; Vietnam, Republican party concerns, national defense, and foreign affairs on NBC; and social welfare, Democratic party affairs, race and civil liberties, and Vietnam on ABC. More time on ABC, in contrast to percentages of stories, was devoted to Republican party affairs than to any other issue area. Only stories about race on CBS; race, agriculture and natural resources, labor-management concerns, and Democratic party affairs on NBC; and agriculture and natural resources and labor-management on ABC failed to receive some positional emphasis more than one time during the campaign.

The picture was very different when issue emphasis was scrutinized in relation to candidate McGovern. Only issue stories about government functioning and partisan affairs on each network received emphasis in McGovern stories more than once during the seventeen-week campaign. McGovern was associated with issues emphasized in a very meager way, indeed.

If one excludes stories about basically partisan affairs for the moment, then issue stories about government functioning—mostly about honesty and morality in government—were the only areas emphasized in association with the Democratic standard-bearer on NBC, CBS, and ABC. Thus one might speculate that candidate McGovern suffered from a lack of issue association in news stories. This is understandable to some extent: an incumbent president is challenged, and the officeholder naturally has an advantage in being associated with all the affairs of state. Yet, such coverage clearly works to the disadvantage of the challenger except under the most catastrophic of conditions for the incumbent. Such a catastrophy was indeed to appear two years later for the incumbent president.

*Positional Emphasis in Issue Stories about Democrats and Republicans*

When positional emphasis of issue stories related to the Democratic and Republican parties was scrutinized, the picture was somewhat different. Issue stories related to the Republican party that received the greatest positional emphasis included stories about government functioning and partisan affairs on CBS and ABC, and the same topics plus foreign affairs and the economy on NBC.

In issue stories related to the Democrats that received positional emphasis by the networks, coverage included stories about government functioning, Vietnam, partisan affairs, and agriculture and natural resources on CBS; about government functioning, the economy, and partisan affairs on NBC; and about partisan affairs, government functioning, the economy, and Vietnam on ABC. In making these assessments, we excluded quite a few issue areas that received coverage by networks only one or two times throughout the campaign period under study. We tried to illustrate general trends rather than individual idiosyncracies of issue coverage in this analysis. By and large, issue areas were given positional emphasis in the same order as their relative frequency and the amount of time devoted to them would suggest.

## SOURCES OF ISSUE STORIES

The way in which issues were presented and the particular context in which information about issues arose may have been influenced considerably by the most important source of information for a story. Some kinds of issues may have been the exclusive province of either Republicans or Democrats. Other issues may have been systematically based on reports that were shown to originate from institutional sources, from interest groups, or from representatives of foreign governments. Subject-matter experts may have been consulted more regularly on some kinds of issues than on others, and ordinary citizens may have been consulted on yet other types of issues. Finally, patterns of coverage may have emerged that indicate that news reporters had almost exclusive dominion over the reporting of yet other kinds of issue stories. In any case, it was important to inspect practices of the way in which sources were consulted so that audience impressions of the informational context in which stories were presented could be more thoroughly appreciated. One might expect television journalists, moreover, to present their sources in a fashion similar to journalists in other media. Explicitly including non-news sources, finally, might have been indicative of the amount of care taken in investigating issues.

Each issue story was classified according to the most important source of information. News reporters were classified as most important sources only when non-reporter sources were not cited or when non-reporter sources were cited very little in relation to the reporter. The first source in a news story about issues was coded as the most important whenever two or more sources (except news reporters) appeared to receive about equal attention. Otherwise, the non-reporter source that received the most attention in the course of a story was considered to be the most important source of story information.

### The Most Important Source of Issue Stories

News reporters served as the most important source of information about issue stories on each of the networks more frequently than any other source. In effect, this means that reporters were the *only* important source presented to the news audience in these stories. Stories on NBC were more likely (37 percent) and stories on CBS less likely (29 percent) to have news reporters as the most important source than were ABC stories (about 30 percent). The amount of time devoted to such stories, moreover, paralleled the percentages (see table 14).

Institutional sources were second most likely to be cited in issue coverage on all three networks. Indeed, assessing sources in terms of the amount of time (rather than the likelihood that a source was cited) suggested that stories in which institutional sources were cited consumed even more time than did stories in which only reporters were the observable sources in issue coverage on CBS and NBC. About 23 percent of the issue stories on CBS, 20 percent on NBC, and 20 percent on ABC included institutions as the most important sources of information. CBS devoted 368 minutes to these stories; NBC, 359 minutes; and ABC stories that had institutional sources consumed 275 minutes of air time during the campaign. This contrasted with CBS and NBC coverage of issues for which reporters were the most important source. CBS devoted 237 minutes to the 29 percent of the issue stories with reporters as most important sources; NBC devoted 312 minutes to the 37 percent of the issue stories with similar sources; and ABC devoted 277 min-

## TABLE 14

Percentages of Stories and Time Devoted to Issue Coverage by Most Important Source of Information and Network

| Problem Area | Reporter % | Reporter Time | Republican % | Republican Time | Democrat % | Democrat Time | Institutional % | Institutional Time | Interest Group % | Interest Group Time | Foreign Rep % | Foreign Rep Time | Citizens % | Citizens Time | Experts % | Experts Time | Others % | Others Time | (N) |
|---|---|---|---|---|---|---|---|---|---|---|---|---|---|---|---|---|---|---|---|
| **CBS** | | | | | | | | | | | | | | | | | | | |
| Social welfare | 41.5 | 10.3 | 10.8 | 15.5 | 8.1 | 6.1 | 21.6 | 9.9 | 13.5 | 6.8 | 0.0 | 0.0 | 0.0 | 0.0 | 5.4 | 10.9 | 0.0 | 0.0 | 37 |
| Agriculture, natural resources | 22.5 | 3.3 | 12.5 | 2.7 | 0.0 | 0.0 | 35.0 | 19.9 | 20.0 | 18.5 | 2.5 | 0.4 | 0.0 | 0.0 | 7.5 | 4.0 | 0.0 | 0.0 | 40 |
| Labor-management | 57.1 | 3.8 | 0.0 | 0.0 | 0.0 | 0.0 | 7.1 | 2.3 | 35.7 | 7.0 | 0.0 | 0.0 | 0.0 | 0.0 | 0.0 | 0.0 | 0.0 | 0.0 | 14 |
| Race, civil liberties | 37.0 | 9.6 | 5.6 | 1.6 | 7.4 | 6.0 | 29.6 | 15.3 | 13.0 | 11.9 | 0.0 | 0.0 | 5.6 | 3.8 | 1.9 | 0.4 | 0.0 | 0.0 | 34 |
| Law and order | 22.6 | 14.8 | 3.7 | 5.8 | 0.0 | 0.0 | 27.5 | 35.8 | 10.1 | 22.6 | 12.8 | 20.0 | 11.0 | 23.2 | 8.3 | 15.8 | 0.0 | 0.0 | 109 |
| Economic, business | 56.8 | 27.8 | 2.3 | 7.6 | 1.7 | 5.3 | 27.8 | 42.7 | 5.7 | 12.3 | 1.7 | 1.3 | 1.7 | 6.3 | 2.3 | 4.3 | 0.0 | 0.0 | 176 |
| Vietnam | 24.4 | 41.1 | 3.4 | 6.7 | 0.0 | 0.0 | 42.3 | 113.2 | 2.1 | 14.3 | 22.2 | 93.4 | 0.4 | 2.3 | 4.7 | 6.9 | 0.4 | 4.5 | 234 |
| Foreign affairs | 34.8 | 30.9 | 0.6 | 4.1 | 0.6 | 0.3 | 10.6 | 16.3 | 3.7 | 5.9 | 47.8 | 105.8 | 0.6 | 1.0 | 1.2 | 4.8 | 0.0 | 0.0 | 161 |
| National defense | 31.9 | 6.9 | 6.4 | 3.8 | 2.1 | 0.8 | 42.6 | 17.4 | 2.1 | 0.4 | 4.3 | 3.2 | 4.3 | 3.7 | 2.1 | 0.5 | 4.3 | 2.2 | 47 |
| Government functioning | 20.3 | 12.8 | 7.6 | 11.8 | 11.4 | 14.7 | 36.7 | 38.8 | 5.1 | 3.6 | 0.0 | 0.0 | 2.5 | 5.3 | 16.1 | 19.4 | 0.0 | 0.0 | 79 |
| Republican party affairs | 13.1 | 24.2 | 53.4 | 161.1 | 4.7 | 17.0 | 12.6 | 35.8 | 9.9 | 46.3 | 0.0 | 0.0 | 1.6 | 9.3 | 4.7 | 23.1 | 0.0 | 0.0 | 191 |
| Democratic party affairs | 16.0 | 41.3 | 4.4 | 18.9 | 65.8 | 278.3 | 3.1 | 13.5 | 6.2 | 18.8 | 0.0 | 0.0 | 0.4 | 3.5 | 4.0 | 13.3 | 0.0 | 0.0 | 225 |
| Others | 41.4 | 9.7 | 3.4 | 2.8 | 3.4 | 0.3 | 31.0 | 7.2 | 10.3 | 2.7 | 0.0 | 0.0 | 0.0 | 0.0 | 10.3 | 7.0 | 0.0 | 0.0 | 29 |
| Total | 28.5 | 236.6 | 10.8 | 249.3 | 12.8 | 328.7 | 23.1 | 368.2 | 7.0 | 170.5 | 10.7 | 224.2 | 2.0 | 58.4 | 4.8 | 110.4 | 0.2 | 6.7 | 1,396 |
| **NBC** | | | | | | | | | | | | | | | | | | | |
| Social welfare | 36.1 | 8.7 | 8.3 | 4.7 | 0.0 | 0.0 | 33.3 | 8.5 | 8.3 | 0.9 | 0.0 | 0.0 | 0.0 | 0.0 | 13.9 | 4.8 | 0.0 | 0.0 | 36 |
| Agriculture, natural resources | 31.6 | 3.0 | 0.0 | 0.0 | 2.6 | 2.5 | 34.2 | 20.7 | 21.1 | 8.4 | 0.0 | 0.0 | 2.6 | 2.2 | 7.9 | 1.6 | 0.0 | 0.0 | 38 |
| Labor-management | 44.4 | 3.4 | 0.0 | 0.0 | 5.6 | 1.9 | 5.6 | 1.8 | 38.9 | 12.6 | 0.0 | 0.0 | 0.0 | 0.0 | 5.6 | 0.6 | 0.0 | 0.0 | 18 |
| Race, civil liberties | 33.3 | 4.6 | 2.0 | 0.3 | 3.9 | 3.1 | 35.3 | 10.5 | 11.8 | 13.4 | 2.0 | 0.4 | 3.9 | 2.5 | 7.8 | 7.5 | 0.0 | 0.0 | 51 |
| Law and order | 36.4 | 16.9 | 0.8 | 5.8 | 0.8 | 0.8 | 28.1 | 40.9 | 2.5 | 6.5 | 17.4 | 29.7 | 7.4 | 13.6 | 6.6 | 12.8 | 0.0 | 0.0 | 121 |
| Economic, business | 54.9 | 32.7 | 0.5 | 2.5 | 1.1 | 2.0 | 26.9 | 46.9 | 11.0 | 25.5 | 1.1 | 0.7 | 7.4 | 9.4 | 2.2 | 3.8 | 0.0 | 0.0 | 182 |
| Vietnam | 41.3 | 73.9 | 1.7 | 6.9 | 1.0 | 5.6 | 31.7 | 22.8 | 2.0 | 8.9 | 19.5 | 103.9 | 0.0 | 0.0 | 3.0 | 14.0 | 0.0 | 0.0 | 303 |
| Foreign affairs | 40.1 | 59.9 | 2.5 | 11.1 | 0.4 | 1.0 | 9.5 | 29.1 | 2.9 | 6.3 | 42.1 | 120.3 | 0.4 | 1.3 | 2.1 | 4.0 | 0.0 | 0.0 | 242 |
| National defense | 37.3 | 8.2 | 3.9 | 2.8 | 0.0 | 0.0 | 47.1 | 22.6 | 3.9 | 4.6 | 5.9 | 1.1 | 2.0 | 2.0 | 0.0 | 0.0 | 0.0 | 0.0 | 51 |

TABLE 14 (continued)

| Problem Area | Reporter % | Reporter Time | Republican % | Republican Time | Democrat % | Democrat Time | Institutional % | Institutional Time | Interest Group % | Interest Time | Foreign Rep % | Foreign Rep Time | Citizens % | Citizens Time | Experts % | Experts Time | Others % | Others Time | (N) |
|---|---|---|---|---|---|---|---|---|---|---|---|---|---|---|---|---|---|---|---|
| **NBC** | | | | | | | | | | | | | | | | | | | |
| Government functioning | 26.2 | 9.8 | 14.8 | 10.2 | 3.3 | 2.4 | 19.7 | 19.8 | 8.2 | 11.4 | 1.6 | 2.6 | 1.6 | 0.3 | 24.6 | 7.8 | 0.0 | 0.0 | 61 |
| Republican party affairs | 28.5 | 33.8 | 46.1 | 170.0 | 5.2 | 15.2 | 10.4 | 25.2 | 4.7 | 17.9 | 0.0 | 0.0 | 1.6 | 8.2 | 3.6 | 10.9 | 0.0 | 0.0 | 193 |
| Democratic party affairs | 22.4 | 42.2 | 4.5 | 22.4 | 62.8 | 264.7 | 2.7 | 5.0 | 4.0 | 19.4 | 0.0 | 0.0 | 1.8 | 8.5 | 1.8 | 3.2 | 0.0 | 0.0 | 223 |
| Others | 55.8 | 15.1 | 0.0 | 0.0 | 0.0 | 0.0 | 14.0 | 5.1 | 0.0 | 0.0 | 4.7 | 0.7 | 9.3 | 8.2 | 16.3 | 7.8 | 0.0 | 0.0 | 43 |
| Total | 37.1 | 312.3 | 8.1 | 236.7 | 10.4 | 299.4 | 20.1 | 359.0 | 5.4 | 135.9 | 12.2 | 259.3 | 1.9 | 56.3 | 4.6 | 78.9 | 0.0 | 0.0 | 1,562 |
| **ABC** | | | | | | | | | | | | | | | | | | | |
| Social welfare | 35.1 | 7.0 | 8.1 | 1.5 | 2.7 | 2.5 | 35.1 | 11.1 | 5.4 | 3.5 | 2.7 | 2.6 | 8.1 | 8.8 | 2.7 | 0.7 | 0.0 | 0.0 | 37 |
| Agriculture, natural resources | 20.8 | 5.1 | 0.0 | 0.0 | 0.0 | 0.0 | 41.7 | 16.9 | 29.2 | 13.4 | 0.0 | 0.5 | 8.3 | 4.2 | 0.0 | 0.0 | 0.0 | 0.0 | 24 |
| Labor-management | 50.0 | 3.5 | 6.3 | 0.4 | 0.0 | 0.0 | 12.5 | 2.5 | 31.3 | 5.1 | 0.0 | 0.0 | 0.0 | 0.0 | 0.0 | 0.0 | 0.0 | 0.0 | 16 |
| Race, civil liberties | 41.7 | 4.4 | 5.6 | 2.7 | 0.0 | 0.0 | 16.7 | 5.4 | 22.2 | 20.4 | 0.0 | 0.0 | 13.9 | 11.9 | 0.0 | 0.0 | 0.0 | 0.0 | 36 |
| Law and order | 32.6 | 21.1 | 1.2 | 0.3 | 0.0 | 0.0 | 24.4 | 21.7 | 7.0 | 4.8 | 18.6 | 25.9 | 7.0 | 10.3 | 9.3 | 12.5 | 0.0 | 0.0 | 86 |
| Economic, business | 44.5 | 16.2 | 0.8 | 2.1 | 0.8 | 2.3 | 27.7 | 34.3 | 14.3 | 25.0 | 1.7 | 0.5 | 1.7 | 3.8 | 7.6 | 2.9 | 0.1 | 0.1 | 119 |
| Vietnam | 34.3 | 54.4 | 2.1 | 6.0 | 0.0 | 0.0 | 34.7 | 74.5 | 2.5 | 14.8 | 22.3 | 84.9 | 0.4 | 2.1 | 3.7 | 18.0 | 0.8 | 0.0 | 242 |
| Foreign affairs | 37.0 | 60.9 | 1.7 | 4.5 | 0.6 | 2.3 | 11.0 | 24.6 | 2.8 | 6.4 | 44.2 | 89.7 | 0.6 | 1.9 | 2.2 | 4.7 | 0.0 | 0.0 | 181 |
| National defense | 35.1 | 10.6 | 2.7 | 0.3 | 0.0 | 0.0 | 45.9 | 11.4 | 1.8 | 0.0 | 8.1 | 3.0 | 5.4 | 4.6 | 2.7 | 1.1 | 0.0 | 0.0 | 37 |
| Government functioning | 32.3 | 15.0 | 6.6 | 8.7 | 14.8 | 11.5 | 7.9 | 25.2 | 1.6 | 2.4 | 0.0 | 0.0 | 0.0 | 0.0 | 16.4 | 9.5 | 0.0 | 0.0 | 61 |
| Republican party affairs | 24.9 | 39.8 | 46.5 | 134.0 | 2.7 | 9.5 | 13.0 | 27.9 | 5.4 | 24.1 | 0.0 | 0.0 | 2.2 | 11.5 | 5.4 | 13.2 | 0.0 | 0.0 | 185 |
| Democratic party affairs | 15.9 | 33.8 | 5.8 | 29.3 | 64.9 | 301.0 | 3.6 | 16.5 | 4.7 | 26.6 | 0.7 | 2.3 | 1.8 | 15.2 | 2.5 | 10.7 | 0.0 | 0.0 | 276 |
| Others | 33.3 | 5.2 | 0.0 | 0.0 | 4.2 | 2.6 | 20.8 | 3.0 | 8.3 | 2.3 | 0.0 | 0.0 | 8.3 | 3.6 | 25.0 | 2.1 | 0.0 | 0.0 | 24 |
| Total | 30.4 | 277.0 | 9.3 | 189.7 | 14.9 | 331.9 | 19.8 | 275.0 | 6.2 | 148.7 | 11.9 | 208.9 | 2.5 | 78.0 | 4.9 | 75.5 | 0.1 | 0.1 | 1,324 |

utes to the 30 percent of the issue stories with reporters as most important sources. It was also clear that ABC stories were about as likely to cite institutional sources as were CBS or NBC stories, but ABC spent less time on stories devoted to issue coverage of any kind. It appeared, reasonably enough, that network reporters were the only observable sources for a large number of fairly short stories, and that, when other sources were cited, stories were lengthier.

Democratic sources were reported somewhat more frequently than were Republican sources on each network. This discrepancy was, however, greater on ABC and less on NBC. Although each network cited partisan sources with about the same frequency, and each network devoted about the same amount of time to issue stories with Democratic sources, CBS gave much more time to stories with Republican sources and ABC much less time to comparable sources than did NBC.

Representatives of foreign countries were also frequent sources of stories about issues, with slightly more than 10 percent of the stories on each network having foreign representatives as most important sources. Interest groups of varying kinds were also fairly frequently cited as most important sources of information for issue stories on each of the networks, with CBS reporting interest groups to a greater extent than ABC or NBC, especially in terms of the amount of time. NBC was more likely, again with respect to the time devoted to such stories, to cite foreign sources than were the other networks and ABC least likely.

Experts were cited next most frequently in network issue coverage, and ordinary citizens least frequently. CBS devoted considerably more time to issue stories with experts as most important sources, although ABC was slightly more likely to attribute stories to experts for its issue coverage. Experts were cited as sources for about one story in twenty on each network, but more than an hour (nearly two hours on CBS) was consumed by issue coverage with experts as the most important source. Again, these findings did not appear unreasonable, since one would assume that information from experts might be more complex than information from other sources.

It was also no surprise that ordinary citizens, Americans who have no particular expertise or station, were consulted as most important sources least frequently of all. Public reactions to events are important in a democratic society. But popular reactions to issues can be accurately measured only by sophisticated scientific

101

surveys. There was reason to believe that the man-in-the-street interview or intellectual speculation about opinion, so popular in the old days of journalism, were therefore more misleading than enlightening in many instances. It must also be noted that the information presented in table 14 concerned the most important source as defined in this study, not the only source of information. It was also clear that each source was reported more frequently than the table suggests when sources were classified in terms of whether they were cited on issue stories at all.

Table 14 also presented information about the most important sources of issue stories by problem area. Patterns in the citation of sources suggested by these data are fairly similar, although some variation is included in specific instances. ABC, for instance, was both more likely to report institutional sources in social welfare stories (both in terms of the proportion of stories and the amount of time devoted to social welfare stories with institutional sources). CBS was also more likely to report partisan sources—and more likely to report Republican than Democratic sources—than NBC or ABC. A similar pattern held with regard to interest groups as attributed sources of information in social welfare stories. In contrast, NBC was more likely than either CBS or ABC to cite experts in its coverage of social welfare, although differences among networks were minimal in the amount of time devoted to such coverage.

Nearly parallel patterns existed for stories about agriculture and natural resources: reporters, institutional sources, and interest groups were likely to be cited. The same general pattern appeared for coverage of labor-management concerns and the economy.

Stories about race and civil liberties tended to use reporters, partisan groups, institutions, interest groups, and ordinary citizens as most important sources. Reporters, interest groups, and institutional sources loomed as most important. Reporters, institutional sources, interest groups, foreign sources, citizens, and experts all served as most important sources of information about law and order stories, and (with the exception of citizens and experts) the same sources frequently played the role of most important source in stories about the economy and foreign affairs. The most important sources of information in stories concerning Vietnam included reporters, Republicans, institutional sources, interest groups, foreign representatives, and experts. The same pattern of sources held for stories about national defense and more general foreign affairs.

Each of the sources, except foreign representatives, served as a most important source of information in issue stories about government functioning. ABC was more likely than the other networks to use reporters and Democrats as sources for issue stories about government functioning, whereas CBS was most likely to cite institutional sources. NBC was most likely to attribute information to Republicans, interest groups, and experts in its coverage of government functioning.

The respective parties served as most important sources of information about Republican and Democratic party affairs, although more time was spent and a greater relative number of stories (and absolute number, as well) were devoted to Democratic coverage with Democratic sources of information than to Republican coverage with Republican sources of information. Relatively little coverage was devoted to partisan stories that included opposition partisans as the most important source of information. NBC was more likely to use reporters as sources of information in partisan stories, and CBS was least likely to do so (even if ABC did not devote quite as much time to stories about Democratic party affairs as CBS). Institutional sources were more frequently cited for Republican party affairs than for issues that related to Democratic party affairs on each network. CBS also used interest groups as sources of information much more frequently than did NBC or ABC in its coverage of Republican affairs.

Ordinary citizens were cited in a few instances concerning partisan affairs; but not a great deal of time or a large number of stories were involved, and the patterns of attribution were very similar for issue stories relating to Republican affairs than they were in coverage of issue stories relating to Democratic affairs. It is important to note that trends in issue coverage that showed the Republican party as receiving more time than the Democratic party were even stronger than would be suggested by the number of minutes associated with each party because the issue stories that related to the GOP received much less coverage than the issue stories related to the Democrats (in both numbers and time). This, in turn, was most likely true because less coverage was devoted to Republicans than to Democrats for reasons suggested in other chapters.

### Use of Republican and Democratic Sources

It was assumed that partisan sources were likely to place an issue in a light that was favorable, or at least neutral, to their own colleagues and unfavorable to the opponents. It was also assumed that differential consultation with partisan sources on the important issues of the day was likely to permit one side greater access to the public arena in order to explain its view. Finally, it was assumed that what benefited one side was at the cost of the other side. For these reasons major party sources were coded whenever they contributed any information to a story. This contrasted with the preceding analysis in which only the source that was most important in a story was coded.

Democratic sources were more likely to be cited than were Republican sources. This was true whether one considered the proportion of stories or the amount of time devoted to those stories. It was also true of coverage on each network. CBS stories cited Republican sources most frequently, and ABC cited Democratic sources most frequently; and CBS devoted the most time to stories that named Democratic sources (see table 15).

Much consultation that party representatives received concerned, not surprisingly, partisan matters. About 60 percent of the stories about Republican affairs on CBS named at least one Republican source, and this was true of 49 percent of the stories on NBC and 51 percent of the stories on ABC. CBS also devoted considerably more time to Republican stories with Republican sources than did the other two networks.

Considerably more attribution was given to Democratic sources about Democratic partisan affairs, however. About 71 percent of the Democratic stories on CBS cited at least one Democratic source, and 66 percent of these stories on NBC and 71 percent on ABC named Democratic sources. Indeed, it was surprising that *even more* stories *failed* to cite at least one source appropriately partisan (i.e., Democratic sources for Democratic stories and Republican sources for Republican stories). The Democrats appeared to enjoy a decisive edge in terms of the extent to which they were consulted as sources about partisan affairs.

At least one Republican source was likely to be named in stories about social welfare, agriculture and natural resources, race and civil liberties, Vietnam, national defense, and the functioning of government. Democratic sources were also cited on these matters, but generally less time was devoted to stories that were attributed to Democratic sources. It must be noted, however, that very little time was devoted to these non-party, non-candidate stories during the campaign. Republican sources were cited on matters of social welfare, Vietnam, and the economy on CBS, Vietnam and foreign affairs on NBC and ABC, and government functioning on all three of the networks in news to which ten minutes or more during the seventeen-

## TABLE 15

### Percentages of Stories and Time Devoted to Issue Coverage That Cited Republican and Democratic Party Sources by Issue Area, Party, and Network

**CBS**

| Problem Area | Other % | Other Time | Republican % | Republican Time | N | Other % | Other Time | Democrat % | Democrat Time | N |
|---|---|---|---|---|---|---|---|---|---|---|
| Social welfare | 86.5 | 30.2 | 13.5 | 19.3 | 37 | 86.5 | 44.9 | 13.5 | 7.6 | 37 |
| Agriculture, natural resources | 87.5 | 46.2 | 12.5 | 2.7 | 40 | 97.5 | 60.3 | 2.5 | 2.4 | 40 |
| Labor-management | 100.0 | 13.0 | 0.0 | 0.0 | 14 | 100.0 | 13.3 | 0.0 | 0.0 | 14 |
| Race, civil liberties | 90.7 | 44.5 | 9.3 | 3.8 | 54 | 92.6 | 42.7 | 7.4 | 4.4 | 54 |
| Law and order | 95.5 | 132.7 | 4.5 | 6.0 | 110 | 96.4 | 117.0 | 3.6 | 7.5 | 110 |
| Economic, business | 97.2 | 97.3 | 2.8 | 10.4 | 176 | 97.7 | 93.9 | 2.3 | 9.1 | 176 |
| Vietnam | 95.3 | 283.2 | 4.7 | 21.9 | 236 | 97.9 | 277.1 | 2.1 | 12.4 | 236 |
| Foreign affairs | 99.4 | 164.9 | 0.6 | 0.6 | 161 | 98.8 | 168.9 | 1.2 | 0.9 | 161 |
| National defense | 91.5 | 34.3 | 8.5 | 4.9 | 47 | 97.9 | 33.3 | 2.1 | 0.8 | 47 |
| Government functioning | 87.3 | 76.7 | 12.7 | 29.6 | 79 | 79.7 | 71.4 | 20.3 | 37.0 | 79 |
| Republican party affairs | 39.8 | 106.4 | 60.2 | 210.3 | 191 | 89.5 | 276.7 | 10.5 | 39.6 | 191 |
| Democratic party affairs | 90.7 | 335.2 | 9.3 | 52.4 | 225 | 28.9 | 78.1 | 71.1 | 287.6 | 225 |
| Other | 96.6 | 26.9 | 3.4 | 2.8 | 29 | 96.6 | 26.6 | 3.4 | 0.3 | 29 |
| Total | 86.6 | 1,391.5 | 13.4 | 364.8 | 1,399 | 84.1 | 1,304.2 | 15.9 | 428.5 | 1,399 |

**NBC**

| Problem Area | Other % | Other Time | Republican % | Republican Time | N | Other % | Other Time | Democrat % | Democrat Time | N |
|---|---|---|---|---|---|---|---|---|---|---|
| Social welfare | 91.7 | 22.9 | 8.3 | 4.7 | 36 | 100.0 | 27.5 | 0.0 | 0.0 | 36 |
| Agriculture, natural resources | 94.7 | 32.5 | 5.3 | 5.8 | 38 | 97.4 | 35.6 | 2.6 | 2.5 | 37 |
| Labor-management | 100.0 | 20.4 | 0.0 | 0.0 | 18 | 94.4 | 18.5 | 5.6 | 1.9 | 18 |
| Race, civil liberties | 96.2 | 41.5 | 3.8 | 2.9 | 52 | 96.2 | 41.3 | 3.8 | 3.1 | 52 |
| Law and order | 99.2 | 121.5 | 0.8 | 5.8 | 122 | 98.4 | 123.3 | 1.6 | 3.9 | 118 |
| Economic, business | 98.9 | 119.2 | 1.1 | 4.4 | 182 | 98.4 | 118.9 | 1.6 | 4.7 | 181 |
| Vietnam | 98.3 | 325.5 | 1.7 | 10.6 | 303 | 99.3 | 335.6 | 0.7 | 0.5 | 298 |
| Foreign affairs | 97.5 | 221.9 | 2.5 | 11.1 | 242 | 99.6 | 232.0 | 0.4 | 1.0 | 232 |
| National defense | 96.1 | 38.5 | 3.9 | 2.8 | 51 | 98.0 | 39.5 | 2.0 | 1.9 | 49 |
| Government functioning | 77.0 | 46.1 | 23.0 | 18.2 | 61 | 91.8 | 56.8 | 8.2 | 7.5 | 61 |
| Republican party affairs | 50.8 | 100.4 | 49.2 | 180.8 | 193 | 91.2 | 249.8 | 8.8 | 31.4 | 187 |
| Democratic party affairs | 91.9 | 323.7 | 8.1 | 41.9 | 223 | 34.1 | 88.3 | 65.9 | 277.3 | 218 |
| Other | 97.7 | 33.6 | 2.3 | 3.4 | 43 | 100.0 | 37.0 | 0.0 | 0.0 | 43 |
| Total | 90.3 | 1,447.7 | 9.7 | 292.3 | 1,564 | 88.4 | | 11.6 | 335.7 | 1,564 |

**ABC**

| Problem Area | Other % | Other Time | Republican % | Republican Time | N | Other % | Other Time | Democrat % | Democrat Time | N |
|---|---|---|---|---|---|---|---|---|---|---|
| Social welfare | 86.5 | 33.4 | 13.5 | 4.5 | 37 | 94.6 | 34.9 | 5.4 | 3.0 | 37 |
| Agriculture, natural resources | 95.8 | 36.8 | 4.2 | 2.8 | 24 | 95.8 | 37.6 | 4.2 | 2.0 | 24 |
| Labor-management | 93.8 | 11.1 | 6.3 | 0.4 | 16 | 100.0 | 11.4 | 0.0 | 0.0 | 16 |
| Race, civil liberties | 94.4 | 42.1 | 5.6 | 2.7 | 36 | 100.0 | 44.8 | 0.0 | 0.0 | 36 |
| Law and order | 98.8 | 96.3 | 1.2 | 0.3 | 86 | 100.0 | 96.6 | 0.0 | 0.0 | 86 |
| Economic, business | 97.5 | 80.4 | 2.5 | 6.9 | 119 | 96.6 | 78.1 | 3.4 | 9.1 | 119 |
| Vietnam | 97.1 | 242.2 | 2.9 | 13.6 | 245 | 98.4 | 248.3 | 1.6 | 7.5 | 245 |
| Foreign affairs | 96.7 | 188.1 | 3.3 | 7.0 | 181 | 99.4 | 192.7 | 0.6 | 2.3 | 181 |
| National defense | 94.6 | 28.3 | 5.4 | 2.7 | 37 | 100.0 | 30.9 | 0.0 | 0.0 | 37 |
| Government functioning | 83.9 | 57.7 | 16.1 | 17.8 | 62 | 83.9 | 61.7 | 16.1 | 14.6 | 62 |
| Republican party affairs | 48.6 | 111.3 | 51.4 | 148.6 | 185 | 92.4 | 230.9 | 7.6 | 26.8 | 185 |
| Democratic party affairs | 88.8 | 370.4 | 11.2 | 67.9 | 277 | 28.9 | 100.5 | 71.1 | 318.9 | 277 |
| Other | 100.0 | 18.9 | 0.0 | 0.0 | 24 | 95.8 | 16.3 | 4.2 | 2.6 | 24 |
| Total | 87.7 | 1,317.0 | 12.3 | 275.1 | 1,329 | 82.4 | | 17.6 | 407.2 | 1,329 |

week campaign was devoted. Democratic sources were named in stories consuming more than ten minutes on even fewer issues. On CBS these stories included Vietnam and government functioning; on ABC they concerned only government functioning. None of the nonpartisan issue areas received as much as ten minutes of coverage on NBC including at least one Democratic source.

### Juxtaposition of Sources in Issue Coverage

CBS issue coverage included the least supporting and the most opposing juxtaposition of information sources. NBC and ABC each included about the same amount of supporting juxtaposition of informational sources, and NBC provided slightly more opposing juxtaposition of informational sources than ABC. ABC provided the least neutral juxtaposition, although differences among networks were very slight in this regard. In general, the networks provided some conflicting points of view in their coverage of issue stories, but each network was more likely to provide information from several sources that were mutually reinforcing or that otherwise failed to contradict one another explicitly. CBS was more critical in its approach to issue stories during the campaign than was NBC or ABC, but differences were small in this regard (see table 16).

More than half of all the issue stories about the major parties, race and civil liberties problems (except on ABC), and foreign affairs included supporting juxtaposition of sources on each network.

More than half of the stories about labor-management and government functioning on NBC included opposing juxtaposition. There were no issue areas in ABC or CBS coverage that included opposing juxtaposition of sources in as many as half of the stories.

At least thirty minutes of coverage was devoted to stories that included opposing juxtaposition about natural resources, law and order, Vietnam, foreign affairs, government functioning, and partisan matters on CBS. Comparable coverage was given to issue stories about law and order, Vietnam, and partisan affairs on NBC, and to Vietnam and partisan affairs on ABC. It was thus evident that CBS provided the most consistent conflict in terms of information about issues.

ABC, in contrast, was more likely than the other networks to provide issue coverage that included supporting juxtaposition. That network gave more than thirty minutes of coverage that included supporting juxtaposition to law and order, the economy, Vietnam, foreign affairs, and major-party matters. Comparable coverage was given to the economy, Vietnam, foreign affairs, and partisan matters on NBC and CBS. Such coverage was also given to law and order on CBS.

Each of the major parties received issue coverage that included more supporting than opposing juxtaposition of informational sources. The Democrats, however, received far more supporting-

TABLE 16

PERCENTAGES OF STORIES AND TIME DEVOTED TO ISSUE COVERAGE THAT INCLUDED
SOURCES PRESENTED AS SUPPORTING, NEITHER SUPPORTING NOR OPPOSING,
AND OPPOSING BY ISSUE AREA AND NETWORK

| Problem Area | SUPPORTING | | NEUTRAL | | OPPOSING | | N |
|---|---|---|---|---|---|---|---|
| | % | Time | % | Time | % | Time | |
| CBS | | | | | | | |
| Social welfare | 30.8 | 4.4 | 23.1 | 3.1 | 46.2 | 27.6 | 13 |
| Agriculture, natural resources | 45.0 | 8.0 | 15.0 | 4.1 | 40.0 | 25.7 | 20 |
| Labor-management | 0.0 | 0.0 | 80.0 | 3.7 | 20.0 | 5.3 | 5 |
| Race, civil liberties | 56.3 | 18.7 | 0.0 | 0.0 | 43.8 | 8.4 | 16 |
| Law and order | 52.3 | 36.1 | 15.9 | 10.2 | 31.8 | 42.0 | 44 |
| Economic, business | 53.3 | 30.1 | 15.6 | 5.5 | 31.1 | 19.2 | 45 |
| Vietnam | 41.1 | 88.6 | 19.6 | 21.4 | 39.3 | 89.0 | 112 |
| Foreign affairs | 55.9 | 43.3 | 11.9 | 8.2 | 32.2 | 42.5 | 59 |
| National defense | 41.2 | 6.8 | 11.8 | 1.0 | 47.1 | 11.9 | 17 |
| Government functioning | 31.4 | 11.4 | 22.9 | 10.7 | 45.7 | 41.5 | 35 |
| Republican party affairs | 51.9 | 99.8 | 17.0 | 30.8 | 31.1 | 92.1 | 106 |
| Democratic party affairs | 62.7 | 142.2 | 9.5 | 26.2 | 27.8 | 105.5 | 126 |
| Other | 28.6 | 4.4 | 42.9 | 1.4 | 28.6 | 1.0 | 7 |
| Total | 49.9 | 493.8 | 15.9 | 126.2 | 34.2 | 511.8 | 605 |
| NBC | | | | | | | |
| Social welfare | 77.8 | 10.5 | 11.1 | 0.3 | 11.1 | 2.1 | 9 |
| Agriculture, natural resources | 50.0 | 7.9 | 30.0 | 4.8 | 20.0 | 5.6 | 10 |
| Labor-management | 37.5 | 6.3 | 0.0 | 0.0 | 62.5 | 10.1 | 8 |
| Race, civil liberties | 60.0 | 13.6 | 13.3 | 2.8 | 26.7 | 11.2 | 15 |
| Law and order | 35.3 | 23.0 | 20.6 | 7.9 | 44.1 | 38.0 | 34 |
| Economic, business | 51.3 | 34.5 | 23.1 | 11.0 | 25.6 | 15.2 | 39 |
| Vietnam | 44.3 | 68.6 | 28.9 | 39.8 | 26.8 | 73.8 | 97 |
| Foreign affairs | 62.7 | 85.0 | 16.9 | 8.8 | 20.5 | 29.9 | 83 |
| National defense | 55.0 | 13.4 | 10.0 | 0.6 | 35.0 | 12.7 | 20 |
| Government functioning | 36.4 | 11.0 | 9.1 | 3.3 | 54.5 | 22.4 | 22 |
| Republican party affairs | 53.5 | 76.3 | 15.5 | 25.6 | 31.0 | 49.1 | 71 |
| Democratic party affairs | 60.5 | 151.2 | 10.9 | 23.7 | 28.6 | 78.8 | 119 |
| Other | 72.7 | 13.4 | 9.1 | 2.4 | 18.2 | 2.4 | 11 |
| Total | 53.5 | 514.9 | 17.3 | 131.1 | 29.2 | 351.4 | 538 |
| ABC | | | | | | | |
| Social welfare | 35.7 | 7.8 | 28.6 | 1.8 | 35.7 | 14.9 | 14 |
| Agriculture, natural resources | 53.3 | 15.9 | 0.0 | 0.0 | 46.7 | 11.8 | 15 |
| Labor-management | 66.7 | 5.3 | 33.3 | 2.0 | 0.0 | 0.0 | 6 |
| Race, civil liberties | 42.9 | 14.8 | 14.3 | 2.7 | 42.9 | 13.1 | 14 |
| Law and order | 60.7 | 31.4 | 21.4 | 6.8 | 17.9 | 10.9 | 28 |
| Economic, business | 62.5 | 32.6 | 10.0 | 3.4 | 27.5 | 22.4 | 40 |
| Vietnam | 42.5 | 49.1 | 20.7 | 19.2 | 36.8 | 78.6 | 87 |
| Foreign affairs | 55.6 | 55.9 | 19.0 | 9.7 | 25.4 | 18.8 | 63 |
| National defense | 45.5 | 7.8 | 27.3 | 1.7 | 27.3 | 4.1 | 11 |
| Government functioning | 40.0 | 17.1 | 20.0 | 9.9 | 40.0 | 18.5 | 25 |
| Republican party affairs | 57.6 | 88.7 | 10.9 | 15.4 | 31.5 | 62.0 | 92 |
| Democratic party affairs | 60.3 | 185.2 | 10.9 | 31.5 | 28.8 | 90.5 | 156 |
| Other | 80.0 | 8.3 | 20.0 | 0.5 | 0.0 | 0.0 | 5 |
| Total | 54.5 | 520.0 | 15.1 | 104.5 | 30.4 | 345.7 | 556 |

source juxtaposition on each network than the Republicans. It was also true that they received more coverage that included opposing juxtaposition than the GOP, but these differences were considerably smaller than the discrepancies in supporting juxtaposition.

CONCLUSION

Party politics, understandably enough, comprised the most frequently discussed issue area in American network news coverage during the 1972 presidential election campaign. Distinctly partisan issues, moreover, were found to receive both absolute emphasis and relative emphasis in comparison with coverage of other issue areas during the campaign.

Vietnam, the economy, and government functioning also received more coverage than other issues. Trends in issue coverage were remarkably parallel in the way that issues were emphasized by each of the networks, although complex patterns of issue coverage emerged once more specific issues were isolated for analysis.

Bad news drove out good news. The major networks must plead guilty to the charge that they presented more "negative" than "positive" coverage of news stories. Much more coverage of issue areas was unfavorable than favorable in its implications for the particular issue, for the administration, and for the parties and the candidates.

But findings also stressed two points: first, most coverage cannot be clearly classified as being favorable or unfavorable; second, the networks followed parallel patterns in the presentation of issue content. If more unfavorable than favorable and more neutral than unfavorable story content was presented in issue coverage, then the networks all tended to follow the same general pattern. This suggests that any overall negative, neutral, or favorable orientation implied by the analysis had more to do with structural bias than with political bias. But these observations were at a highly general level in the sense that they referred to styles of issue coverage without regard to particular differences and nuances in the way that particular issues may be presented.

CBS was most critical and also included the greatest amount of variation in the way it covered issue stories when compared with NBC and ABC. CBS was much more critical in its coverage of the functioning of government and of issues relating to the Republican party and campaign, two issue areas that related to problems surrounding Watergate. CBS also presented more variation in sources of information and the perspectives that these sources presented in the sense that CBS more frequently provided conflicting information in its stories about issues. Thus CBS employed a "negative" style of coverage, and employed it more in stories about Republicans than about Democrats.

ABC included more crowds and pictures in its coverage of all the issue areas than the other networks, and NBC was rather bland in its coverage of issues during the campaign. Some basis for allegations of bias may exist in the way that the networks covered partisan issues. CBS was more unfavorable and less favorable to the Republicans than the other networks; it was also less unfavorable and more neutral in its coverage of the Democrats than either NBC or ABC. These partisan implications coincided with the generally more acerbic coverage that CBS devoted to other specific issue areas as well.

But having demonstrated what appears to be a modicum of bias in CBS coverage of issues, we find it imperative to place the findings in perspective and to consider what alternative and plausible explanations might account for this coverage. Clearly, we are dealing with *trends* in coverage that are not starkly different among networks. We would be well advised, therefore, not to exaggerate the differences that existed among the networks and the amount of partisan bias suggested by these differences. To the extent that the negative flavor of CBS issue coverage emerged from issues related to government functioning and Republican party policies, for instance, the negativism may be influenced by greater coverage and general attention devoted to Watergate by CBS than by the other networks.

* Detailed statistical tabulations are available from the author upon request.

1. A large body of literature could be cited in this regard. Particularly important is Philip E. Converse, "Information Flow and the Stability of Partisan Attitudes," in Campbell et al., eds., *Elections and the Political Order*, pp. 136-57; Edward C. Dreyer, "Media Use and Electoral Choices: Some Political Consequences of Information Exposure," *Public Opinion Quarterly* 35 (Winter 1971-72): 544-53; Gerald Pomper, Richard Boyd, and John Kessel, articles and comments in *American Political Science Review* 66 (June 1972): 416-70; Harold Mendelsohn and Irving Crespi, *Polls, Television, and the New Politics* (Scranton: Chandler, 1970); Benjamin D. Singer, "Mass Media and Communications Processes in the Detroit Riot of 1967," *Public Opinion Quarterly* 34 (1970): 236-345; Ulf Himmelstrand, *Social Pressures, Attitudes, and Democratic Processes* (Stockholm: Almquist and Wiksell, 1960); and Hinckley et al., "Information and Voting."

2. In particular, see J. McGinniss, *The Selling of the President, 1968* (New York: Simon and Schuster, 1970); Lang and Lang, *Politics and Television*; Michael Jay Robinson, "Public Affairs Television and the Growth of Political Malaise: The Case of 'The Selling of the Pentagon,'" Ph.D. diss. (University of Michigan, 1972), especially pp. 49-82, 140-86; McCombs and Shaw, "The Agenda-Setting Function of Mass Media."

3. B. Roper, *A Ten-Year View of Public Attitudes toward Television*; and more recently, *A Survey of Public Attitudes*, part 1.

4. For example, see Efron, *The News Twisters*; and Robert Cirino, *Don't Blame the People* (Los Angeles: Diversity Press, 1971), for statements of these respective positions.

5. A more complete explication of coding rules and conventions is presented in Judge and Hofstetter, *Content Analysis of Taped Television Stories*.

6. Campbell et al., *The American Voter*.

7. See ibid.; and the second of two reports on this project, *Television and Civic Education: Popular Views, Uses, and Impact of Video News in the 1972 Campaign* (Washington, D.C.: American Enterprise Institute, forthcoming).

8. The reader should reflect on these coding rules *very carefully* lest he misinterpret some aspects of the following analysis. A more complete set of rules and examples is provided in Judge and Hofstetter, *Content Analysis of Taped Television Stories*.

9. See, for instance, Efron, *The News Twisters*.

10. Winnick, "Critique of *The News Twisters*."

# 5. Political Parties in 1972 Campaign Coverage

INTRODUCTION

Political parties serve many functions for individual voters. Among other things, parties form the backbone of American organized politics. Local parties are close to the people both in geography and commonly held partisan positions on important policy questions of the day. Local party organizations, as distinct from candidate campaign organizations, are relatively permanent institutions that try to win power if they are out of office, or try to maintain power in tens of thousands of elective contests.[1] National party organizations assume particular significance during election campaigns.[2]

Perhaps parties play the most important role for individual citizens by serving as a reference group.[3] When asked to state their partisan affiliation, most Americans identify themselves with one of the two major parties or as an "independent." Americans tend to see themselves as "Democrats," or "Republicans," or "independents" in a partisan sense. Indeed, even children see themselves as "little" Democrats, Republicans, or independents.

Available studies suggest that a sense of partisan affiliation is initially acquired early in life. As the child ages, vague, highly affective attitudes assume greater significance and acquire greater support from other kinds of attitudes. Beliefs and values, for instance, tend to become integrated into a miniature political ideology during adolescence and young adulthood.[4]

Regardless of disagreements concerning just how changeable partisan identification is, two conclusions are inescapable. (1) Partisan sentiments are initially formed during childhood and adolescence. The most influential agent in the early acquisition of partisanship is probably the family. In this sense sons are more like their fathers than speculation about youthful rebellion may imply. (2) Partisan sentiments are subject to modification and change as a consequence of new information about political and social life.[5] Changes in partisan sentiment are probably less frequent than modification of partisan views. This is particularly true over the short run because a complete changeabout in one's sense of party affiliation requires changes in a large number of other partisan attitudes as well. Nonetheless, many people do change their partisanship.

Television news relates to individual partisanship by being the most important medium that transmits information about "the Democrats," "the Republicans," and their policies. Beliefs, values, and feelings are doubtlessly affected by treatment of the parties during a campaign. Americans typically have many groups with which they positively or negatively identify; thus the association of these groups with parties is possibly of great significance in the formation of popular images. Television news also informs citizens about the issue positions of parties, and disagreement concerning issues is an important reason for defecting from partisan loyalties.[6]

## PARTY STORIES

Stories that mentioned one or the other of the major parties were classified as having a party emphasis (*in addition* to whatever other emphases were discerned). Each party story was then classified according to which party enjoyed the more prominent emphasis. If the Democratic party was judged to have been emphasized to a greater extent than the Republican party, for instance, then a story would be classified as having a Democratic emphasis. If stories emphasized both parties about the same and if a candidate from one of the parties was also present, then the candidate's party was coded. If stories treated the major parties alike, the first party mentioned was coded. In general, length of coverage, association with a candidate, and position were all assumed to be indicators of emphasis related to impact so that a citizen was more likely to be influenced by what was emphasized more.[7]

Democrats received considerably greater exposure than Republicans during the campaign on each network's evening news programs. On CBS and NBC Democrats were emphasized in about 55 percent of the stories about the major parties. Democrats received an even larger share of the party stories, 63 percent, on ABC. The amount of time devoted to coverage of the major parties paralleled the proportion of stories emphasizing each party. About 422 minutes were devoted to coverage of the Democrats and 353 minutes to coverage of the Republicans on CBS, 376 minutes to coverage of the Democrats and 283 minutes to coverage of the Republicans on NBC, and 461 minutes to coverage of the Democrats and 243 minutes to coverage of the Republicans on ABC. Thus the Democrats appeared to have received an advantage from news coverage in terms of the level of exposure. Yet, caution suggests that attention should be given to more qualitative aspects of this exposure.

*Favorable and Unfavorable Stories about the Parties*

Stories about the parties were coded according to whether they reflected favorably, neutrally, or unfavorably on the Democratic and Republican parties. Stories were judged to be favorable when they associated desirable, fortunate, or otherwise good attributes with a party. Likewise, stories were judged to be unfavorable when undesirable, unfortunate, or otherwise bad items were associated with a party. The extent to which stories were favorable or unfavorable was assessed by judging whether predominantly good or predominantly bad things were associated with each party. Stories that were ambiguous or that contained about the same amount of good and bad associations were classified as neutral. As with most of the codes in this study, coders were instructed to classify questionable stories in a neutral category rather than to risk error by forcing ambiguous stories into a favorable or unfavorable category.

An NBC story illustrates what was considered to have been a favorable story about the Democratic campaign and party. The story portrayed Democratic party candidate George McGovern in front of a friendly audience, and included statements of confidence that the Democrats would win. The story also included assertions by the reporter that a number of Democrats were more conservative than might be assumed, and that this could lead to trouble for the Democrat. The implication was that McGovern would lose votes, and that he was trying to persuade people that he was not a "wild radical" who had taken over the party. In the judgment of coders, the confidence that Democrats would win outweighed doubts about support for McGovern by the allegedly conservative voters in West Virginia.

Another NBC story was coded as unfavorable to the Republican party and campaign because it explicitly tied socially undesirable behavior—physical violence and esoteric forms of spying—to major participants in the Committee to Re-Elect the President. Most of the Watergate coverage was also interpreted in the same vein. Revelations about Watergate, even prior to the 1972 election, were generally unfavorable to Republican aspirations to power.

Between 400 and 450 stories about the parties appeared on weekday evening network news during the campaign, and about 80 percent of these were judged to be neutral with regard to each of the parties. CBS devoted the largest block of time to news about both major parties, and NBC allocated the least time. ABC carried the most stories, and NBC carried the fewest.

Republicans and Democrats received about the same proportion of favorable and unfavorable stories on each network, although stories about Republicans were slightly more likely to be favorable than stories about Democrats. Stories about Republicans were also less likely to be unfavorable than stories about Democrats, at least on NBC and ABC. These differences were, however, negligible (see table 17).

Favorable stories about the Republican party consumed more time on each of the networks than comparable stories about the Democrats, but discrepancies between the parties were least on ABC and greatest on NBC. In contrast, more time was devoted to Republican stories that were unfavorable on CBS (127 minutes) than to Democratic stories that were unfavorable (114 minutes). Time consumed by stories that were unfavorable to the Democratic party was greater on NBC and ABC than by comparable stories about the Republican party. In each instance, however, more time was devoted to unfavorable reports about each party than favorable reports, especially on CBS. The ratio of favorable to unfavorable party coverage was greatest on ABC and least on CBS. Thus CBS coverage might be viewed as being most antagonistic to the parties.

Favorable coverage of both parties increased in terms of both the proportion of stories and the amount of time allotted as the election neared. Unfavorable coverage, however, decreased for the Democrats while it increased for the Republicans. Thus a viewer might have received the impression that the fortunes of the Democratic party were increasing relative to the fortunes of the Republican party. This impression might have offset the slight advantage that the Republicans maintained in overall favorable coverage. Again, great similarities appeared in network profiles of party coverage, and discrepancies were so slight that conclusions supporting assertions of bias can be drawn from these data only in the most tenuous way.

Patterns of partisan advantage polarized slightly when favorable, neutral, and unfavorable implications for parties in stories that emphasize one group over the other were inspected.* Stories about the Republican party were both more favorable and more unfavorable with regard to the Republicans than were stories about the Democratic party. Similarly, stories about the Democratic party were both more favorable and unfavorable about the Democrats than were stories about the Republican party. Many more stories were neutral (presumably being much more difficult to evaluate and less relevant to political parties) with regard to the opposition party

## TABLE 17

Percentages of Stories and Time Devoted to Favorable, Neutral, and Unfavorable Democratic and Republican Party Coverage by Network, Party, and Period in Campaign

| Period in Campaign | Republican Party | | | | | | | Democratic Party | | | | | | |
|---|---|---|---|---|---|---|---|---|---|---|---|---|---|---|
| | Favorable | | Neutral | | Unfavorable | | N | Favorable | | Neutral | | Unfavorable | | N |
| | % | Time | % | Time | % | Time | | % | Time | % | Time | % | Time | |
| **CBS** | | | | | | | | | | | | | | |
| July | 3.1 | 4.1 | 92.7 | 182.0 | 4.2 | 10.5 | 96 | 4.2 | 14.1 | 78.1 | 129.0 | 17.7 | 53.5 | 96 |
| August | 6.3 | 16.7 | 83.6 | 187.9 | 10.2 | 24.4 | 128 | 3.1 | 5.2 | 85.3 | 197.4 | 11.6 | 28.5 | 129 |
| September | 7.9 | 9.9 | 73.7 | 89.6 | 18.4 | 27.6 | 76 | 5.3 | 9.9 | 81.3 | 103.0 | 13.3 | 13.8 | 75 |
| October | 12.8 | 31.3 | 70.7 | 130.0 | 16.5 | 64.0 | 133 | 9.8 | 20.3 | 82.0 | 187.0 | 8.3 | 17.9 | 133 |
| Total | 7.9 | 61.9 | 79.9 | 589.5 | 12.2 | 126.5 | 433 | 5.8 | 49.5 | 82.0 | 616.5 | 12.2 | 113.7 | 433 |
| **NBC** | | | | | | | | | | | | | | |
| July | 3.7 | 3.3 | 93.9 | 144.1 | 2.4 | 13.0 | 82 | 2.4 | 12.8 | 86.6 | 119.1 | 11.0 | 28.6 | 82 |
| August | 10.1 | 21.1 | 79.8 | 161.3 | 10.1 | 17.9 | 119 | 5.1 | 6.8 | 84.7 | 170.7 | 10.2 | 20.6 | 118 |
| September | 9.6 | 11.5 | 75.9 | 90.8 | 14.5 | 21.2 | 83 | 4.8 | 7.7 | 77.1 | 92.4 | 18.1 | 23.5 | 83 |
| October | 13.7 | 30.2 | 73.4 | 115.6 | 12.9 | 30.0 | 124 | 5.6 | 13.6 | 83.9 | 143.9 | 10.5 | 18.3 | 124 |
| Total | 9.3 | 66.2 | 79.9 | 511.9 | 10.3 | 82.1 | 408 | 4.7 | 40.9 | 83.3 | 526.2 | 12.0 | 91.0 | 407 |
| **ABC** | | | | | | | | | | | | | | |
| July | 7.0 | 15.8 | 89.6 | 171.6 | 3.5 | 10.4 | 115 | 6.1 | 21.8 | 75.4 | 136.5 | 18.4 | 37.6 | 114 |
| August | 6.7 | 10.4 | 80.7 | 133.7 | 12.6 | 24.8 | 119 | 5.8 | 12.4 | 79.2 | 136.6 | 15.0 | 23.8 | 120 |
| September | 13.8 | 25.4 | 70.2 | 100.2 | 16.0 | 21.9 | 94 | 3.2 | 5.5 | 84.9 | 117.8 | 11.8 | 22.4 | 93 |
| October | 11.8 | 25.8 | 75.6 | 136.4 | 12.6 | 27.4 | 119 | 10.7 | 32.0 | 78.5 | 134.8 | 10.7 | 27.1 | 121 |
| Total | 9.6 | 77.4 | 79.4 | 541.9 | 11.0 | 84.5 | 447 | 6.7 | 71.8 | 79.2 | 525.8 | 14.1 | 110.9 | 448 |

when party emphasis was not controlled. Differences were doubtless due in part to these trends.

Between 10 and 16 percent of the stories about the Republican party were favorable to the GOP, and 13 to 17 percent were unfavorable. Eight to 10 percent of the stories about the Democratic party were favorable, and 13 to 16 percent were unfavorable. CBS devoted nearly twice as much time to Republican stories that were unfavorable to Republicans than either of the other networks (nearly ninety minutes of unfavorable coverage concerned the Republican party, as opposed to about forty minutes on NBC and ABC). CBS was also more critical in stories about Democrats in which Democrats received unfavorable evaluations, although ABC carried nearly as much time unfavorable to Democrats in such stories. NBC was not too far behind ABC.

### Positive and Negative Evaluation of the Campaigns

Stories about the Nixon and McGovern campaigns were also classified as favorable, unfavorable, or neutral. A story was considered favorable if it portrayed the campaign in a positive light, or if the story portrayed success, increasing support, enthusiasm, or high levels of morale among its partisans. Conversely, a story about the campaign was considered unfavorable if the story portrayed the campaign in unsuccessful or unenthusiastic terms, or if it showed decreasing support or low levels of morale. Stories were considered neutral if unambiguous classifications could not be made, either because stories contained about the same amount of favorable and unfavorable material or because stories contained material that was neither clearly favorable nor unfavorable (see table 18).

The Nixon campaign was viewed more favorably and less unfavorably than the McGovern campaign on each of the major networks. This was true regardless of whether the number of stories or the amount of time was used as an indicator of coverage (except for NBC stories, in which slightly more time was devoted to favorable McGovern campaign stories than to favorable Nixon stories; but this difference was only about eight minutes throughout the entire campaign period). CBS broadcasts committed nearly twice as much time to favorable Nixon campaign coverage than to favorable McGovern campaign coverage. The extent of the Nixon margin over favorable McGovern campaign coverage was less, but still substantial, on ABC.

CBS broadcast the most favorable Nixon coverage, NBC the least favorable; and CBS was also by far the most critical of the Nixon

TABLE 18

Percentages of Stories and Time Devoted to Favorable, Neutral, and Unfavorable Nixon and McGovern Coverage by Network and Period in Campaign

| Period in Campaign | Nixon Campaign | | | | | | | McGovern Campaign | | | | | | |
|---|---|---|---|---|---|---|---|---|---|---|---|---|---|---|
| | Favorable | | Neutral | | Unfavorable | | (N) | Favorable | | Neutral | | Unfavorable | | (N) |
| | % | Time | % | Time | % | Time | | % | Time | % | Time | % | Time | |
| **CBS** | | | | | | | | | | | | | | |
| July | 23.8 | 7.3 | 61.9 | 33.6 | 14.3 | 1.2 | 21 | 13.1 | 19.0 | 65.6 | 96.9 | 21.3 | 31.3 | 61 |
| August | 22.2 | 21.1 | 64.4 | 46.3 | 13.3 | 11.4 | 45 | 14.6 | 8.8 | 58.5 | 49.2 | 26.8 | 24.0 | 41 |
| September | 25.8 | 17.0 | 54.8 | 22.0 | 19.4 | 14.2 | 31 | 10.5 | 8.9 | 68.4 | 41.2 | 21.1 | 12.0 | 38 |
| October | 33.3 | 38.4 | 39.2 | 28.5 | 27.5 | 46.9 | 51 | 13.0 | 9.8 | 57.4 | 45.3 | 29.6 | 25.3 | 54 |
| Total | 27.0 | 83.9 | 53.4 | 130.4 | 19.6 | 73.7 | 148 | 12.9 | 46.5 | 62.4 | 232.6 | 24.7 | 92.8 | 194 |
| **NBC** | | | | | | | | | | | | | | |
| July | 25.0 | 5.1 | 68.8 | 25.4 | 6.3 | 0.6 | 16 | 19.6 | 22.4 | 60.9 | 55.4 | 19.6 | 20.6 | 46 |
| August | 17.6 | 12.1 | 64.7 | 37.8 | 17.6 | 7.4 | 34 | 20.9 | 11.4 | 53.5 | 37.8 | 25.6 | 19.4 | 43 |
| September | 18.2 | 12.2 | 57.6 | 28.4 | 24.2 | 13.6 | 33 | 20.0 | 12.6 | 62.9 | 34.8 | 17.1 | 13.1 | 35 |
| October | 28.1 | 28.3 | 63.2 | 38.3 | 8.8 | 3.7 | 57 | 21.4 | 19.1 | 58.9 | 43.5 | 19.6 | 16.3 | 56 |
| Total | 22.9 | 57.7 | 62.9 | 130.0 | 14.3 | 25.3 | 140 | 20.6 | 65.5 | 58.9 | 171.5 | 20.6 | 69.4 | 180 |
| **ABC** | | | | | | | | | | | | | | |
| July | 47.1 | 13.3 | 41.2 | 11.8 | 11.8 | 4.0 | 17 | 14.0 | 23.2 | 59.3 | 95.9 | 26.7 | 39.4 | 86 |
| August | 41.4 | 17.5 | 55.2 | 23.7 | 3.4 | 2.3 | 29 | 11.6 | 9.4 | 58.1 | 48.3 | 30.2 | 10.0 | 43 |
| September | 36.6 | 26.5 | 53.7 | 37.3 | 9.8 | 8.7 | 41 | 1.9 | 1.9 | 73.6 | 63.5 | 24.5 | 14.2 | 53 |
| October | 22.0 | 19.5 | 60.0 | 37.3 | 18.0 | 21.0 | 50 | 13.2 | 15.6 | 60.4 | 56.1 | 26.4 | 27.8 | 53 |
| Total | 33.6 | 76.8 | 54.7 | 110.0 | 11.7 | 36.0 | 137 | 10.6 | 50.2 | 62.6 | 263.9 | 26.8 | 91.4 | 235 |

campaign. About twice as much favorable as unfavorable time was devoted to coverage of the Nixon campaign effort on NBC and ABC but not on CBS, although the total amount of time consumed by Nixon campaign coverage varied appreciably by network. NBC broadcast the least unfavorable Nixon coverage (and the least total coverage about Nixon campaign stories), and CBS broadcast the most.

NBC broadcasts devoted more time to favorable McGovern stories and less time to unfavorable McGovern stories than the other networks. CBS devoted the most time to unfavorable stories about McGovern (slightly more than ABC). Both CBS and ABC maintained very similar profiles of favorable, neutral, and unfavorable McGovern campaign coverage. NBC deviated from this pattern by portraying the McGovern campaign in a much more favorable light than the other two networks. Nearly as much favorable as unfavorable coverage was given to the McGovern campaign on NBC news, whereas substantially more unfavorable than favorable coverage appeared on the other networks. NBC was also less critical about the Nixon campaign efforts, but was also less favorable about them as well. Clearly, the Nixon campaign maintained some advantage on all three networks.

The networks, with the exception of ABC, tended to depict the Nixon campaign in increasingly favorable terms as the campaign progressed. The proportion of time devoted to unfavorable stories also increased. Little overall change occurred in the amount of coverage devoted to favorable and unfavorable McGovern campaign stories during the same period. McGovern received an initial burst of favorable coverage in July followed by a paucity of favorable coverage. Then his fortunes began to improve. The increase in positive campaign reports was not, however, very substantial. No such dip occurred in coverage of campaign stories that reflected unfavorably on McGovern's campaign efforts.

A similar pattern held when campaign stories about Nixon and McGovern efforts were separated according to the party emphasized in the story.* Republican party stories about the Nixon campaign and Democratic party stories about the McGovern campaign were either favorable or unfavorable to a lesser extent than the stories reported above (with the exception of ABC favorable McGovern coverage). But Republican stories with a Republican party emphasis were considerably more unfavorable than favorable in relation to the McGovern campaign effort. Democratic stories were even more unfavorable than favorable in relation to the Nixon campaign effort. The number of stories was not very large in either case, but

Nixon partisans appeared to have received a clear advantage in the way that implications were drawn in campaign reporting of the respective parties if not of the opposition party.

MODES OF PRESENTATION

The way in which party stories were presented is significant for many of the same reasons that the way in which stories about candidates and issues were presented is significant. The partisan meaning of a story was very likely influenced by the images associated with parties. Stories that included pictures, film, action settings, closeups and flashbacks, large, active, and supportive crowds, supporter enthusiasm, and antagonism to the opposition were presumed to have a greater impact on viewers than stories that did not contain these features. Similarly, stories presented early in a broadcast were assumed to have greater impact than stories appearing later. An attempt was made to gauge the impact of a story on the viewer, given only characteristics of news stories.

*Pictures*

Pictures appeared in over 75 percent of the stories about parties. ABC stories about the major parties most frequently included pictures, and CBS employed pictures in its party coverage least frequently. About 95 percent of the party stories on ABC contained pictures, whereas 77 (Republican stories) to 82 (Democratic stories) percent of the CBS party stories did. Democratic party stories were slightly more likely than Republican party stories to include pictures on each of the networks, although these differences were not as great as the differences among the networks in the use of pictures. The amount of time devoted to stories with pictures paralleled the overall coverage for the two parties. Each of the networks devoted more time to the Democrats than to the Republicans, and this differential was greatest for ABC and least for CBS. Thus there was somewhat greater variation in the time devoted to stories with pictures for the Democratic (455 minutes) and the Republican (233 minutes) parties on ABC than there was in CBS and NBC coverage that included pictures. CBS allotted 381 minutes to the Democrats and 304 minutes to the Republicans, and NBC allotted 353 minutes to the Democrats and 264 minutes to the Republicans when the amount of time devoted to stories with pictures was measured (see table 19).
The propensity for each network to include pictures in coverage of the two major parties increased as the campaign reached a climax,

## TABLE 19

### PERCENTAGES OF STORIES AND TIME DEVOTED TO DEMOCRATIC AND REPUBLICAN PARTY COVERAGE WITH AND WITHOUT PICTURES BY NETWORK AND PERIOD IN CAMPAIGN

| PERIOD IN CAMPAIGN | CBS | | | | | NBC | | | | | ABC | | | | |
|---|---|---|---|---|---|---|---|---|---|---|---|---|---|---|---|
| | Pictures % | Time | No Pictures % | Time | N | Pictures % | Time | No Pictures % | Time | N | Pictures % | Time | No Pictures % | Time | N |
| **Republican Party** | | | | | | | | | | | | | | | |
| July | 77.3 | 25.5 | 22.7 | 4.0 | 22 | 90.0 | 15.5 | 10.0 | 0.6 | 10 | 91.7 | 17.2 | 8.3 | 1.5 | 12 |
| August | 66.5 | 124.9 | 34.5 | 31.8 | 84 | 76.9 | 124.3 | 23.1 | 12.7 | 78 | 88.2 | 91.1 | 11.8 | 8.5 | 68 |
| September | 89.3 | 46.1 | 10.7 | 5.1 | 28 | 93.9 | 43.4 | 6.1 | 0.8 | 33 | 100.0 | 46.8 | 0.0 | 0.0 | 30 |
| October | 86.4 | 106.5 | 13.6 | 8.2 | 59 | 86.2 | 80.3 | 13.8 | 5.2 | 65 | 100.0 | 78.2 | 0.0 | 0.0 | 57 |
| Total | 76.7 | 303.5 | 23.3 | 49.2 | 193 | 83.9 | 263.5 | 16.1 | 19.3 | 186 | 94.6 | 233.3 | 5.4 | 10.0 | 167 |
| **Democratic Party** | | | | | | | | | | | | | | | |
| July | 74.6 | 146.4 | 25.4 | 15.5 | 71 | 81.4 | 125.0 | 18.6 | 16.6 | 70 | 87.1 | 171.1 | 12.9 | 4.5 | 101 |
| August | 80.0 | 63.9 | 20.0 | 10.4 | 45 | 85.4 | 58.4 | 14.6 | 5.0 | 41 | 98.1 | 75.1 | 1.9 | 1.8 | 53 |
| September | 83.3 | 65.9 | 16.7 | 9.9 | 48 | 98.0 | 81.6 | 2.0 | 0.8 | 51 | 100.0 | 98.1 | 0.0 | 0.0 | 63 |
| October | 90.4 | 104.4 | 9.6 | 5.3 | 73 | 100.0 | 88.1 | 0.0 | 0.0 | 58 | 100.0 | 110.1 | 0.0 | 0.0 | 62 |
| Total | 82.3 | 380.7 | 17.7 | 41.0 | 237 | 90.9 | 353.1 | 9.1 | 22.4 | 220 | 95.0 | 454.5 | 5.0 | 6.3 | 279 |

despite the fact that less total time was given to these stories. Table 19 shows that the proportion of stories with pictures increased from 10 to 20 percent on each network, with the exception of a few irregularities in Republican party coverage on CBS and NBC. GOP picture coverage on these two networks dipped, but only slightly, during the last month of the campaign; so that although twice as many stories were broadcast about the Republican party during October-early November as in September, a slightly smaller proportion of them contained pictures.

By far the greatest pictorial exposure was given to each of the parties during the month of their national conventions, when exposure was measured in terms of the total time allotted to each party. The Republicans received 125, 124, and 91 minutes of coverage with pictures in August on CBS, NBC, and ABC, respectively. The Democrats received 146, 125, and 171 minutes of coverage in July on the respective networks.

During campaign periods in which each party received the most coverage, ABC provided the Republican party with less and the Democratic party with more attention. It was also clear that the networks allocated time to stories containing pictures in ways that maximized the drama and excitement arising from national party conventions. Indeed, the amount of attention given to parties surpassed that allotted to them even in the month preceding the election itself.

### Other Visuals

Similar tendencies existed for network coverage of the major parties when the use of film, action settings, closeups, and flashbacks was scrutinized. Democrats received greater exposure in stories with film and action settings than Republicans. The difference was greatest on ABC and least on CBS. Parallel tendencies also occurred in the use of closeups and flashbacks on each network.*

### Positional Emphasis

It was assumed that stories broadcast early in a news program received greater attention by viewers than those broadcast later. Stories about Democrats and Republicans were coded according to whether they occurred within the first five stories of the broadcast or later.[8]

About 40 percent of the CBS stories about Republicans occurred during the first five stories of broadcasts in comparison with 52

121

percent of the CBS stories about the Democrats. On NBC 38 percent of the Republican and 41 percent of the Democratic stories were among the first five stories, and 38 percent of the Republican and 50 percent of the Democratic stories were among the first five on ABC. About twice as much time was devoted to stories about Democrats as to stories about Republicans in this high-emphasis position on ABC and CBS.

The relative size of these discrepancies was also reflected in the amount of time given to the major parties. Although twice as much time was devoted to Democratic as to Republican party stories on ABC and CBS, the discrepancy between parties was considerably smaller on NBC (181 minutes for Democrats compared with 119 minutes for Republicans).

The tendency for Democrats to receive positional emphasis declined during the campaign period on each of the networks. Whereas 73 percent of the July Democratic party stories were among the first five stories on CBS, only 32 percent of October-November Democratic stories were. Comparable declines in story emphasis occurred for the Republicans on each of the networks, although these declines were not as precipitous. One of the reasons for this appeared to be that the Republican party was not nearly as likely as the Democratic party to receive emphasis in stories in the initial period. However, even these patterns may betray the reality of network story emphasis evident in table 20. Time and relative frequency of stories about Republicans that received positional emphasis followed opposite patterns. The larger the percentage of GOP stories emphasized, the less time devoted to them.

The total amount of time devoted to major parties in stories that were emphasized paralleled the number of stories broadcast about each party. More stories and time were devoted to each party during the conventions. Similarly, more stories and time were devoted to the Republican party (if not the Democratic party) closer to the election in October than at any other time, except during the conventions.

Thus it appeared that stories about the Democratic party included more pictures, film, action settings, closeups, and flashbacks than stories about the Republican party. The Democrats also had stories about their party broadcast among the first five stories more often than the Republicans. The Democrats tended to benefit more, however, in stories carried by ABC than in stories carried by the other networks. The differences in the amount of time devoted to stories about each party was even greater than the differences in propor-

## TABLE 20

### Percentages of Stories and Time Devoted to Stories among First Five in Broadcasts and Others in Democratic and Republican Party Coverage by Party, Network, and Period in Campaign

| PERIOD IN CAMPAIGN | CBS | | | | | NBC | | | | | ABC | | | | |
|---|---|---|---|---|---|---|---|---|---|---|---|---|---|---|---|
| | First | | Last | | N | First | | Last | | N | First | | Last | | N |
| | % | Time | % | Time | | % | Time | % | Time | | % | Time | % | Time | |
| **Republican Party** | | | | | | | | | | | | | | | |
| July | 40.9 | 9.0 | 59.1 | 20.5 | 22 | 50.0 | 7.3 | 50.0 | 8.9 | 10 | 33.3 | 4.9 | 66.7 | 13.8 | 12 |
| August | 42.9 | 57.9 | 57.1 | 98.8 | 84 | 43.6 | 71.3 | 56.4 | 65.7 | 78 | 48.5 | 53.1 | 51.5 | 46.5 | 68 |
| September | 46.4 | 21.5 | 53.6 | 29.8 | 28 | 27.3 | 15.5 | 72.7 | 28.7 | 33 | 33.3 | 21.9 | 66.7 | 24.8 | 30 |
| October | 32.2 | 34.6 | 67.8 | 80.5 | 59 | 33.8 | 24.8 | 66.2 | 60.7 | 65 | 28.1 | 22.8 | 71.9 | 55.4 | 57 |
| Total | 39.3 | 123.0 | 60.1 | 229.7 | 193 | 37.6 | 118.8 | 62.4 | 164.0 | 186 | 37.7 | 102.8 | 62.3 | 140.5 | 167 |
| **Democratic Party** | | | | | | | | | | | | | | | |
| July | 73.2 | 122.3 | 26.8 | 39.5 | 71 | 67.1 | 103.8 | 32.9 | 37.9 | 70 | 66.3 | 124.9 | 33.7 | 50.8 | 101 |
| August | 60.0 | 44.2 | 40.0 | 30.1 | 45 | 43.9 | 31.8 | 56.1 | 31.6 | 41 | 54.7 | 49.4 | 45.3 | 27.5 | 53 |
| September | 45.8 | 36.0 | 54.2 | 39.8 | 48 | 19.6 | 18.6 | 80.4 | 63.8 | 51 | 33.3 | 27.4 | 66.7 | 70.7 | 63 |
| October | 31.5 | 31.8 | 68.5 | 77.9 | 73 | 25.9 | 27.3 | 74.1 | 60.8 | 58 | 35.5 | 36.1 | 64.5 | 74.1 | 62 |
| Total | 52.3 | 234.3 | 47.7 | 187.4 | 237 | 40.9 | 181.4 | 59.1 | 194.1 | 220 | 49.8 | 237.8 | 50.2 | 223.0 | 279 |

tions of stories. Differences in total time paralleled differences in relative frequency, despite the fact that differences in relative frequency were smaller.

### Context of Party Stories

The way that a party and campaign was portrayed and the images that resulted were influenced in large part by the context associated with a campaign and party effort during an election. Were crowds numerous and large? Were they favorable? Enthusiastic? Highly active? Were campaign representatives shown "giving hell" to the opposition? Did the story suggest that support was increasing or decreasing for the campaign effort?

*Crowd size.* (See table 21.) Stories that contained crowds of 100 or more people were classified as large; stories that portrayed twenty to ninety-nine supporters were classified as medium; and stories that included fewer than twenty supporters (or none) were classified as small.

Large crowds appeared in about one-third of the stories about the Republican party on each network. The proportion of stories about the Democratic party that contained large crowds varied somewhat. Large crowds appeared in about 39 percent of the Democratic party stories on CBS, 29 percent of the stories on NBC, and 31 percent of the stories on ABC. Thus the Republicans received a slight edge on NBC and ABC, and the Democrats received a slight edge on CBS. These differences were, however, very slight.

Approximately the same amount of time was given to stories that showed large crowds associated with Democratic and Republican partisans on NBC, whereas much more time was given to such stories about the Democrats on CBS and ABC. In large part these differences appeared to be due to the greater amount of overall time allocated to stories about Democrats in general. The differences paralleled discrepancies in the number of stories broadcast about each part. Crowds more frequently accompanied stories about each of the parties as the campaign drew to a close. But once again, it was difficult to distinguish differences in the amount of time due to more frequent coverage of the Democrats and differences due to bias in coverage.

*Other contextual attributes.* Stories about the Democratic party were more likely to include highly active crowds than were stories about the Republican party when time was considered. Republicans were most likely to be cast in an active crowd on CBS and least likely to

## TABLE 21

### Percentages of Stories and Time Devoted to Republican and Democratic Party Coverage in Stories with Large, Medium, and Small Crowds by Network and Period in Campaign

| Period in Campaign | CBS | | | | | | | NBC | | | | | | | ABC | | | | | | |
|---|---|---|---|---|---|---|---|---|---|---|---|---|---|---|---|---|---|---|---|---|---|
| | Large | | Medium | | Small | | N | Large | | Medium | | Small | | N | Large | | Medium | | Small | | N |
| | % | Time | % | Time | % | Time | | % | Time | % | Time | % | Time | | % | Time | % | Time | % | Time | |
| **Republican Party** | | | | | | | | | | | | | | | | | | | | | |
| July | 0.0 | 0.0 | 18.2 | 4.3 | 81.8 | 18.8 | 11 | 0.0 | 0.0 | 50.0 | 5.8 | 50.0 | 8.5 | 6 | 16.7 | 2.2 | 33.3 | 4.8 | 50.0 | 4.6 | 6 |
| August | 30.0 | 40.7 | 30.0 | 44.2 | 40.0 | 34.6 | 50 | 30.6 | 42.9 | 26.5 | 36.4 | 42.9 | 37.7 | 49 | 29.4 | 26.7 | 26.5 | 16.1 | 44.1 | 29.8 | 34 |
| September | 31.8 | 12.4 | 22.7 | 13.4 | 45.5 | 19.0 | 22 | 50.0 | 21.3 | 10.0 | 4.0 | 40.0 | 12.6 | 20 | 36.8 | 15.4 | 21.1 | 9.4 | 42.1 | 16.7 | 19 |
| October | 48.9 | 41.3 | 20.0 | 38.4 | 31.1 | 22.8 | 45 | 35.5 | 23.4 | 32.3 | 21.4 | 32.3 | 21.9 | 31 | 45.2 | 26.4 | 22.6 | 16.2 | 32.3 | 23.0 | 31 |
| Total | 34.4 | 94.4 | 24.2 | 100.4 | 41.4 | 95.2 | 128 | 34.0 | 87.7 | 26.4 | 67.6 | 39.6 | 80.7 | 106 | 35.6 | 70.8 | 24.4 | 46.5 | 40.0 | 74.1 | 90 |
| **Democratic Party** | | | | | | | | | | | | | | | | | | | | | |
| July | 12.0 | 26.7 | 28.0 | 43.5 | 60.0 | 71.3 | 50 | 9.5 | 18.3 | 21.4 | 28.4 | 69.0 | 58.6 | 42 | 6.8 | 10.8 | 35.6 | 51.9 | 57.6 | 77.1 | 59 |
| August | 35.5 | 25.3 | 29.0 | 16.4 | 35.5 | 20.2 | 31 | 10.7 | 8.6 | 46.4 | 25.0 | 42.9 | 19.7 | 28 | 31.0 | 24.0 | 31.0 | 18.1 | 37.9 | 20.8 | 29 |
| September | 36.7 | 27.7 | 26.7 | 16.5 | 36.7 | 17.7 | 30 | 36.8 | 30.5 | 31.6 | 25.2 | 31.6 | 17.7 | 38 | 36.1 | 30.4 | 30.6 | 28.2 | 33.3 | 27.1 | 36 |
| October | 64.9 | 66.0 | 15.8 | 18.7 | 19.3 | 13.0 | 57 | 51.2 | 45.3 | 23.3 | 19.0 | 25.6 | 16.3 | 43 | 54.0 | 57.8 | 28.0 | 28.9 | 18.0 | 16.9 | 50 |
| Total | 38.7 | 145.7 | 23.8 | 95.2 | 37.5 | 122.2 | 168 | 28.5 | 102.8 | 29.1 | 97.6 | 42.4 | 112.3 | 151 | 30.5 | 123.1 | 31.6 | 127.0 | 37.9 | 141.8 | 174 |

appear in this context on ABC. Stories about the Democratic party were most likely to include highly active crowds on ABC and least likely to on NBC. Discrepancies in treatment were least on CBS and NBC and greatest on ABC.

Democratic party stories were more likely to include enthusiastic supporters than Republican party stories when time was used as an indicator. Partisan differences diminished, however, when the proportion of stories including enthusiastic supporters was scrutinized. Overall patterns of change in supporter enthusiasm proved to be irregular for each party during the campaign.

Antagonism to the opposition was also much more apparent in stories about the Democratic party than in stories about the Republican party. These differences paralleled differences in supporter enthusiasm that appeared in major-party stories, although differences in antagonism to the opposition were considerably greater in magnitude than differences in enthusiasm.*

Thus Democrats appeared to receive some advantage in portraits of crowd activity, enthusiasm, and antagonism to the opposition. The advantages, moreover, appeared to be slightly greater on ABC, although patterns were parallel in all cases. It was a simple matter to assume that differences in party campaign strategies could well account for these patterns.

*Crowd favorability.* Stories about the major parties and campaign organizations were also classified according to whether crowds in the stories were favorable or not. A story was classified as including a favorable crowd when crowds in the pictures performed activities predominantly favorable to the campaign. Favorable types of activities included applause, acclaimation, milling about a candidate or his representative in a supportive way, and other activities clearly construed as supportive to the campaign.

Stories that could not be clearly classified in a favorable way were included in a "not favorable" classification. It is important to note that this category included stories that are neutral or ambiguous with respect to crowd favorability about the campaign as well as stories that were clearly unfavorable to the campaign efforts of the parties.

Crowds were more frequently favorable in stories about Republican party efforts than in stories about Democratic party efforts.* On CBS about 71 percent of the stories about the Republican party, in comparison with 62 percent of the stories about the Democratic party, included predominantly favorable crowds. On NBC 74 percent of the stories about the Republican party, in comparison with 66 percent of the stories about the Democratic party, contained favorable crowds, and 69 percent of the Republican stories and 60 percent of the Democratic stories on ABC showed predominantly favorable crowds. These differences, however, masked discrepancies between the parties, since approximately twice as much *time* was devoted to stories that included crowds predominantly favorable to Democrats.

Finally, as the election approached, stories about Democrats increasingly showed crowds that were favorable, and stories about Republicans decreasingly showed favorable crowds. Although some variation occurred in this pattern, when time rather than relative frequency devoted to favorable crowd reactions was considered, the same general pattern emerged. The Democrats were portrayed in more favorable crowd contexts than were the Republicans, and the disparities increased rather then decreased as the campaign drew to a close.

*Shifts in support for the campaigns.* Each story about the campaign was coded according to whether it showed support declining, increasing, or staying at the same level (see table 22). Stories that emphasized growing support, success, attainment of a goal, and addition of particular groups to the party's coalition were coded as indicating increasing support. The opposite pattern—declining support, failure to meet a goal, confusion or disarray, loss of a group to the opposition—were considered to indicate decreasing support. Stories that could not be classified clearly were considered neutral.

Many stories could also be classified in terms of both the Democratic and Republican parties, depending on whether the stories referred explicitly to support levels for each campaign. A story about success of the Democrats might be classified as a failure for the Republicans, for instance, if it showed that the Democrats had won away some key GOP groups. But the same story could also be classified as neutral with regard to the Republicans if no explicit mention was made of the Republicans or if implications were ambiguous. In general, neither gains nor losses by one side were necessarily considered to be losses or gains by the other side unless explicitly noted.

Stories about the parties and campaigns indicated that the Democrats were shown as increasing their support slightly more frequently than the Republicans on CBS and NBC, whereas the Republicans were slightly favored on ABC. The differences were slight and, for

127

## TABLE 22

### PERCENTAGES OF STORIES AND TIME DEVOTED TO INCREASING, NO CHANGE, AND DECREASING SUPPORT FOR NIXON AND MCGOVERN CAMPAIGNS IN CANDIDATE AND PARTY COVERAGE BY CANDIDATE AND PERIOD IN CAMPAIGN

| PERIOD IN CAMPAIGN | STORIES ABOUT DEMOCRATIC PARTY AND CAMPAIGN | | | | | | | STORIES ABOUT REPUBLICAN PARTY AND CAMPAIGN | | | | | | |
|---|---|---|---|---|---|---|---|---|---|---|---|---|---|---|
| | Increasing % | Time | No Change % | Time | Decreasing % | Time | (N) | Increasing % | Time | No Change % | Time | Decreasing % | Time | (N) |
| **CBS** | | | | | | | | | | | | | | |
| July | 2.5 | 2.6 | 91.7 | 189.1 | 5.8 | 15.5 | 120 | 1.6 | 1.7 | 98.4 | 215.6 | 0.0 | 0.0 | 125 |
| August | 4.6 | 12.4 | 94.0 | 233.6 | 1.3 | 6.7 | 151 | 2.0 | 7.0 | 98.0 | 245.7 | 0.0 | 0.0 | 151 |
| September | 4.3 | 3.7 | 89.4 | 123.3 | 6.4 | 13.7 | 94 | 7.2 | 9.4 | 91.8 | 136.3 | 1.0 | 0.4 | 97 |
| October | 4.4 | 13.1 | 92.2 | 269.3 | 3.3 | 11.5 | 180 | 3.3 | 12.5 | 93.9 | 274.6 | 2.8 | 6.8 | 180 |
| Total | 4.0 | 31.8 | 92.1 | 815.3 | 3.9 | 47.4 | 545 | 3.3 | 30.6 | 95.7 | 872.2 | 1.1 | 7.2 | 553 |
| **NBC** | | | | | | | | | | | | | | |
| July | 9.8 | 22.4 | 82.4 | 140.1 | 7.8 | 15.8 | 102 | 2.9 | 4.8 | 97.1 | 176.5 | 0.0 | 0.0 | 105 |
| August | 7.6 | 15.4 | 90.3 | 214.5 | 2.1 | 6.3 | 145 | 2.1 | 3.4 | 97.9 | 230.0 | 0.0 | 0.0 | 144 |
| September | 3.8 | 7.0 | 91.3 | 131.3 | 4.8 | 6.4 | 104 | 5.8 | 9.2 | 93.3 | 133.6 | 1.0 | 1.9 | 104 |
| October | 6.2 | 17.8 | 90.7 | 195.2 | 3.1 | 7.1 | 161 | 4.3 | 11.5 | 92.5 | 198.3 | 3.1 | 9.8 | 161 |
| Total | 6.8 | 62.7 | 89.1 | 681.1 | 4.1 | 35.5 | 512 | 3.7 | 28.9 | 95.1 | 738.4 | 1.2 | 11.7 | 514 |
| **ABC** | | | | | | | | | | | | | | |
| July | 4.3 | 11.7 | 88.4 | 195.0 | 7.2 | 15.5 | 138 | 2.9 | 6.8 | 97.1 | 222.5 | 0.0 | 0.0 | 140 |
| August | 5.7 | 13.3 | 92.1 | 170.1 | 2.1 | 6.7 | 140 | 2.9 | 9.1 | 97.1 | 181.1 | 0.0 | 0.0 | 140 |
| September | 3.6 | 3.2 | 87.4 | 144.6 | 9.0 | 16.9 | 111 | 10.6 | 23.0 | 87.6 | 144.2 | 1.8 | 3.3 | 113 |
| October | 3.0 | 6.9 | 93.9 | 224.8 | 3.0 | 9.6 | 164 | 2.5 | 6.4 | 96.3 | 231.1 | 1.2 | 3.3 | 163 |
| Total | 4.2 | 35.2 | 90.8 | 734.5 | 5.1 | 48.7 | 553 | 4.3 | 45.3 | 95.0 | 778.8 | 0.7 | 6.6 | 556 |

TABLE 22 (Continued)

| PERIOD IN CAMPAIGN | STORIES ABOUT McGOVERN | | | | | | | STORIES ABOUT NIXON | | | | | | |
|---|---|---|---|---|---|---|---|---|---|---|---|---|---|---|
| | Increasing % | Time | No Change % | Time | Decreasing % | Time | (N) | Increasing % | Time | No Change % | Time | Decreasing % | Time | (N) |
| **CBS** | | | | | | | | | | | | | | |
| July | 3.1 | 2.4 | 87.7 | 136.2 | 9.2 | 12.8 | 65 | 4.8 | 0.3 | 95.2 | 26.7 | 0.0 | 0.0 | 21 |
| August | 13.3 | 12.1 | 84.4 | 58.0 | 2.2 | 4.2 | 45 | 1.2 | 2.6 | 98.8 | 154.2 | 0.0 | 0.0 | 84 |
| September | 2.2 | 2.8 | 84.8 | 55.7 | 13.0 | 13.7 | 46 | 7.1 | 1.9 | 92.9 | 49.3 | 0.0 | 0.0 | 28 |
| October | 7.0 | 11.4 | 88.7 | 91.0 | 4.2 | 5.7 | 71 | 3.5 | 3.0 | 94.7 | 108.4 | 1.8 | 0.5 | 57 |
| Total | 6.2 | 28.8 | 86.8 | 340.9 | 7.0 | 36.3 | 227 | 3.2 | 7.8 | 96.3 | 338.6 | 0.5 | 0.5 | 190 |
| **NBC** | | | | | | | | | | | | | | |
| July | 10.4 | 21.0 | 80.6 | 104.9 | 9.0 | 12.8 | 67 | 11.1 | 2.2 | 88.9 | 10.8 | 0.0 | 0.0 | 9 |
| August | 24.4 | 13.3 | 73.2 | 47.3 | 2.4 | 2.9 | 41 | 1.3 | 0.4 | 98.7 | 133.7 | 0.0 | 0.0 | 77 |
| September | 6.0 | 5.1 | 86.0 | 68.4 | 8.0 | 6.2 | 50 | 6.1 | 2.4 | 93.9 | 41.8 | 0.0 | 0.0 | 33 |
| October | 12.5 | 16.9 | 83.9 | 66.8 | 3.6 | 2.4 | 56 | 6.3 | 9.0 | 92.2 | 72.9 | 1.6 | 1.5 | 64 |
| Total | 12.6 | 56.3 | 81.3 | 287.4 | 6.1 | 24.3 | 214 | 4.4 | 14.0 | 95.1 | 259.2 | 0.5 | 1.5 | 183 |
| **ABC** | | | | | | | | | | | | | | |
| July | 3.0 | 6.3 | 88.9 | 150.1 | 8.1 | 12.2 | 99 | 18.2 | 4.8 | 81.8 | 11.7 | 0.0 | 0.0 | 11 |
| August | 11.3 | 11.3 | 84.9 | 62.5 | 3.8 | 3.1 | 53 | 1.5 | 3.6 | 98.5 | 94.3 | 0.0 | 0.0 | 67 |
| September | 4.9 | 2.8 | 85.2 | 74.6 | 9.8 | 14.8 | 61 | 17.2 | 6.3 | 82.8 | 37.9 | 0.0 | 0.0 | 29 |
| October | 3.3 | 2.1 | 90.2 | 96.5 | 6.6 | 9.3 | 61 | 0.0 | 0.0 | 100.0 | 72.2 | 0.0 | 0.0 | 53 |
| Total | 5.1 | 22.6 | 87.6 | 383.7 | 7.3 | 39.4 | 274 | 5.0 | 14.6 | 95.0 | 216.2 | 0.0 | 0.0 | 160 |

all practical purposes, inconsequential. The Democrats, however, were consistently viewed as losing support more frequently than the Republicans. Republican efforts appeared to be maintaining support in about 95 percent of all the stories about the campaign, whereas an ebb and flow of support was somewhat more commonly portrayed for the Democratic campaign.

More time was devoted to stories on ABC that portrayed Republicans increasing in support, and more time was devoted on NBC and CBS to Democratic successes in gaining support, although partisan differences were very small in this regard on CBS. In sharp contrast, the amount of time devoted to showing Democrats losing support ranged from three times that showing Republicans in comparable situations on NBC to about eight times that for Republicans on ABC. CBS devoted about seven minutes to stories that showed the Republicans losing support in comparison with forty-seven minutes that showed the Democrats losing support.

In absolute terms a decreasing amount of time was devoted to stories that showed the Democratic party losing support as the election approached, and an increasing amount of time was given to stories that showed the Republicans both losing and gaining support. Patterns were, however, irregular because not many stories were classified as indicating clearcut gains or losses for either side. Except on ABC, the Democratic presidential hopeful was portrayed as either holding his own or gaining support. It would appear, however, that network news coverage of the erosion of Democratic support—increasing as the campaign's end approached—outweighed the erosion of Repubican support because more total time was devoted to these stories. ABC portrayed Republican support in the most positive vein; NBC portrayed Democratic support in the most positive vein; and CBS fell somewhere in between.

If one scrutinized stories emphasizing either McGovern or Nixon, a somewhat different pattern emerged.* Stories about McGovern on CBS showed both more increasing and declining support during the campaign, and McGovern stories on NBC and ABC showed decreasing support as the campaign reached a climax. In contrast, stories about Nixon showed increasing support as the campaign progressed. Very few stories appeared that indicated a shift away from the Nixon campaign. Indeed, ABC did not broadcast a single story that emphasized Nixon and that showed a shift away from him in support. (On CBS, only one minute was devoted to two stories showing a shift in support away from the Nixon camp, whereas five and one-half minutes were devoted to such stories on NBC.)

Patterns of shifting support that were portrayed in weekday evening news stories were extremely complex. It appeared that McGovern and the Democrats both benefited and suffered from such coverage. The Democrats received more benign treatment on NBC, and the Republicans received the most favorable treatment on ABC. Relatively small numbers of stories were included in this analysis, but it appeared that significant differences existed by network. Democrats tended to benefit from other coverage, especially visuals and crowds during the campaign. But more similarities than differences appeared in coverage by CBS, NBC, and ABC.

PARTY AND CAMPAIGN LINKAGES

Each of the parties comprises a coalition of groups.[9] These groups comprise a set of reference points for individual citizens in the conduct of their political affairs.[10] A party solidifies its support by emphasizing ties to reference groups that are particularly associated with it; these groups sensitize individual members to positive aspects of the party and to negative aspects of the opposition.

An attempt was made to classify stories about the Democratic and Republican parties according to the explicit appearance of such groups. Very few explicit linkages could be inferred from network news stories about the parties, and thus the following analysis should be regarded as suggestive rather than conclusive.

### Group Linkages

Each story about a party was classified according to whether one or more of the reference groups were explicitly associated with the campaign of the party. These associations, or linkages, were classified as positive, negative, neutral, or not present. In most cases linkages with reference groups did not exist. The few cases of negative association between candidates and reference groups that were uncovered have been included with neutral stories in a "not positive" class for the sake of tabulation. Consequently, positive stories and all other stories form the basis for the analysis of reference groups. (See table 23.)

Democrats were associated with nonwhites, blue-collar workers, union members, and non-party supporters more frequently than Republicans. Nonwhites, blue-collar workers, and union members are also considered by most analysts to be important members of the Democratic coalition; and although the Democratic associations were relatively more frequent than association of these groups with the Republicans, the differences were not very large. The vast bulk

## TABLE 23

Linkage to Reference Groups in Republican and Democratic Party Stories by Time and Network

| Reference Group | CBS Linked % | Time | Not Linked % | Time | N | NBC Linked % | Time | Not Linked % | Time | N | ABC Linked % | Time | Not Linked % | Time | N |
|---|---|---|---|---|---|---|---|---|---|---|---|---|---|---|---|
| Republican party association with nonwhites | 5.7 | 20.5 | 94.3 | 332.2 | 193 | 2.7 | 10.1 | 97.3 | 272.7 | 186 | 5.4 | 14.5 | 94.6 | 228.8 | 167 |
| Democratic party association with nonwhites | 5.9 | 41.7 | 94.1 | 380.0 | 237 | 4.1 | 23.7 | 95.9 | 351.8 | 220 | 6.1 | 33.0 | 93.9 | 427.7 | 279 |
| Republican party association with non-Protestants | 4.1 | 23.6 | 95.9 | 329.0 | 193 | 1.1 | 5.3 | 98.9 | 277.5 | 186 | 1.8 | 5.0 | 98.2 | 238.3 | 167 |
| Democratic party association with non-Protestants | 2.1 | 12.6 | 97.9 | 409.1 | 237 | 1.8 | 11.5 | 98.2 | 364.0 | 220 | 2.5 | 13.5 | 97.5 | 447.2 | 279 |
| Republican party association with blue-collar workers | 1.0 | 1.9 | 99.0 | 350.8 | 193 | 1.6 | 5.4 | 98.4 | 277.4 | 186 | 1.8 | 9.3 | 98.2 | 234.0 | 167 |
| Democratic party association with blue-collar workers | 8.0 | 43.2 | 92.0 | 378.5 | 237 | 11.4 | 56.1 | 88.6 | 319.5 | 220 | 5.7 | 40.4 | 94.3 | 420.3 | 279 |
| Republican party association with union membership | 3.1 | 7.7 | 96.9 | 345.0 | 193 | 4.3 | 14.3 | 95.7 | 268.5 | 186 | 3.0 | 7.8 | 97.0 | 235.5 | 167 |
| Democratic party association with union membership | 13.1 | 73.9 | 86.9 | 347.8 | 237 | 15.5 | 73.2 | 84.5 | 302.3 | 220 | 11.8 | 63.2 | 88.2 | 397.6 | 279 |
| Republican party association with southerners | 7.3 | 30.4 | 92.7 | 322.2 | 193 | 5.4 | 27.7 | 94.6 | 255.1 | 186 | 6.6 | 18.4 | 93.4 | 224.9 | 162 |
| Democratic party association with southerners | 6.8 | 29.3 | 93.2 | 392.4 | 237 | 3.6 | 13.9 | 96.3 | 361.6 | 220 | 8.2 | 47.7 | 91.8 | 413.1 | 279 |
| Republican party association with social minorities | 3.1 | 16.8 | 96.9 | 335.9 | 193 | 2.2 | 9.2 | 97.8 | 273.6 | 186 | 0.6 | 1.5 | 99.4 | 241.8 | 167 |
| Democratic party association with social minorities | 3.0 | 17.8 | 97.0 | 403.9 | 237 | 2.7 | 9.6 | 97.3 | 366.0 | 220 | 1.4 | 4.8 | 98.6 | 456.0 | 279 |
| Republican party association with party workers | 30.1 | 126.8 | 69.9 | 225.9 | 193 | 23.1 | 79.1 | 76.9 | 203.7 | 186 | 28.1 | 79.2 | 71.9 | 164.1 | 167 |
| Democratic party association with party workers | 23.2 | 132.3 | 76.8 | 289.4 | 237 | 22.7 | 110.1 | 77.3 | 265.4 | 220 | 20.8 | 110.5 | 79.2 | 350.3 | 279 |
| Republican party association with non-party workers | 11.9 | 41.2 | 88.1 | 311.5 | 193 | 15.1 | 56.6 | 84.9 | 226.2 | 186 | 13.2 | 52.4 | 86.8 | 190.9 | 167 |
| Democratic party association with non-party workers | 17.7 | 86.0 | 82.3 | 335.7 | 237 | 16.8 | 74.1 | 83.1 | 301.5 | 220 | 15.4 | 96.3 | 84.6 | 364.5 | 279 |

of the news stories, moreover, did not link any of these groups explicitly to either of the parties' campaign efforts.

Table 23 indicates that differences in the amount of time devoted to each party were considerably greater than indicated by the percentages of stories in each of the above groups. Social minorities —protesters, homosexuals, groups that advocate the legalization of marijuana and other causes—and party workers were also more frequently associated with the Democratic party in terms of exposure measured by minutes. Of course, it is necessary to note that at least as much time was devoted to Democratic party stories that *failed* to link any of the groups with the Democrats as was devoted to stories that failed to link the groups with the Republican party. (Much more time, of course, was devoted to the Democrats in general, although the number of linkages to partisan groups was generally small.)

Republicans were more frequently associated with party workers than Democrats; but it must be recalled that more time was devoted to coverage relating the Democratic party to party workers, because more total time was devoted to stories about the Democrats. Party workers were the only group that the Republican campaign effort was related to more frequently than the Democratic campaign effort. This was the case on each network. Republicans were more frequently associated with non-Protestants on CBS (not on NBC or ABC), with southerners on CBS and NBC (not on ABC), and with social minorities on CBS (not on NBC or ABC). The Democratic campaign did receive more coverage in association with social minorities on each network when measured in terms of time.

Other data* show that the Democrats were more frequently associated with the less affluent and Republicans with the affluent on each network. Differences in time involved in this coverage, however, were slight because very few stories were carried on any of the networks in which the affluence of the crowd was clearly apparent. Democrats were also associated with urbanites more frequently than Republicans on CBS (but not on NBC or ABC). Republicans were more frequently associated with young people, and more time was devoted to such stories about Republicans on each network except NBC. As expected, Democrats were more frequently associated with liberals and Republicans with conservatives on each network, although the amount of time involved in these stories was very small for both parties and campaign efforts.

Thus it appeared that the Democratic campaign effort was associated with at least some of its traditional support base on each of

133

the networks—nonwhites, blue-collar workers, and union members. Republicans cut into several possible Democratic bastions in a consistent fashion, however, by being linked with southerners and young people. Republicans were also associated more frequently with conservatives and suburbanites, an important traditional base of support for the GOP. In addition, the GOP was associated with party workers more frequently in comparison with the Democrats, and the Democrats were associated more frequently with non-party supporters and with liberals. None of these trends was very surprising given the outcome of the 1972 election. And although not many stories included explicit group association, it was clear that the images suggested by the associations that occurred may well have contributed to eroding Democratic and coalescing Republican ranks.

### Partisan Linkages

Each story about Republican and Democratic campaign efforts was also classified according to whether the story showed an association, dissociation, or no linkage to other persons in each party at the national, state, or local levels (see table 24). It was assumed that an association (for example, welcoming a candidate or his representatives, doing things that identified positively with him, or showing support for the campaign effort) bolstered implied support, whereas dissociation (avoiding a candidate or his representatives, doing things that identified negatively with him, or showing hostility for the campaign effort) undermined implied support for the campaign effort.

Republicans were associated with national figures in their party less frequently than were Democrats. This was true on each network, although inter-party discrepancies were least on CBS. Considerably more time, moreover, was devoted to stories that associated national Democratic figures with the Democratic presidential campaign than national Republican figures with the Republican presidential campaign. Similarly, more time was devoted to showing dissociation from the Republican camp on NBC and from the Democratic camp on CBS and ABC, although the differences in proportions were not large. CBS focused most on Republican associations and dissociations (about 27 percent of party stories), and ABC focused least on such stories (a mere 7 percent of the party stories). Each network devoted about 25 to 30 percent of its stories about the Democratic party to association or dissociation of national leaders with the Democratic cause; but nearly all this attention was devoted to stories that stressed association rather than dissociation.

Associations and dissociations between parties and state and local leaders were also subjected to scrutiny. Although few stories concerned these relationships, Democratic stories clearly showed a greater extent of both dissociation and association. More attention was paid to Democratic squabbles than to intra-party conflicts

TABLE 24

PERCENTAGES OF STORIES AND TIME DEVOTED TO LINKAGE OF PARTIES
TO NATIONAL POLITICIANS IN DEMOCRATIC AND REPUBLICAN PARTY COVERAGE
BY NETWORK AND PERIOD IN CAMPAIGN

| PERIOD IN CAMPAIGN | Associated % | Associated Time | Dissociated % | Dissociated Time | None % | None Time | N |
|---|---|---|---|---|---|---|---|
| | | | Democratic Party | | | | |
| | | | CBS | | | | |
| July | 35.5 | 75.5 | 3.2 | 4.6 | 61.3 | 65.8 | 62 |
| August | 27.5 | 21.6 | 0.0 | 0.0 | 72.5 | 46.2 | 40 |
| September | 21.1 | 14.9 | 2.6 | 0.4 | 76.3 | 46.1 | 38 |
| October | 8.1 | 9.0 | 0.0 | 0.0 | 91.9 | 91.1 | 62 |
| Total | 22.8 | 121.0 | 1.5 | 5.1 | 75.7 | 249.3 | 202 |
| | | | NBC | | | | |
| July | 36.2 | 54.5 | 6.9 | 10.0 | 56.9 | 58.6 | 58 |
| August | 25.0 | 13.1 | 2.8 | 2.1 | 72.2 | 44.3 | 36 |
| September | 19.0 | 14.3 | 11.9 | 7.7 | 69.0 | 49.1 | 42 |
| October | 8.0 | 4.8 | 2.0 | 0.2 | 90.0 | 76.4 | 50 |
| Total | 22.6 | 86.8 | 5.9 | 19.9 | 71.5 | 228.4 | 186 |
| | | | ABC | | | | |
| July | 28.1 | 49.5 | 4.5 | 7.1 | 67.4 | 102.5 | 89 |
| August | 14.3 | 12.0 | 2.4 | 1.4 | 83.3 | 57.1 | 42 |
| September | 22.4 | 20.5 | 6.1 | 5.2 | 71.4 | 55.9 | 49 |
| October | 14.3 | 19.3 | 0.0 | 0.0 | 85.7 | 78.6 | 56 |
| Total | 21.2 | 101.2 | 3.4 | 13.7 | 75.4 | 294.1 | 236 |
| | | | Republican Party | | | | |
| | | | CBS | | | | |
| July | 18.2 | 1.9 | 9.1 | 1.1 | 72.7 | 12.8 | 11 |
| August | 26.5 | 22.9 | 6.1 | 5.1 | 67.3 | 77.0 | 49 |
| September | 21.4 | 11.2 | 0.0 | 0.0 | 78.6 | 16.2 | 14 |
| October | 15.9 | 10.3 | 6.8 | 2.9 | 77.3 | 55.4 | 44 |
| Total | 21.2 | 46.3 | 5.9 | 9.1 | 72.9 | 161.4 | 118 |
| | | | NBC | | | | |
| July | 16.7 | 3.1 | 16.7 | 3.1 | 66.7 | 5.2 | 6 |
| August | 12.1 | 5.3 | 9.1 | 6.3 | 78.8 | 51.2 | 33 |
| September | 26.3 | 7.1 | 0.0 | 0.0 | 73.7 | 19.3 | 19 |
| October | 8.2 | 8.7 | 6.1 | 6.8 | 85.7 | 50.1 | 49 |
| Total | 13.1 | 24.3 | 6.5 | 16.1 | 80.4 | 125.9 | 107 |
| | | | ABC | | | | |
| July | 12.5 | 1.4 | 12.5 | 2.4 | 75.0 | 10.4 | 8 |
| August | 6.7 | 2.2 | 0.0 | 0.0 | 93.3 | 42.5 | 30 |
| September | 5.3 | 0.5 | 0.0 | 0.0 | 94.7 | 25.8 | 19 |
| October | 5.1 | 2.6 | 0.0 | 0.0 | 94.9 | 50.7 | 39 |
| Total | 6.3 | 6.7 | 1.0 | 2.4 | 92.7 | 129.4 | 96 |

in the Republican campaign by each of the networks. This was particularly true for the Democratic campaign in its relation to local political leaders. But there was also greater coverage of association. Less than one-tenth of the network party coverage about Democrats stressed the association between the Democratic campaign and local Democratic leaders on each network. This coverage greatly outweighed stories showing dissociation.*

Thus it appeared that the Democratic campaign effort benefited more from the frequent and lengthy ties to Democratic leaders, and less frequent dissociation from them, than the GOP campaign. The relationship between Democrats and local leaders was particularly important. Stories concerning linkages between the parties and national, state, and local leaders were not frequently reported, in comparison with other kinds of stories about the parties. But the similarities in each network's reporting association and dissociation in each partisan camp suggested little selectivity in network programming.

SOURCES OF MAJOR-PARTY STORIES

Credibility of sources may be expected to vary in stories about the major parties and campaign efforts. Maximum opportunity was afforded film editors to package stories from partisan sources in a variety of ways. Critical or supportive second sources, for instance, might have been consulted, and these sources included in a way that was inimical or helpful to party interests emphasized in a story. Scrutinizing patterns of sources, finally, says something about the way in which the networks went about reporting political news. If hostile sources appeared more frequently in stories about Republicans than Democrats, for instance, then it might be assumed that the networks were less charitable to the GOP. Similarities in sources used by CBS, NBC, and ABC, however, would suggest that structural or situational rather than partisan bias was at fault.

Stories about Democratic and Republican parties and campaign efforts were classified according to the most important and the second most important sources of information for each story. Sources employed in the classification scheme included network reporters, Republican and Democratic partisans, other party partisans, institutional representatives, interest groups, foreign representatives (usually foreign officials), citizens, and experts. Coding of party sources followed prior conventions in all respects.

*General Sources*

Stories about the Republican and Democratic parties were classified according to most important and second most important sources in table 25. It was evident that political partisans played roles as story sources about the parties to a disproportionate degree. This was also true of secondary sources, although the basic pattern

## TABLE 25

### Percentages of Stories and Time Devoted to Democratic and Republican Party Stories by Cited Sources of Information and Network

| Sources | CBS Republican % | Time | CBS Democratic % | Time | N | NBC Republican % | Time | NBC Democratic % | Time | N | ABC Republican % | Time | ABC Democratic % | Time | N |
|---|---|---|---|---|---|---|---|---|---|---|---|---|---|---|---|
| **Most Important Source** | | | | | | | | | | | | | | | |
| Reporter | 47.7 | 36.0 | 52.3 | 31.8 | 65 | 53.8 | 33.5 | 46.2 | 42.2 | 93 | 50.0 | 38.6 | 50.0 | 33.2 | 82 |
| Republican party | 86.8 | 169.2 | 13.2 | 27.2 | 114 | 92.6 | 180.4 | 7.4 | 11.5 | 94 | 81.9 | 125.2 | 18.1 | 34.6 | 94 |
| Democratic party | 3.7 | 13.6 | 96.3 | 303.6 | 163 | 2.1 | 3.5 | 97.9 | 269.6 | 142 | 1.7 | 6.5 | 98.3 | 307.6 | 181 |
| Other party | 0.0 | 0.0 | 0.0 | 0.0 | 0 | 0.0 | 0.0 | 0.0 | 0.0 | 0 | 0.0 | 0.0 | 0.0 | 0.0 | 0 |
| Institutions | 69.2 | 57.9 | 30.8 | 18.8 | 39 | 62.2 | 35.0 | 37.8 | 19.4 | 37 | 61.9 | 34.4 | 38.1 | 29.7 | 42 |
| Interest groups | 63.0 | 42.1 | 37.0 | 19.4 | 27 | 62.5 | 17.6 | 37.5 | 13.5 | 16 | 40.9 | 17.5 | 59.1 | 31.2 | 22 |
| Foreign reps. | 0.0 | 0.0 | 100.0 | 1.5 | 1 | 0.0 | 0.0 | 0.0 | 0.0 | 0 | 0.0 | 0.0 | 0.0 | 0.0 | 0 |
| Citizens | 66.7 | 12.1 | 33.3 | 5.9 | 6 | 14.3 | 0.3 | 85.7 | 15.3 | 7 | 42.9 | 9.7 | 57.1 | 10.4 | 7 |
| Experts | 60.0 | 21.7 | 40.0 | 13.3 | 15 | 70.6 | 12.4 | 29.4 | 3.9 | 17 | 44.4 | 11.4 | 55.6 | 11.2 | 18 |
| Total | 44.9 | 352.7 | 55.1 | 421.7 | 430 | 45.8 | 282.8 | 54.2 | 375.5 | 406 | 37.5 | 243.3 | 62.5 | 457.8 | 445 |
| **Second Most Important Source** | | | | | | | | | | | | | | | |
| Reporter | 43.7 | 96.2 | 56.3 | 142.1 | 135 | 41.7 | 85.5 | 58.3 | 123.4 | 115 | 35.2 | 87.1 | 64.8 | 168.3 | 142 |
| Republican party | 60.9 | 42.1 | 39.1 | 29.8 | 23 | 68.2 | 41.3 | 31.8 | 21.4 | 22 | 62.5 | 15.8 | 37.5 | 13.1 | 16 |
| Democratic party | 13.3 | 18.1 | 86.7 | 102.6 | 45 | 15.8 | 14.8 | 84.2 | 76.7 | 38 | 8.5 | 10.2 | 91.5 | 88.3 | 47 |
| Other party | 0.0 | 0.0 | 100.0 | 0.5 | 1 | 0.0 | 0.0 | 0.0 | 0.0 | 0 | 0.0 | 0.0 | 100.0 | 1.7 | 1 |
| Institutions | 70.6 | 23.9 | 29.4 | 10.0 | 17 | 60.0 | 17.8 | 40.0 | 7.8 | 10 | 47.4 | 19.7 | 52.6 | 24.4 | 19 |
| Interest groups | 40.0 | 16.8 | 60.0 | 11.9 | 10 | 25.0 | 2.1 | 75.0 | 6.0 | 4 | 45.5 | 13.8 | 54.5 | 16.6 | 11 |
| Foreign reps. | 0.0 | 0.0 | 0.0 | 0.0 | 0 | 100.0 | 7.1 | 0.0 | 0.0 | 2 | 50.0 | 1.4 | 50.0 | 1.8 | 2 |
| Citizens | 66.7 | 12.0 | 33.3 | 4.1 | 6 | 50.0 | 0.3 | 50.0 | 2.7 | 2 | 42.9 | 9.4 | 57.1 | 11.1 | 7 |
| Experts | 75.0 | 25.2 | 25.0 | 7.4 | 8 | 27.3 | 4.4 | 72.7 | 14.4 | 11 | 66.7 | 2.8 | 33.3 | 0.6 | 3 |
| Total | 42.7 | 234.3 | 57.3 | 308.4 | 246 | 40.2 | 173.3 | 59.8 | 252.4 | 204 | 33.9 | 160.4 | 66.1 | 325.8 | 248 |

was more muted in these instances. The Democrats enjoyed their own partisan sources in stories more frequently on NBC and ABC, and the Republicans were the most important source for their own stories more frequently on NBC than on the other networks. On each network about 60 to 70 percent of the stories that had institutional sources were about the Republicans; this may have been a reflection of the participation of public officials in the Republican national campaign.

Interest group, citizen, and expert sources appeared more frequently in Republican than in Democratic stories on CBS, and more frequently in Democratic than in Republican stories on ABC. Interest groups and experts (but not citizens) were more frequent story sources on NBC about Republicans. More time was devoted to stories about the GOP with expert and institutional sources than was devoted to Democrats. When reporters were sources, each party received about equal attention. A great deal of the Democratic party's coverage emanated from its own partisan sources. Indeed, it appeared that the advantage Democrats enjoyed by way of greater overall coverage could be accounted for in large part by their own partisan sources. Democrats received nearly twice as much coverage (in terms of minutes) when their own partisans were sources than the Republicans received when theirs were.

Differences tended to be maintained when the second most important source of each story was scrutinized. A larger proportion of stories with reporters as second most important source (when some other second source did not exist) were about Democrats than about Republicans. Democrats, moreover, served less frequently as secondary sources in GOP stories than Republicans served as secondary sources in Democratic party stories. Interest groups served as secondary sources in stories about Democrats more frequently, and institutions were more frequently associated with the GOP as secondary sources on CBS and NBC (but not on ABC). Only about half of the stories about the parties on each network included more than one source. Over half of these secondary sources, moreover, were network reporters, so that the actual number of nonreporter sources that appeared in a story about the parties was narrowly circumscribed.

### Juxtaposition of Sources

Whenever more than one source was used in reporting a story, the second source could support, oppose, or have little significance for the information supplied by the initial source. Stories about the parties that had two or more sources were classified according to whether the second source tended to support, oppose, or have no clear relation to the first source (see table 26). It was assumed that supporting juxtaposition of sources tended to reinforce the impressions created by a story and therefore to be favorable to the story's object. In contrast, opposing juxtaposition was assumed to counterbalance whatever favorable images may have been created by a story's initial source and therefore to be unfavorable to the story's subject. Neutral or ambiguous juxtaposition was assumed to have neither favorable nor unfavorable implications for the story's source.

The Democratic party received more supporting, and nearly the same proportion of stories that included opposing, juxtaposition as the Republican party. More total time, however, was devoted to both supporting and opposing juxtaposition in stories about Democrats than in stories about Republicans. Patterns of juxtaposition were similar on each network; however, CBS broadcast fewer stories with supporting, and more stories with opposing, juxtaposition about each party than the other networks. NBC broadcast fewer stories with opposing juxtaposition, and CBS broadcast fewer stories with supporting juxtaposition about the Republicans. NBC presented more stories that contained supporting juxtaposition about the Democrats, and NBC and ABC broadcast about the same proportion of stories with opposing juxtaposition about the Democratic party.

The proportion of stories that included supporting juxtaposition increased over time for both Republican and Democratic parties on CBS and NBC, while a decrease in such stories occurred on ABC. Opposing juxtaposition occurred more frequently in CBS and ABC stories about the two major parties, although considerable irregularity in these patterns occurred. Opposing juxtaposition was less frequently observed nearer the end of the campaign on ABC and more frequently on CBS and NBC in stories about Republicans; a slight increase in stories that contained opposing juxtaposition occurred in stories about the Democrats.

Thus Republicans and Democrats both appeared to benefit most from NBC stories and least from CBS stories. Democrats, moreover appeared to benefit slightly more than Republicans from the frequency and length of stories that included supporting and opposing juxtaposition. The ratio of supporting to opposing juxtaposition in stories was slightly less favorable to the GOP. These ratios were least favorable for each of the parties in CBS coverage, and relatively less favorable for Republicans than Democrats.

## TABLE 26

#### PERCENTAGES OF STORIES AND TIME DEVOTED TO CONFLICTING, SUPPORTING, AND NEUTRAL EXPLICIT SOURCES OF INFORMATION IN DEMOCRATIC AND REPUBLICAN PARTY STORIES BY PARTY, NETWORK, AND PERIOD IN CAMPAIGN

| PERIOD IN CAMPAIGN | REPUBLICAN PARTY | | | | | | | DEMOCRATIC PARTY | | | | | | |
|---|---|---|---|---|---|---|---|---|---|---|---|---|---|---|
| | Supporting % | Supporting Time | Neutral % | Neutral Time | Opposing % | Opposing Time | N | Supporting % | Supporting Time | Neutral % | Neutral Time | Opposing % | Opposing Time | N |
| **CBS** | | | | | | | | | | | | | | |
| July | 36.4 | 10.0 | 36.4 | 6.6 | 27.3 | 6.6 | 11 | 54.8 | 56.8 | 7.1 | 6.4 | 38.1 | 55.2 | 42 |
| August | 49.0 | 44.0 | 16.3 | 19.5 | 34.7 | 44.3 | 49 | 37.9 | 21.1 | 27.6 | 14.6 | 34.5 | 23.4 | 29 |
| September | 25.0 | 3.9 | 41.7 | 9.7 | 33.3 | 12.9 | 12 | 47.8 | 19.0 | 4.3 | 0.4 | 47.8 | 27.0 | 23 |
| October | 57.6 | 29.1 | 3.0 | 0.4 | 39.4 | 47.3 | 33 | 70.2 | 50.2 | 4.3 | 6.6 | 25.5 | 29.6 | 47 |
| Total | 47.6 | 87.0 | 17.1 | 36.3 | 35.2 | 111.0 | 105 | 55.3 | 147.1 | 9.9 | 28.0 | 34.8 | 135.1 | 141 |
| **NBC** | | | | | | | | | | | | | | |
| July | 60.0 | 5.3 | 20.0 | 3.1 | 20.0 | 2.3 | 5 | 60.5 | 62.5 | 11.6 | 10.9 | 27.9 | 30.7 | 43 |
| August | 57.6 | 39.0 | 12.1 | 10.4 | 30.3 | 29.4 | 33 | 57.9 | 23.1 | 21.1 | 6.3 | 21.1 | 7.2 | 19 |
| September | 45.5 | 9.2 | 36.4 | 7.7 | 18.2 | 3.8 | 11 | 56.7 | 34.5 | 10.0 | 6.9 | 33.3 | 16.5 | 30 |
| October | 65.6 | 37.9 | 6.3 | 2.5 | 28.1 | 22.3 | 32 | 64.3 | 34.1 | 3.6 | 1.8 | 32.1 | 15.7 | 28 |
| Total | 59.3 | 91.4 | 13.6 | 23.7 | 27.2 | 57.9 | 81 | 60.0 | 154.3 | 10.8 | 26.0 | 29.2 | 70.1 | 120 |
| **ABC** | | | | | | | | | | | | | | |
| July | 80.0 | 6.1 | 20.0 | 2.3 | 0.0 | 0.0 | 5 | 60.0 | 66.7 | 10.0 | 15.2 | 30.0 | 35.4 | 60 |
| August | 52.9 | 40.9 | 14.7 | 7.6 | 32.4 | 20.2 | 34 | 64.3 | 39.0 | 25.0 | 11.2 | 10.7 | 7.5 | 28 |
| September | 37.5 | 11.8 | 25.0 | 7.7 | 37.5 | 13.1 | 16 | 50.0 | 42.3 | 10.5 | 6.8 | 39.5 | 27.4 | 38 |
| October | 65.5 | 27.8 | 6.9 | 4.2 | 27.6 | 19.1 | 29 | 59.0 | 40.8 | 7.7 | 2.0 | 33.3 | 32.0 | 39 |
| Total | 56.0 | 86.0 | 14.3 | 21.8 | 29.8 | 52.5 | 84 | 58.2 | 188.8 | 12.1 | 35.2 | 29.7 | 102.4 | 165 |

*Sources of Story Juxtaposition*

Each story classified as including supporting, neutral, or opposing juxtaposition was also tabulated by the most important initial source. This was done to study the source of each kind of juxtaposition in news about parties. Partisan sources and sources classified as interest groups and situations were the only non-network sources that appeared very frequently when this analysis was conducted.* Partisan sources, as expected, provided supporting juxtaposition in stories about their own partisans and opposing juxtaposition in stories about the opposition.

There was, however, a considerable amount of opposing juxtaposition in stories about one's own camp among partisan sources. On CBS 28 percent of Republican stories with Republican sources contained opposing juxtaposition; comparable figures were 25 percent on ABC and 21 percent on NBC; these rates were nearly the same in coverage of Democrats. Much more time was devoted to stories about the Democratic camp that contained opposing juxtaposition than to similar stories about the Republican camp, or to stories about the Republican camp that contained opposing juxtaposition from partisan colleagues. This appeared, however, to be due to the greater time devoted to coverage of Democrats rather than to partisan bias.

*Favorability of Partisan Stories by Source*

Sources of stories about the Republican and Democratic parties and campaign efforts were also tabulated in order to gauge the extent to which different sources were associated with favorable and unfavorable stories about the parties (see table 27). Network reporters were the most important reported sources of very few stories favorable to either campaign effort. NBC reporters were cited as sources in the largest proportion of stories favorable to Republicans (5 percent), and CBS reporters were sources in the largest proportion of stories favorable to Democrats (3 percent); but these discrepancies were not great. Reported partisan sources were associated with party coverage favorable to the respective parties, but again, not overwhelmingly. About 13 percent of CBS coverage of Republican stories with reported Republican sources, for instance, was favorable (compared with NBC and ABC with 18 and 24 percent). About 11 percent of the Democratic party stories on CBS with cited Democratic sources were favorable (compared with 12 percent on NBC and 14 percent on ABC). At the same time, stories with cited opposition sources were less unfavorable than might have been

## TABLE 27

### Percentages of Stories and Time Devoted to Party Coverage by Source of Story and Network

#### CBS

| Sources | Republican Party | | | | | | | Democratic Party | | | | | | |
|---|---|---|---|---|---|---|---|---|---|---|---|---|---|---|
| | Favorable % | Favorable Time | Neutral % | Neutral Time | Unfavorable % | Unfavorable Time | (N) | Favorable % | Favorable Time | Neutral % | Neutral Time | Unfavorable % | Unfavorable Time | (N) |
| Reporter | 4.5 | 3.9 | 86.4 | 52.9 | 9.1 | 11.4 | 66 | 3.1 | 1.9 | 93.8 | 61.4 | 3.1 | 4.8 | 65 |
| Republican | 13.2 | 28.4 | 76.3 | 142.8 | 10.7 | 25.1 | 114 | 1.8 | 3.9 | 84.2 | 167.1 | 14.0 | 25.3 | 114 |
| Democratic | 4.9 | 13.6 | 84.8 | 275.6 | 10.4 | 29.8 | 164 | 11.0 | 32.5 | 73.0 | 220.9 | 15.9 | 65.5 | 164 |
| Other Party | 0.0 | 0.0 | 100.0 | 3.3 | 0.0 | 0.0 | 1 | 0.0 | 0.0 | 100.0 | 3.3 | 0.0 | 0.0 | 1 |
| Institutions | 0.0 | 0.0 | 74.4 | 42.6 | 25.6 | 32.3 | 39 | 2.5 | 3.4 | 90.0 | 66.9 | 7.5 | 6.7 | 40 |
| Interest Groups | 18.5 | 9.3 | 70.4 | 46.7 | 11.1 | 5.4 | 27 | 0.0 | 0.0 | 85.2 | 56.6 | 14.8 | 4.8 | 27 |
| Foreign Reps. | 0.0 | 0.0 | 100.0 | 1.5 | 0.0 | 0.0 | 1 | 0.0 | 0.0 | 100.0 | 1.5 | 0.0 | 0.0 | 1 |
| Citizens | 0.0 | 0.0 | 83.3 | 15.3 | 16.7 | 2.8 | 6 | 16.7 | 3.5 | 66.7 | 12.1 | 16.7 | 2.4 | 6 |
| Experts | 20.0 | 6.6 | 53.3 | 8.8 | 26.7 | 19.6 | 15 | 6.7 | 4.4 | 86.7 | 26.4 | 6.7 | 4.2 | 15 |
| Total | 7.9 | 61.9 | 79.9 | 589.5 | 12.2 | 126.5 | 433 | 5.8 | 49.5 | 82.0 | 616.5 | 12.2 | 113.7 | 433 |

#### NBC

| Sources | Republican Party | | | | | | | Democratic Party | | | | | | |
|---|---|---|---|---|---|---|---|---|---|---|---|---|---|---|
| | Favorable % | Favorable Time | Neutral % | Neutral Time | Unfavorable % | Unfavorable Time | (N) | Favorable % | Favorable Time | Neutral % | Neutral Time | Unfavorable % | Unfavorable Time | (N) |
| Reporter | 5.4 | 6.8 | 92.5 | 68.1 | 2.2 | 0.7 | 93 | 0.0 | 0.0 | 90.3 | 64.0 | 9.7 | 11.6 | 93 |
| Republican | 18.1 | 32.9 | 71.3 | 136.0 | 10.6 | 23.0 | 94 | 1.1 | 0.6 | 87.2 | 167.0 | 11.7 | 24.3 | 94 |
| Democratic | 2.8 | 7.4 | 87.5 | 237.0 | 9.7 | 31.4 | 144 | 11.9 | 38.2 | 77.6 | 194.6 | 10.5 | 40.8 | 143 |
| Other Party | 0.0 | 0.0 | 100.0 | 2.3 | 0.0 | 0.0 | 1 | 0.0 | 0.0 | 100.0 | 2.3 | 0.0 | 0.0 | 1 |
| Institutions | 0.0 | 0.0 | 72.2 | 35.0 | 27.8 | 16.3 | 36 | 0.0 | 0.0 | 91.7 | 49.1 | 8.3 | 2.3 | 36 |
| Interest Groups | 25.0 | 7.1 | 62.5 | 19.6 | 12.5 | 4.5 | 16 | 6.3 | 2.2 | 81.3 | 26.6 | 12.5 | 2.4 | 16 |
| Foreign Reps. | 0.0 | 0.0 | 0.0 | 0.0 | 0.0 | 0.0 | 0 | 0.0 | 0.0 | 0.0 | 0.0 | 0.0 | 0.0 | 0 |
| Citizens | 42.9 | 7.0 | 57.1 | 8.7 | 0.0 | 0.0 | 7 | 0.0 | 0.0 | 71.4 | 10.8 | 28.6 | 4.8 | 7 |
| Experts | 41.2 | 4.9 | 35.3 | 5.2 | 23.5 | 6.2 | 17 | 0.0 | 0.0 | 58.8 | 11.6 | 41.2 | 4.7 | 17 |
| Total | 9.8 | 66.2 | 79.9 | 511.9 | 10.3 | 82.1 | 408 | 4.7 | 40.9 | 83.3 | 526.2 | 12.0 | 91.0 | 407 |

#### ABC

| Sources | Republican Party | | | | | | | Democratic Party | | | | | | |
|---|---|---|---|---|---|---|---|---|---|---|---|---|---|---|
| | Favorable % | Favorable Time | Neutral % | Neutral Time | Unfavorable % | Unfavorable Time | (N) | Favorable % | Favorable Time | Neutral % | Neutral Time | Unfavorable % | Unfavorable Time | (N) |
| Reporter | 3.7 | 3.5 | 88.9 | 59.9 | 7.4 | 6.0 | 81 | 1.2 | 1.9 | 87.7 | 58.3 | 11.1 | 9.7 | 81 |
| Republican | 23.7 | 39.1 | 64.5 | 95.0 | 11.8 | 23.6 | 93 | 0.0 | 0.0 | 78.7 | 122.0 | 21.3 | 37.7 | 94 |
| Democratic | 2.8 | 10.0 | 85.6 | 267.8 | 11.7 | 36.3 | 180 | 14.0 | 58.1 | 76.5 | 221.4 | 9.5 | 32.9 | 179 |
| Other Party | 20.0 | 3.1 | 60.0 | 6.0 | 20.0 | 2.7 | 5 | 20.0 | 3.1 | 80.0 | 8.7 | 0.0 | 0.0 | 5 |
| Institutions | 5.0 | 4.6 | 75.0 | 38.9 | 20.0 | 12.9 | 40 | 2.4 | 2.5 | 90.2 | 50.3 | 7.3 | 7.5 | 41 |
| Interest Groups | 22.7 | 10.6 | 68.2 | 35.1 | 9.1 | 2.8 | 22 | 4.5 | 1.9 | 72.7 | 36.3 | 22.7 | 10.4 | 22 |
| Foreign Reps. | 0.0 | 0.0 | 0.0 | 0.0 | 0.0 | 0.0 | 0 | 0.0 | 0.0 | 0.0 | 0.0 | 0.0 | 0.0 | 0 |
| Citizens | 14.3 | 4.0 | 85.7 | 16.1 | 0.0 | 0.0 | 7 | 14.3 | 4.2 | 57.1 | 9.2 | 28.6 | 6.7 | 7 |
| Experts | 22.2 | 2.5 | 77.8 | 20.1 | 0.0 | 0.0 | 18 | 0.0 | 0.0 | 66.7 | 19.6 | 33.3 | 3.0 | 18 |
| Total | 9.6 | 77.4 | 79.4 | 538.9 | 11.0 | 84.5 | 446 | 6.7 | 71.8 | 79.4 | 525.8 | 13.9 | 107.9 | 447 |

expected. About 10 percent of the Republican stories on CBS and NBC and 12 percent of the stories on ABC were unfavorable to Republicans, and 14, 12, and 21 percent of the stories with cited Republican sources on CBS, NBC, and ABC, respectively were unfavorable to Democrats. Again, caution suggests that strong conclusions ought not to be drawn from such small differences.

Stories with reported institutional sources were more unfavorable to Republicans than to Democrats on each network, and stories with reported interest group sources were more favorable to Republicans and somewhat more unfavorable to Democrats. Stories with experts cited as sources were more favorable to Republicans and unfavorable to Democrats (except on NBC, where a minor discrepancy in this pattern could be noted).

Thus a highly complex pattern of reported sources emerges from table 27. Stories with reporters as the only sources cited were more neutral, although some differences among the networks could be observed. Partisan sources were both most favorable and most unfavorable about respective campaign efforts. In general, it appeared that the Republicans may have benefited slightly from their overall treatment, but that this benefit was marginal at best.

CONCLUSIONS

It is not clear that either the Democrats or the Republicans were favored by network news coverage in 1972. Coverage patterns did not appear consistently corrosive to the interests of either major campaign. However, considerably greater coverage was devoted to stories about the Democratic party and its campaign effort.

Differences in the style and tone of campaign coverage did appear: CBS, for instance, was more critical of campaign efforts, but this criticism was apparent in its stories about each party. CBS, moreover, was also more favorable to each party in some indicators than were other networks; these differences were fairly small in any case. Thus the more political polarized coverage of the 1972 campaign by CBS did not seem to adversely affect either party very much.

A news coverage pattern emerged from the analysis similar to the coverage pattern for major-party candidates. The Democrats benefited from the mode of story presentation and context of news stories, and the Republicans benefited slightly more from the "softer" judgmental measures of story content. These stories involved general evaluations of party coverage and the character of group associations with the campaigns. Democrats benefited from some aspects of story sources used and the ways in which these sources were employed, but conclusions based on these data remain less clear.

The similarities in news coverage patterns about the parties in terms of general evaluations (overall favorability and evaluation of the campaigns), modes of presentation (use of pictures, 'film, action settings, closeups, flashbacks, and positional emphasis), context of stories (crowd size, crowd activity, supporter enthusiasm, antagonism to the opposition, favorable or unfavorable character of the crowds, and shifts in support), and group connections suggest that differences were more closely associated with structural or situational rather than partisan bias in network coverage. The same generalization is true for the use of sources, since benefits to either party based on sources, evaluations of what the sources say, or evaluations of the stories in which the sources appear were only marginally different for the major parties. (Democrats received more attention from their own sources than did Republicans from theirs, but respective partisan sources were also more frequently critical in tone.) CBS appeared to include more material in stories that challenged initial sources than the other networks, and NBC provided the most benign coverage of the parties in this regard. Again, these differences followed from the generally more critical stance that CBS took toward campaign coverage; but, and this must be emphasized, CBS was more critical than the other networks in its coverage of both parties.

*Detailed statistical tabulations are available from the author upon request.

1. Frank J. Sorauf, *Party Politics in America*, 2d ed. (Boston: Little, Brown & Co., 1972), chaps. 3 and 4.

2. Ibid., chap. 5; Hugh A. Bone, *Political Party Management* (Morristown, N.J.: General Learning Press, 1973).

3. Campbell et al., *The American Voter*.

4. An excellent critical review is present in David O. Sears, "Political Behavior," in Lindzey and Aronson, *Applied Social Psychology*, vol. 5, *The Handbook of Social Psychology*, especially pp. 370-99.

5. Ibid.; Converse, "Information Flow and the Stability of Partisan Attitudes"; Hinckley et al., "Information and the Vote."

6. Mendelsohn and Crespi, *Polls, Television, and the New Politics*, especially pp. 170-317.

7. A detailed discussion of coding rules and conventions is presented in Judge and Hofstetter, *Content Analysis of Taped Television Stories*.

8. Ibid.

9. See John H. Kessel, *The Goldwater Coalition* (Indianapolis: Bobbs-Merrill, 1968).

10. Herbert McClosky and Harold Dahlgreen, "Primary Group Influence on Party Loyalty," *American Political Science Review* 54 (1969): 757-76; Michael Parenti, "Ethnic Politics and the Persistence of Ethnic Identification," *American Political Science Review* 51 (1967): 717-26; and Robert Axelrod, "Where the Voters Come from: An Analysis of Electoral Coalitions, 1952-1968," *American Political Science Review* 66 (1972): 11-20.

# 6. Alternative Techniques of Analysis: Ratings and Themes

## INTRODUCTION

In preceding chapters conclusions about network news content and style of presentation have been based on relatively well-defined judgments. Very specific categories were defined explicitly for most variables. A full range of rules and conventions was developed and then inculcated in coders' minds through a lengthy process of repetition and practice. A continuous system of monitoring was also used so that coders were under constant supervision; points of ambiguity or error could be cleared up by the staff supervisor. Indeed, training and monitoring of coders actually consumed more time than the coding of news content and presentation; the final documentation for this coding involved many pages of detailed rules and conventions for coding and a vast array of examples.[1] Such content coding was designed to identify aspects of news content and presentation in a relatively precise and rigorous way. This kind of coding, however, assumed that one held a theory identifying each item of content or presentation style coded as important in some way.

### Technical Concerns

Some critics will take issue with content coding as outlined in the first five chapters of this book and with conclusions drawn based on the content coding. These critics may argue that such coding "doesn't really get at what I mean by news bias," or "I don't really care what these indicators show, I still think that. . . . " In part such criticisms suggest that although content coding may be extremely accurate in what it measures, the coding does not really measure many facets of content discussed when one speaks of bias. In other words, the content codes are not completely valid as measures of bias, even when considered collectively.[2] In part this entire question raises philosophical issues concerning what kinds of evidence can be considered to "count for or against" political bias in news coverage. We deal with these concerns in the introductory and concluding chapters of this book. And in part these criticisms may also suggest that other, more valid measures of content and style of presentation need to be derived in order to accurately measure bias.[3]

### Errors in Measurement

Other technically sophisticated critics may take issue with the content coding on still other grounds. Each particular technique of measurement (or gauging news content and style of presentation, in the present instance) had two kinds of errors associated with it: (1) errors directly related to the particular technique; and (2) more general, more pervasive errors related to failure to utilize a number of different measurements. Single techniques of measurement were, of course, susceptible to both kinds of errors. The content coding present so far is fairly narrow in the sense that it involved only one way of coding news content and presentation, and it is susceptible to both kinds of errors.[4]

The second group of critics may also be suggesting that more confident findings were possible if yet different coding techniques were used and if these revealed confirming results. If several different techniques—each having a different kind of error specifically associated with it—were used to code content and presentation, and if each technique confirmed the others, we would be more confident that findings were not due to the more specific kinds of error. We would also learn which specific measures appeared to agree and which ones failed to reach specific conclusions.[5] In any case, the use of alternative measures (multiple methods) is clearly good scientific procedure and was therefore employed in this study.

### Two Alternative Analysis Techniques

Rating scales and analysis of textual themes were two independent techniques of content analysis used in this study as a hedge against error. Findings from analyses of rating scales and the thematic analysis are summarized in this chapter.

*Ratings of content and presentation.* Applying rating scales to news story content and style of presentation provides one alternative technique employed in this study. Rating scales were used to elicit holistic, evaluative responses from trained coders on the content and style of presentation of each of the news stories.[6] Staff coders were presented with a set of forty-nine polar adjectives and were asked to rate each story. Some adjectives were used to rate all news stories. Others were used to rate only party stories, only candidate stories, or only issue stories because the particular polar adjective used was assumed to be specifically applicable to some aspect of only these types of stories.[7]

The polar adjectives appeared under each type of category in the form of a seven-point scale (in semantic differential format). Figure 1 presents an example of several rating scales applied to all news stories.

**Presentation**

Partial    \_\_\_\_ \_\_\_\_ \_\_\_\_ \_\_\_\_ \_\_\_\_ \_\_\_\_ \_\_\_\_    Impartial

Complex    \_\_\_\_ \_\_\_\_ \_\_\_\_ \_\_\_\_ \_\_\_\_ \_\_\_\_ \_\_\_\_    Simple

**Content**

Good    \_\_\_\_ \_\_\_\_ \_\_\_\_ \_\_\_\_ \_\_\_\_ \_\_\_\_ \_\_\_\_    Bad

Interesting    \_\_\_\_ \_\_\_\_ \_\_\_\_ \_\_\_\_ \_\_\_\_ \_\_\_\_ \_\_\_\_    Boring

Fig. 1. Four rating scales used in coding all news stories

Coders were instructed to check the blank on each rating scale that corresponded most closely with their own reaction to either the story's content or the style of presentation. The middle blank was used for neutral ratings. In all cases of doubt or ambiguity, coders were instructed to check the neutral blank. Ratings for each story were completed immediately after viewing the story.

It is important to note that rating scales are considered by some social scientists to be notoriously unreliable. Thus the analysis was viewed as supplementary, and conclusions were evaluated in this light. Coders had difficulty coding the same content in exactly the same way at several different times; two coders, presumably trained in identical fashion, did not always agree on ratings given to stories as much as they agreed on other kinds of content measures (for example, content codes used earlier in this study). Thus agreement between the conclusions reached in this chapter and in other chapters provides strong confirmation to our conclusions.

A number of steps were taken to improve the reliability of content and style ratings.[8] After a period of intensive training, three different coders rated all content and presentation on each scale in an independent fashion. At a later time a total score was computed combining the three independent scores by computer. Adding together three independent ratings constrained the kinds of errors due to idiosyncracies of individual coders. Summation of ratings, therefore, raised the overall reliability of rating scales considerably. Close monitoring of coding and periodic troubleshooting sessions were also employed at regular intervals in order to decrease error. Persons with extremely strong ideological views and those with both conservative and liberal bents were, of course, eliminated from the coding staff. Finally, several items with very low reliability were not used in the analysis.

### Two Strategies for Rating Stories

Stories were rated on the forty-nine scales in several ways, with two major rating categories used at the most general level in this phase of the analysis. Stories were first rated in terms of their content as independently as possible of the way that the stories were presented. Some stories had inherently unfavorable implications for one or the other of the major parties or their candidate. Most stories about Watergate, for instance, reflected unfavorably on Republican efforts in 1972 and the Nixon candidacy; and most stories about the Eagleton resignation reflected unfavorably on Democratic campaign efforts and the McGovern candidacy. Implications from these stories were relatively independent of the way in which they were presented.

Stories were then rated in terms of the way that they were presented (their style of presentation) as independently as possible of story content. Some stories were presented in ways unfavorable to one candidate or the other, one party or the other, or whatever was emphasized, almost regardless of content. Sarcasm or an intense emphasis on irony, for instance, may have been used to give an otherwise neutral story a distinctly favorable or unfavorable air, so that the audience may have received an unfavorable or a favorable impression despite the neutral story content. One might expect that style of presentation weighed more heavily as reporters, commentators, and anchormen departed from relatively straight, descriptive news reporting.

Other strategic decisions led us to apply one set of ratings to all news stories and another to stories that emphasized only candidates, parties or campaign efforts, or issues. In one set of ratings (called global story ratings) the overall characteristics of story content and style of presentation were rated without respect to the specific candidate, party, or issue emphasis.

A second set of ratings was applied more specifically to stories that emphasized a major-party candidate, issue, or party or campaign effort. One set of ratings for content and another for style of presentation were developed for stories concerning each of these specific topics.

It is important to note that global ratings applied to the general story context. Global ratings were assessed for stories about Nixon, McGovern, and the two major parties. These ratings should be interpreted as indicators of the more general context in which mention of the candidates or of the parties and campaign efforts occurred. Ratings of candidates, parties and campaign efforts, or issues should be interpreted as indicative of the more specific content and style of presenting these subjects in this presentation.

*Thematic analysis.* An additional analysis of candidate, party and campaign, and issue imagery was also based on another method of classifying news content. Rather than classifying entire stories according to a predetermined set of rules and conventions—as each of the methods previously employed required—content was classified according to specific themes appearing within stories.

A theme consisted of a part of a sentence or an entire sentence. The specific themes selected for this analysis included combinations of subject, verb, and object about one of the 134 "target topics" selected to represent various characteristics of the major analysis categories.[9] These categories—candidates, issues, the parties or campaigns— had been related by other scholars to citizens' voting behavior in American elections. The specific subject, verb, and object did not need to be present explicitly in a phrase in order for content to have been classified as a theme. Rather, the structure and function of a phrase in the sentence required only that subject, verb, and object were all present implicitly.

The coding procedure used in classifying thematic content represents an attempt to maximize coder reliability, roughly paralleling procedures for coding ratings. Over 100,000 lines of English-language news text (excluding commercials and human interest and feature stories) were analyzed sentence by sentence. Classification of thematic content involved two distinct processes.

(1) Each phrase was identified. Then, the list of 134 "target topics" was inspected to determine whether the phrase was relevant to one of the topics. Phrases not defined by the list were discarded. The majority of phrases present in news content were not relevant to the list of "target topics" and were discarded. Many phrases, even in politically relevant news stories, did not bear explicitly on political content. It is always possible that the coding of thematic material omitted some phrases directly pertinent to the campaign. But all phrases that were tied explicitly to candidates, campaign issues, and parties or campaigns were included in the analysis. A broad set of general coding categories was first established. More detailed topics were defined within these categories. The 134 target topics were developed by a further refinement of these more-detailed topics so that phrases could be fit into them. Issue topics, which were most likely to omit some material relevant to the election, were most

149

broadly defined. Thus it is unlikely that politically relevant material was excluded on a systematic basis.

(2) Each theme was further classified according to the text and the role it played in the story. This included classification according to whether themes provided a favorable, neutral (or ambiguous), or unfavorable implication for the "target topic." Locating and classifying themes according to various "target topics" was difficult and, as in any measurement process, may have been subject to some error. But classifying thematic content as favorable, neutral, or unfavorable with regard to "target topics" was a far more difficult process and more subject to error. Space does not allow a detailed discussion of rules and conventions for classification of thematic material.[10]

In general, whenever positive, successful, good, and other cultural values were attributed to a "target topic" in a theme, the theme was classified as favorable. Whenever negative, unsuccessful, bad, and other negative cultural values were attributed to a "target topic" in a theme, the themes were classified as unfavorable. Neutral classification was employed when neither favorable nor unfavorable qualities were attributed to a "target topic" by a theme, or when things attributed to a "target topic" by a theme were ambiguous with regard to cultural value. In many instances judgments about both the evaluative character of themes and the source were based on the larger context in which the theme occurred. Coders were instructed to read entire stories and passages within stories in order to classify thematic content more accurately and reliably.

Once all themes in a story were classified with regard to source and evaluative character, they were summed for the story. The individual themes within a story were aggregated to the story as a unit of analysis; once again, statistical analysis was based on story characteristics rather than on some other unit of analysis.

Possible errors in classification arose from sources quite different from the sources of errors in preceding analyses. Coding errors arose at the subsentence level of the theme rather than at the story level. One would expect errors based on *random* aspects of coding to diminish as themes were combined into increasingly general story aggregates. Thus aggregation of themes should have made the analysis less subject to random error than it otherwise would be.

Themes relating to "target topics" that concerned candidates, parties or campaigns, or issues, were combined into very general classifications of thematic content. Thus the original number of "themes" was grossly reduced and became more comprehensible and manageable for purposes of statistical analysis.

In some cases collapsing themes about "target topics" into more general categories also involved combining themes not mutually exclusive, so that inflated estimates of the number of themes relating to general topics resulted. Estimates of the number of themes related to parties and campaigns were probably most inflated, and estimates of the number of themes related to candidates were less inflated. Themes related to issue topics were unaffected because these topics were mutually exclusive. It was assumed that, although the inflated estimates of thematic content led to overestimates of the absolute number of themes in some cases, the inflation did not affect *relative* thematic content about candidates or parties in an irregular way. If the frequency of themes about McGovern, for instance, was inflated, then the frequency of themes about Nixon was also inflated, with the rates of inflation similar for each candidate. Similar assumptions were made about thematic material relating to the Democratic and Republican parties. These assumptions were supported by inspection of the distributions of thematic content for some of the specific "target topics."

Concerning viewers, we assumed that popular impressions about candidates, parties, and issues were based on theme patterns that appeared in network news programs. Regardless of whether news-watching was viewed as "work" or "play," thematic content provided images related to candidates, parties, and issues. Patterns in thematic content should be reflected in the politically defined themes used as a basis for this analysis. Political bias would then be inherent in differential patterns of thematic stories, once structural bias was taken into account.

## MAJOR-PARTY CANDIDATES

### Candidate Ratings

Candidate Nixon fared slightly better than candidate McGovern in terms of the global ratings of story content in which the candidates were mentioned. But mean (average) ratings in table 28 suggest that global ratings did not differ sharply. Fairly consistent but small discrepancies in content appeared on each network.

The content of stories in which Nixon appeared suggests that support for his candidacy was increasing to a greater extent than support for McGovern's candidacy. The impression that a viewer might have received of Nixon, moreover, emphasized efficiency and, to a lesser extent, goodness, in contrast to the impression of McGovern that emphasized inefficiency and, to a lesser extent, badness. Candidate

151

Nixon did, however, consistently appear in stories rated as containing considerably more boring content than did candidate McGovern.

Differences existed among networks in the way that stories about Nixon and McGovern were rated; but these inter-network differences were not very substantial in most cases. Discrepancies were greatest on ABC and least on NBC for most of the rating scales. Both ABC and CBS McGovern stories received more negative ratings than NBC stories, and ABC Nixon stories tended to receive the most favorable ratings. By and large, NBC stories were rated as more boring than stories about either of the candidates on the other networks (except McGovern coverage on ABC), although, once again, differences were small.

TABLE 28

MEAN GLOBAL RATINGS OF STORY CONTENT AND STYLE OF PRESENTATION IN NIXON AND MCGOVERN COVERAGE BY NETWORK AND RATING Scale

| RATING [a] | CBS | | NBC | | ABC | |
|---|---|---|---|---|---|---|
| | Nixon | McGovern | Nixon | McGovern | Nixon | McGovern |
| *Story Content* | | | | | | |
| Boring | 9.1 | 8.7 | 9.9 | 8.9 | 9.5 | 8.9 |
| Decreasing support | 11.9 | 12.2 | 11.7 | 11.9 | 11.5 | 12.1 |
| Inefficient | 11.8 | 12.3 | 12.0 | 12.2 | 11.5 | 12.2 |
| Bad | 12.2 | 12.3 | 12.3 | 12.2 | 12.0 | 12.5 |
| *Style of presentation* | | | | | | |
| Impartial | 12.6 | 12.6 | 13.2 | 12.3 | 13.0 | 12.2 |
| Simple | 11.1 | 10.5 | 11.9 | 10.2 | 11.3 | 10.7 |
| Unenthusiastic | 10.9 | 10.7 | 11.3 | 10.7 | 11.0 | 10.8 |
| Slow | 12.4 | 12.5 | 12.6 | 12.7 | 12.5 | 12.7 |
| Unfavorable | 12.2 | 12.3 | 12.2 | 12.2 | 11.8 | 12.7 |
| Unemotional | 13.8 | 13.0 | 14.1 | 13.3 | ˙13.9 | 13.2 |
| Uncritical | 11.7 | 11.8 | 12.3 | 11.9 | 12.6 | 12.4 |
| (Number) | (176) | (198) | (154) | (163) | (148) | (198) |

[a]Adjectives represent the polar adjectives that stand at the high end of the bipolar set of adjectives, so that categories that contain larger means manifest more of the characteristic listed in the row. Neutral and ambiguous ratings are scored as neutral and placed at the middle of the respective scales, so that extreme ratings are "dampened." The effects of this coding are to diminish extremely high and low ratings and, thereby, to make conclusions more conservative.

Ratings of presentation style mirrored ratings of content in the sense that discrepancies between stories grouped by candidate were small but fairly consistent for the three networks. Coverage of both candidates (interestingly enough from the point of view of this study) was rated as being relatively "impartial," although coverage of stories that included mention of Nixon on NBC and ABC were relatively less partial than stories that included mention of McGovern. Stories about McGovern and Nixon on CBS received equal ratings of impartiality in presentation.

The average style of presentation ratings (means) in table 28 suggest that Nixon coverage was more simplified, less enthusiastic, faster, and less emotional than McGovern coverage on each network. Nixon stories were less critical in presentation on both NBC and ABC than were McGovern stories, but slightly more critical on CBS. McGovern was presented either less favorably or no more favorably than Nixon on each network.

Discrepancies between candidate ratings were least for CBS stories and greatest for NBC and ABC stories. The greatest difference in story ratings appeared for the simple-complex rating of story presentation, and the largest difference in average ratings occurred on NBC. McGovern coverage appeared in a much more complex setting than did Nixon coverage. NBC and ABC coverage of McGovern was rated as considerably more partial than was coverage of Nixon, whereas no difference in the level of average partiality for Nixon and McGovern CBS stories appeared. Coverage of both candidates received high average ratings in lacking emotionalism on the emotional-unemotional rating scale, although coverage of McGovern was rated as being considerably more emotional then coverage of Nixon on each network.

Nixon story coverage was rated as most partial, complex, enthusiastic, fast, emotional, and critical on CBS. CBS and NBC stories about Nixon received equal average ratings as being most unfavorable. Similarly, coverage of Nixon stories on NBC was most impartial, simplified, unenthusiastic, slow, and unemotional, and coverage of Nixon stories on ABC was most uncritical. Coverage of McGovern stories on CBS was most impartial, fast, emotional, and critical; comparable coverage on NBC was most complex, favorable, and unemotional; and coverage on ABC was most partial, simplified, unenthusistic, unfavorable, and uncritical.

Ratings of content and style of presentation were also made with a narrower focus on attributes of Nixon and McGovern (see table 29). In the case of the preceding global ratings, any mention of a candidate or a party in any story—no matter how tangential to the candidate or to the election for that matter—was rated. These stories did not necessarily focus on Nixon or McGovern. The following analysis should sharpen our image of candidate coverage.

Nixon and McGovern coverage was rated in relation to a number of traits associated with candidates for public office. The traits selected were assumed to be characteristics that the electorate mentions with some frequency in their voting decisions or characterizations that would appear to bear on the way a candidate was assessed.

Nixon was rated as being stronger, more unlikeable, more competent, more insincere, less honest, less kind, more selfish, more mild, and more passive than McGovern on all three networks. The image of a fairly tough, practical, effective, competent, but unlovable candidate was associated with Nixon. CBS and NBC candidate coverage presented Nixon as slightly less inspiring, less kind, and more stupid than McGovern, and ABC coverage presented McGovern as slightly less inspiring, more kind, and more stupid than Nixon. But most of these differences were small indeed.

TABLE 29

MEAN CANDIDATE RATINGS OF CONTENT AND STYLE OF PRESENTATION IN
NIXON AND MCGOVERN STORIES BY NETWORK AND RATING SCALE

| RATING [a] | CBS | | NBC | | ABC | |
|---|---|---|---|---|---|---|
| | Nixon | McGovern | Nixon | McGovern | Nixon | McGovern |
| *Story Content* | | | | | | |
| Strong | 13.6 | 12.4 | 13.8 | 12.7 | 13.7 | 12.4 |
| Unlikeable | 11.6 | 11.4 | 11.6 | 11.2 | 11.5 | 11.4 |
| Competent | 12.9 | 12.5 | 13.0 | 12.7 | 13.2 | 12.4 |
| Insincere | 11.9 | 11.1 | 11.9 | 11.2 | 11.8 | 11.1 |
| Honest | 11.9 | 12.2 | 11.9 | 12.2 | 11.8 | 12.2 |
| Uninspiring | 11.7 | 11.6 | 11.6 | 11.5 | 11.6 | 11.7 |
| Kind | 12.2 | 12.3 | 12.2 | 12.5 | 12.1 | 12.4 |
| Selfish | 11.9 | 11.7 | 11.9 | 11.6 | 11.9 | 11.6 |
| Stupid | 11.3 | 11.2 | 11.4 | 11.1 | 11.2 | 11.3 |
| Mild | 10.8 | 10.6 | 10.9 | 10.7 | 10.7 | 10.6 |
| Passive | 9.7 | 8.9 | 10.0 | 8.9 | 9.7 | 9.1 |
| *Style of Presentation* | | | | | | |
| Unfavorable | 11.6 | 11.9 | 11.4 | 11.6 | 11.2 | 12.1 |
| Corrosive | 11.6 | 11.9 | 11.1 | 11.6 | 11.1 | 12.2 |
| Uncritical | 12.7 | 12.3 | 13.2 | 12.6 | 13.4 | 12.9 |
| Complex | 10.9 | 12.5 | 10.5 | 12.5 | 11.2 | 12.2 |
| Uninteresting | 9.8 | 9.0 | 10.2 | 9.2 | 9.9 | 9.2 |
| (Number) | (176) | (198) | (154) | (163) | (148) | (198) |

[a]See note to table 28.

The extent to which average ratings of Nixon were similar on each network was remarkable, given the amount of variation possible. The same similarity in ratings was also apparent for McGovern. Thus very little difference among networks was discernible in the kind of traits associated with each candidate in story content. The strong, efficient, effective, competent image was associated with Nixon and juxtaposed against the lovable, kindly, but ineffective, foolish, weak, inefficient, incompetent image associated with McGovern.

The greatest discrepancies between Nixon and McGovern coverage occurred in ratings of strength, sincerity, and passiveness. CBS story content was rated as showing slightly less difference between the candidates in content ratings than NBC or ABC. This may be because CBS presented stories that muted the differences between candidates or because of some other reason.[11] From analysis of style of presentation, below, it did not appear that CBS stories were more complex and, hence, less stereotypic of the candidates.

Nixon stories were presented in a consistently more favorable, less corrosive, less critical, less complex, and less interesting way than McGovern stories. This was true on all three networks; differences in presentation between the candidates, moreover, were considerably larger than were candidate differences in ratings of content. ABC stories about Nixon were most favorable, uncritical, and complex in terms of presentation. CBS stories about Nixon were most unfavorable, corrosive, critical, and interesting. NBC stories about Nixon were least complex and most uninteresting, and (along with ABC) most supportive.

CBS stories about McGovern were most critical, interesting, and (along with NBC) most complex, and ABC stories about McGovern were most unfavorable, corrosive, uncritical, simple, and (along with NBC) uninteresting. (NBC stories about McGovern were rated most favorable and supportive in presentation.)

Differences in presentation were greatest between the candidates for story complexity and level of interest. McGovern stories were consistently presented in a more complex and a much more interesting way than Nixon stories. McGovern was portrayed in a more corrosive manner than Nixon on ABC (the difference in presentation of Nixon and McGovern was in the same direction but was not as great on CBS and NBC). McGovern was also presented in a very unfavorable way relative to Nixon on CBS and NBC.

### Thematic Treatment of Candidates

Themes that were related to fifty-four "target topics," all of which concerned news coverage of major-party candidates, were combined in order to provide an aggregate indicator of the character of network coverage during the 1972 campaign. Considerable disparities in the amount of favorable thematic material carried in candidate stories were discerned, but the disparities were parallel on each network. A brief verbal summary of results is presented.*

Generally, Nixon received more favorable coverage than McGovern. The Democratic standard-bearer was more likely to receive coverage that contained neutral themes than was his GOP opponent. McGovern coverage was also characterized by a greater average number of themes—primarily neutral and unfavorable to his candidacy—than Nixon.

A strong case for political bias did not appear to be supported by analysis of either candidate ratings or themes. Nixon was rated more favorably than McGovern in most instances. But differences among networks were slight. Nixon stories contained a larger average number of favorable and about the same number of unfavorable general candidate themes than did McGovern stories. But each network carried more favorable Nixon than McGovern thematic content, more neutral McGovern than Nixon thematic content, and about the same amount of unfavorable Nixon and McGovern thematic content. The amazing degree of similarity among network thematic and rating profiles about candidate coverage suggests that one basis for political bias (sharp and consistent differences among networks) was not apparent in the evening news.

### Party Ratings

A high degree of agreement existed in the average global ratings of story content concerning major parties on all three networks. Stories about Republicans were rated more boring than stories about Democrats. The Republican party was also seen as losing support, and as being more efficient and "bad" on each of the networks, when compared with the Democratic party.

Slight variation occurred among networks in the way story content about the major parties was rated. CBS party coverage was, for instance, least boring. This was true of coverage concerning both the Republican and Democratic parties. CBS stories also showed the greatest drop in support for the Republicans, and were (along with NBC stories) likely to show the GOP to be inefficient and bad. ABC, in contrast, was most likely to show increased support for the Republicans and to include content in its stories that suggested the GOP was efficient and good.

Stories whose content portrayed the Democratic party as inefficient (but more inefficient than the GOP) were rated as equal on all three networks. Stories about the Democrats were most boring in presentation and showed the greatest decline in support on ABC. Finally, ABC presented the Democratic party in the worst light. Although differences were very small, it appears that both CBS and NBC provided more favorable coverage of the Democratic party in news content.

In table 30 it is important to observe that the overall differences in average ratings are slight but consistent. A similar set of conclusions can be reached with regard to ratings of network styles of presentation in stories about the Democratic and Republican parties.

Coverage of stories about Republicans was most partial, enthusiastic, emotional, and critical on CBS, and most impartial, favorable,
and uncritical on ABC. NBC stories about the GOP were least
enthusiastic, slowest, and unemotional. NBC and ABC presented
stories that were equally complex, and NBC and CBS presented
stories that were equally unfavorable about Republican party fortunes.

The Democrats, in contrast, fared best on CBS. In general, CBS
stories about the Democrats were rated as most impartial, complex
(along with NBC), enthusiastic, fast, favorable, and emotional. At the
same time, however, CBS coverage of the Democratic party was most
critical. ABC coverage of the Democrats was most partial, simple,
slow, unenthusiastic (along with NBC), unfavorable, and uncritical.
NBC coverage of the Democrats was least emotional.

TABLE 30

MEAN GLOBAL RATINGS OF CONTENT AND STYLE OF PRESENTATION IN DEMOCRATIC
AND REPUBLICAN PARTY COVERAGE BY NETWORK AND RATING SCALE

| RATING [a] | CBS | | NBC | | ABC | |
|---|---|---|---|---|---|---|
| | Republican | Democratic | Republican | Democratic | Republican | Democratic |
| *Story Content* | | | | | | |
| Boring | 8.5 | 8.5 | 9.5 | 8.8 | 9.2 | 8.9 |
| Decreasing support | 12.2 | 12.0 | 12.1 | 12.0 | 12.0 | 12.1 |
| Inefficient | 11.9 | 12.2 | 11.9 | 12.2 | 11.7 | 12.2 |
| Bad | 12.8 | 12.2 | 12.8 | 12.3 | 12.6 | 12.5 |
| *Style of Presentation* | | | | | | |
| Impartial | 12.2 | 12.6 | 12.4 | 12.5 | 12.6 | 12.3 |
| Simple | 10.1 | 10.0 | 11.3 | 10.0 | 11.3 | 10.3 |
| Unenthusiastic | 10.5 | 10.5 | 11.2 | 10.6 | 10.9 | 10.6 |
| Slow | 12.7 | 12.6 | 12.8 | 12.7 | 12.6 | 12.7 |
| Unfavorable | 12.7 | 12.2 | 12.7 | 12.3 | 12.5 | 12.5 |
| Unemotional | 13.4 | 12.8 | 13.8 | 13.2 | 13.6 | 13.1 |
| Uncritical | 11.4 | 11.3 | 12.0 | 11.5 | 12.1 | 12.2 |
| (Number) | (193) | (237) | (187) | (220) | (168) | (279) |

[a]See note to table 28.

Although critical, CBS coverage appeared to have been slightly
more favorable to the Democratic party and the McGovern candidacy
than coverage on the other networks. CBS coverage was generally
more complex, and therefore multifaceted, in character, more interesting (perhaps because it was invested with greater complexity, emo-
tion, and speed in delivery), and generally more favorable. ABC
coverage of the Republican party and the Nixon candidacy appeared
to have been somewhat more favorable. But differences in ratings
were small. Indeed, very little variance in the ratings was explained
by candidate or party classifications among networks when analysis
of variance was conducted. Second, complete consistency in average

ratings did not, of course, appear in these data. Thus, although trends in coverage may be noted, a strong case for network bias could hardly be based on these data.

Stories about the parties were also rated on a number of traits that relate to images people associate with the electoral politics (see table 31). The networks portrayed the Democratic party as less successful, weaker, but more honest, less selfish, and less stupid than the Republican party. ABC portrayed the Democrats as slightly more passive than the Republicans, and CBS and NBC portrayed the contrary.

Average ratings of content about each party were remarkably similar for CBS, NBC, and ABC, but a fair amount of difference between parties did emerge with regard to most of the ratings on each network. Differences between the parties were greatest for ratings of success, weakness, and honesty. The Democrats were rated as successful, strong, but less honest.

TABLE 31

MEAN RATINGS OF CONTENT AND STYLE OF PRESENTATION IN REPUBLICAN AND DEMOCRATIC PARTY STORIES BY NETWORK AND RATING SCALE

| RATING[a] | CBS | | NBC | | ABC | |
|---|---|---|---|---|---|---|
| | Republican | Democratic | Republican | Democratic | Republican | Democratic |
| *Story Content* | | | | | | |
| Unsuccessful | 11.5 | 12.3 | 11.3 | 12.2 | 11.3 | 12.4 |
| Passive | 8.8 | 8.7 | 9.0 | 8.7 | 8.8 | 8.9 |
| Weak | 11.3 | 12.2 | 11.2 | 12.2 | 11.0 | 12.5 |
| Honest | 11.0 | 12.1 | 11.1 | 12.0 | 11.1 | 12.1 |
| Selfish | 12.2 | 11.8 | 12.1 | 11.8 | 12.1 | 11.8 |
| Stupid | 11.8 | 11.5 | 11.8 | 11.6 | 11.7 | 11.6 |
| *Style of Presentation* | | | | | | |
| Unfavorable | 12.5 | 12.1 | 12.4 | 12.0 | 12.2 | 12.3 |
| Corrosive | 12.3 | 12.0 | 12.2 | 12.0 | 11.9 | 12.3 |
| Uncritical | 12.0 | 12.2 | 12.4 | 12.3 | 12.6 | 12.8 |
| Complex | 12.4 | 12.4 | 11.5 | 12.4 | 11.7 | 12.1 |
| Uninteresting | 9.3 | 9.2 | 9.7 | 9.2 | 9.7 | 9.4 |
| (Number) | (193) | (237) | (187) | (220) | (168) | (279) |

[a]See note to table 28.

CBS portrayed the Republicans as least successful, least passive (along with ABC), weakest, least honest, most selfish, and most stupid (along with NBC). The Democrats were portrayed on CBS as most active and strongest (along with NBC), and least stupid. NBC stories suggested that the Democrats were most successful, and they were portrayed as about equally selfish on all three networks. It is important not to make too much of these comparisons, however, since differences were slight in most instances.

Ratings of style of presentation in network coverage of stories that emphasized major parties were quite similar to ratings of content. Reporting about the Republican party was consistently more unfavorable and uninteresting than was reporting about the Democratic party on each network. CBS coverage of Republican party stories was most unfavorable, and ABC coverage was most favorable. NBC coverage of Democratic stories was most favorable, and ABC coverage was most unfavorable. However, differences in neither set of story presentation ratings were very large.

CBS coverage of the GOP was the most corrosive and critical, but it was also the most complex and interesting. ABC coverage of the GOP was, at the same time, most supportive, uncritical, and (along with NBC) most uninteresting. NBC coverage of the Republicans was the most simple and least complex. In contrast, coverage of the Democratic party was the most supportive on CBS and NBC. CBS coverage of the Democrats was also the most critical, complex, and interesting (along with NBC), and ABC reporting about the Democrats was most corrosive, uncritical, simple, and uninteresting.

### Thematic Treatment of Parties and Campaigns

Themes relating to twenty "target topics" about major parties and campaigns were aggregated to provide a general indicator of the thematic treatment that the parties and campaigns received during the election. The "target topics" included mention of parties' leaders, government leaders (at the national, state, and local levels, as well as administrative personnel who are partisan), issues relevant to the parties, or campaigns of the major parties, campaign organizations and leaders, party leaders, other candidates, and party or campaign linkages to policy positions and issues.*

Republicans benefited by receiving more favorable themes in the average news story than Democrats. The Democrats also received more unfavorable and neutral thematic coverage than their Republican adversaries on NBC and ABC. CBS devoted slightly more unfavorable and neutral coverage to the GOP. But CBS also devoted more favorable coverage to the GOP.

Neither ratings of content and style of presentation in stories about the major parties nor investigation of the thematic content of these stories provided strong evidence of partisan bias. Results were neither consistently favorable nor unfavorable to either major party on any one network; but when some degree of consistency occurred, parallel patterns appeared in CBS, NBC, and ABC coverage.

159

ISSUE RATINGS AND THEMATIC CONTENT

Issue coverage was also evaluated in terms of the issues and specific linkages to major-party candidates. A major assumption in this analysis was that references to candidates occurring within the context of a story about issues helped to influence popular perceptions of the candidates. Thus issue coverage including references to candidates must affect the images that people have of these political actors, as well as the issues.

### Ratings of Candidates in Issue Stories

An abbreviated set of rating scales was used to evaluate the content and style of presentation of issue stories with regard to major-party candidates (see table 32). It turned out that the content rating scale designed to assess liberalism-conservatism was unreliable in assessing story content due to coders' inabilities to discern such traits. Indeed, the liberal-conservative dimension is very poorly defined in the beliefs of the American public.[12]

TABLE 32

MEAN ISSUE STORY RATINGS OF CONTENT AND STYLE OF PRESENTATION CONCERNING NIXON AND MCGOVERN BY NETWORK AND RATING SCALE

| RATING [a] | CBS | | NBC | | ABC | |
|---|---|---|---|---|---|---|
| | Nixon | McGovern | Nixon | McGovern | Nixon | McGovern |
| *Story Content* | | | | | | |
| Bad | 12.3 | 12.9 | 12.4 | 12.8 | 12.2 | 12.9 |
| *Style of Presentation* | | | | | | |
| Unfavorable | 12.3 | 12.9 | 12.4 | 12.8 | 12.2 | 12.9 |
| Unsupportive | 12.4 | 12.8 | 12.4 | 12.8 | 12.2 | 12.8 |
| Uncritical | 11.9 | 12.7 | 12.1 | 12.3 | 12.4 | 12.7 |
| Complex | 12.1 | 12.1 | 11.9 | 12.0 | 12.2 | 11.8 |
| Uninteresting | 9.9 | 10.3 | 10.3 | 10.3 | 10.3 | 10.4 |
| (Number) | (176) | (198) | (154) | (163) | (148) | (198) |

[a]See note to table 28.

Issue stories appeared to contain implications for the McGovern candidacy that were consistently bad, in comparison with the implications of issue coverage for Nixon. Although sharp differences in the good-bad rating did not appear with regard to either candidate, issue stories reported on CBS and ABC appeared to have slightly worse implications for McGovern than did comparable coverage on NBC. Candidate Nixon, at the same time, appeared in issue stories with the least favorable ratings on NBC and the most favorable ratings on ABC, although, once again, the magnitude of differences in these ratings was not great.

In terms of presentation, issue linkage to Nixon was rated more favorably, more supportively, but also more critically than was issue linkage to McGovern. This coverage was the most unfavorable to Nixon on NBC and most favorable on ABC, and CBS coverage was the most unsupportive (along with NBC), most critical, but also most interesting. ABC issue coverage linked to Nixon was the most favorable, supportive, uncritical, complex, and uninteresting (along with NBC).

Presentation of issues in relation to McGovern, moreover, was the most unfavorable on CBS and ABC, and the most favorable on NBC (once again, differences were very slight among networks in those ratings). All three networks linked issues to McGovern in an equally unsupportive way; this coverage was rated as the most critical on NBC, the most complex on CBS, and the most interesting on NBC (along with CBS). McGovern issue coverage was the least complex on ABC; issue ties to McGovern were equally critical on CBS and ABC. Again, network differences were much smaller than the differences in average ratings between candidates on each individual network.

### Thematic Treatment of Issues

Themes related to the general categories of local, state, national, and international "target topics" were aggregated into a single "general issue" classification for purposes of analysis in this section. We were concerned in this analysis more narrowly with how issues were treated at a very general level of concern.

The maxim that bad news drives out good news was reaffirmed in terms of the way that issue content appeared in news stories during the campaign. But it was also clear that favorable thematic content displaced neutral thematic content, since not only did a larger average number of unfavorable than favorable themes appear in news coverage but a larger average number of favorable than neutral themes appeared in the same coverage.*

Issue coverage was also related to the major-party candidates. Such coverage shades impressions about the positions of candidates on issues, and about their capabilities to handle complex domestic and foreign affairs. Issue imagery, moreover, was but one more source of general candidate imagery that doubtlessly combined with impressions from yet other sources to form the collections of images that citizens developed and maintained about the candidates.

Nixon was associated with greater average amounts of favorable thematic issue content than McGovern (on CBS and NBC) and about the same average amount of issue content on ABC. But the same was

161

also true of unfavorable issue themes: Nixon was associated with a greater average number of unfavorable issue themes than McGovern on each of the networks. Nixon was also associated with more neutral thematic content than his Democratic adversary. But a moderately parallel pattern of favorable, neutral, and unfavorable thematic issue content was apparent.*

Issue coverage again affirmed a central finding that has repeatedly emerged in this study. The networks cover issues in much the same way. And although more unfavorable than favorable issue coverage was broadcast during the 1972 election, substantial proportions of the total issue coverage were neutral.

CONCLUSION

Average ratings of news content and style of presentation in stories about the candidates, parties, and issues linked to candidates and parties have been summarized in this chapter. On many of the softer indicators, Nixon and the Republicans appeared in at least as favorable terms as McGovern and the Democrats. Nixon was harsher, yet more competent; McGovern was kinder, yet less competent. With many exceptions it appears that ABC presented news in content and style that was slightly more favorable to Nixon and the Republicans than to McGovern and the Democrats, and CBS presented news in content and style that was slightly more favorable to McGovern and the Democrats than to Nixon and the Republicans. NBC appeared to have been closer to CBS than to ABC in ratings of its overall content and style of presentation in this regard, although NBC fairly consistently received ratings that attributed an uninteresting, bland character to its coverage.

Nonetheless, differences in coverage of candidates and parties—whether in terms of global ratings of all stories or specific ratings applied to candidate, party, or issue stories—were small. Very little association appeared between the average ratings when comparing parties or candidates, although greater differences appeared between average ratings of parties and candidates than among the networks in the way that candidates and parties were covered. It is therefore difficult to make a very strong case that any particular network was politically biased in its coverage of the candidates or parties—or, at least, that this bias was very great or marked in its character. It is important to note that coverage did vary by time of campaign, according to the very limited analysis that we have been able to present in this chapter. It is therefore important that future studies of the relation between television news coverage and politics not be confined to the normal campaign period from Labor Day until the election.

Nor did systematic and clear evidence for political bias in coverage of the Democratic or the Republican parties, the Nixon or McGovern candidacies, or issues emerge from the analysis of the thematic content of the evening news. The complexity of news story characteristics, for one thing, was very great. Candidate Nixon received more favorable coverage, for instance, than candidate McGovern, and (except for CBS) McGovern received more unfavorable coverage than Nixon. But candidate Nixon was much more likely to be associated with unfavorable issue themes than was candidate McGovern. The GOP was also more likely to be associated with favorable, and the Democratic party with unfavorable, themes during the campaign; but the bulk of the unfavorable associations with the Democrats occurred during July, whereas the unfavorable associations with the GOP ran throughout the campaign.

More detailed scrutiny of thematic content associated with issues than was reported here, moreover, revealed that the bulk of issue themes was unfavorable, and that only a few issues were given substantial unfavorable coverage throughout the entire campaign period.* The amount of unfavorable coverage did not change a great deal as the campaign progressed, but the only overall increase in unfavorable coverage was on CBS. CBS was most unfavorable, although differences in the average number of favorable and neutral themes per story were not large among the networks.

Differences in network coverage, moreover, were slight in comparison with differences due to time, candidate, party, or issue. Thus, once again, little systematic evidence of a partisan bias was present in our overview of ratings and thematic analysis. We can increase our confidence that partisan bias did not dominate network coverage of the 1972 presidential campaign. Very different methods in measuring news content were employed, and our general conclusions received reaffirmation.

* Detailed statistical tabulations are available from the author upon request.

1.  Judge and Hofstetter, *Content Analysis of Taped Television Stories.*

2.  Hosti, *Content Analysis for the Social Sciences and Humanities,* pp. 142-49; see also Donald T. Campbell, "Recommendations for APA Test Standards Regarding Construct Trait or Discriminant Validity," *American Psychologist* 14 (1960): 546-53.

3.  See Winnick, "Critique of *The News Twisters,*" in this regard.

4.  Donald T. Campbell and Donald W. Fiske, "Convergent and Discriminant Validation by the Multitrait-Multimethod Matrix," *Psychological Bulletin* 56 (1959): 81-105.

5.  Ibid.

6. An excellent rationale for rating scales appears in Rhea Seagull, "Bias on Television News: Its Measurement and Perception" (Philadelphia: Master's thesis proposal, Annenberg School of Communications, University of Pennsylvania, 1972); see also Charles E. Osgood et al., "Evaluation Assertion Analysis," *Litera* 3 (1956): 47-102.

7. Judge and Hofstetter, *Content Analysis of Taped Television Stories*.

8. For an analysis of the reliability of measures employed in this study, see Hofstetter and Judge, *Reliability of Television Election News Coverage Content Coding*.

9. Hosti, *Content Analysis*, pp. 116-17.

10. See Deborah Evans, C. Richard Hofstetter, and William Oiler, *Thematic Content of Evening Network News Programs during the 1972 Presidential Campaign, Working Paper Number 3 in the Television Election News Coverage Project (TENCP)* (Columbus: Ohio State University, Polimetrics Laboratory Report No. 13, mimeo., 1974).

11. Inspection of item variances does not support this explanation.

12. Converse, "Information and Partisan Attitudes."

# 7. Specific Issues and Sources in News Coverage

INTRODUCTION

This chapter probes more deeply into two subjects discussed in earlier chapters: (1) the way in which individual reporters covered issues, and (2) the way in which networks handled specific issues. We will scrutinize specific sources and specific issues more closely than we did earlier, but this chapter remains an overview rather than an exhaustive analysis.[1]

Conclusions in the preceding chapters were based on very abstract classifications of news content. The analysis has been very abstract and general in order to include all stories. But inclusiveness may mask important findings that relate to more specific, less abstract matters.

On the other hand, the cost of focusing on very specific issues in an exclusive way may bias the systematic character of a scientific investigation. If very general categories were not used, some stories doubtless would be omitted from analysis. Distorted conclusions might result if arbitrariness entered into the decision to omit stories that did not concern a particular topic, for instance, and if the omitted stories were then related to politics differently than were the included stories. Some stories must be selected and other stories omitted from any analysis. Some characteristics of these stories were judged to be relevant and other characteristics irrelevant. Thus exclusive studies may be particularly useful whenever the analyst desires to select news stories that are especially relevant for his concerns, and inclusive studies may be particularly useful whenever the analyst desires to be assured that his selections are not distorting conclusions. The weakness of exclusive studies lies in the danger of bias that may distort conclusions, and the weakness of inclusive studies lies in the danger of masking conclusions that are particularly relevant.

Such paradoxes are by no means "solved" in non-quantitative studies of media content. Indeed, if anything, the kinds of biases that exist are masked by a veneer of ambiguity. A deep-seated concern for error characterizes the more quantitative scientific studies, and, hence, in these studies the likelihood is greater that many subtle biases will be recognized than in the literary, sometimes more polemical studies.

In this analysis the focus was on several network reporters, commentators, and anchormen, but by no means on all of them. Specific issues were included, and a variety of issues that some might argue should be extensively discussed were excluded.[2] The somewhat arbitrary criteria of frequency of stories and appearances by reporters and of the general interest and popular concern for issues was used in choosing specific sources and issues for analysis. Interest and concern were surmised from news coverage, campaign polls, and national convention platforms. Reporters who did not have major responsibility for at least ten stories during the campaign period, for example, were usually not included, just as issues that failed to receive attention in at least ten stories on one of the major networks were usually not included.

However, some issues receiving less coverage were included, and some receiving more coverage were omitted. In general, specific issues studied in chapter one were included in statistical tabulations but not discussed in the text. These issues were generally about the major parties and Vietnam. For example, the issue of amnesty received little coverage but was nonetheless discussed and debated in partisan circles. Amnesty was also identified, in at least some people's minds, with one of the candidates. Large portions of the public, moreover, held rather intense views on the subject.

It must be reiterated that the criteria used for including or excluding issues and reporters were more arbitrary than in previous chapters. Certainly this was true in comparison with the way that the more general issue and source categories have been defined previously. Yet this more particularistic descriptive analysis allowed focus on more specific topics that many felt were especially significant in the 1972 presidential campaign.

All of the stories under analysis were coded in terms of the way in which they were judged to relate to specific issues, the administration, and the Republican and Democratic campaign efforts. If stories had predominantly favorable or unfavorable implications for issues, the administration, and the campaigns, they were coded accordingly. If the stories had neutral or ambiguous implications, a neutral code was used; and if the stories failed to relate to the specific issues, the administration, or the campaigns, they were also classified as neutral. Thus the neutral classification was somewhat inflated in terms of the absolute proportion of stories it included. This should not, however, affect conclusions based on comparisons of favorable and unfavorable classifications of stories.

REPORTERS AND THE ISSUES

The twenty-eight network reporters who appeared most frequently during the seventeen-week period were included in the following analysis. This criterion of inclusion, as noted, was fairly arbitrary; but all the network anchormen, news commentators, and reporters who had regular beats in Washington and at other key places in the country during the campaign, or who reported much news that was politically relevant, were included. Most likely, if error in selection of sources appeared, the error resided in selecting too many rather than too few reporters.

Tabulations of favorable, neutral, and unfavorable characteristics of stories were computed separately for each reporter who played a role in reporting the story. If, for instance (as frequently occured), the anchorman as well as another reporter in the field participated in the coverage of a story, then story evaluations were attributed to each man. Multiple classification of stories was allowed in the analysis because it was usually difficult, if not impossible, to distinguish exactly what kind of contribution each of several sources made to a story. Classifying stories by each source most likely resulted in conservative estimates of the extent to which coverage by any given individual was extreme—either in a favorable or unfavorable way—because the contributions of additional, possibly more moderate sources, were included in overall story evaluations.

### Straight News

Looking first at sources of straight news—stories that were not commentaries—anchormen varied in the extent to which their issue-reporting was favorable, neutral, and unfavorable. Approximately 2 percent of Cronkite's (CBS) issue coverage was favorable. Chancellor (NBC) and Smith (ABC) provided nearly twice as much favorable coverage in terms of percentages. Reasoner (ABC) fell between Smith and Cronkite, with about 3 percent of the issue stories being favorable. Smith was more likely than the other anchormen to report unfavorable issue stories; but his co-anchorman, Reasoner, was least likely of all to report such stories. Differences in the percentages of stories (or, as interpreted in a strict statistical sense, differences in the likelihood that an anchorman reported a specific story) that were favorable or unfavorable were relatively small, and it is probably more informative to scrutinize the amount of time devoted to favorable and unfavorable issue stories by the anchormen than their relative frequencies. (See table 33.)

167

## TABLE 33

PERCENTAGES OF STORIES AND TIME DEVOTED TO FAVORABLE, NEUTRAL, AND UNFAVORABLE
COVERAGE OF ISSUES IN STRAIGHT NEWS BY SOURCE AND NETWORK

| Network and Reporter | Favorable | | Neutral | | Unfavorable | | N |
|---|---|---|---|---|---|---|---|
| | % | Time | % | Time | % | Time | |
| **CBS** | | | | | | | |
| Cronkite[a] | 2.0 | 11.7 | 86.2 | 675.0 | 11.9 | 157.0 | 615 |
| Schorr | 0.0 | 0.0 | 85.0 | 83.6 | 15.0 | 24.1 | 40 |
| Collingwood | 7.5 | 2.5 | 86.6 | 66.5 | 6.0 | 4.2 | 67 |
| Kalb | 0.0 | 0.0 | 91.4 | 60.5 | 8.6 | 5.0 | 35 |
| Plante | 0.0 | 0.0 | 80.0 | 19.6 | 20.0 | 13.8 | 10 |
| Morton | 0.0 | 0.0 | 83.3 | 55.7 | 16.7 | 9.4 | 30 |
| Scheiffer | 0.0 | 0.0 | 76.0 | 27.9 | 24.0 | 10.1 | 25 |
| Pierpoint | 5.6 | 1.4 | 88.9 | 30.8 | 5.6 | 2.3 | 18 |
| Dick | 0.0 | 0.0 | 90.9 | 24.8 | 9.1 | 1.7 | 11 |
| Rather | 1.4 | 0.4 | 88.4 | 101.0 | 10.1 | 21.8 | 69 |
| Hermann | 0.0 | 0.0 | 84.6 | 24.2 | 15.4 | 3.7 | 13 |
| Mudd | 4.0 | 5.7 | 85.9 | 200.9 | 10.2 | 43.4 | 177 |
| Pappas | 0.0 | 0.0 | 92.9 | 36.6 | 7.1 | 1.4 | 14 |
| Total | 2.7 | 60.8 | 86.4 | 3,002.7 | 10.8 | 638.1 | 2,742 |
| **NBC** | | | | | | | |
| Chancellor | 3.8 | 52.5 | 84.9 | 872.1 | 11.3 | 172.9 | 914 |
| Utley | 3.8 | 7.8 | 88.6 | 75.2 | 7.6 | 15.6 | 79 |
| Jones | 0.0 | 0.0 | 87.5 | 33.0 | 12.5 | 5.3 | 16 |
| Dancy | 7.1 | 3.6 | 85.7 | 57.9 | 7.1 | 5.6 | 28 |
| Delaney | 9.1 | 2.1 | 72.7 | 22.8 | 18.2 | 3.2 | 11 |
| Nesson | 0.0 | 0.0 | 84.6 | 25.0 | 15.4 | 4.2 | 13 |
| Mackin | 5.9 | 2.0 | 94.1 | 28.5 | 0.0 | 0.0 | 17 |
| Stern | 0.0 | 0.0 | 80.0 | 37.6 | 20.0 | 11.1 | 20 |
| Lord | 0.0 | 0.0 | 78.6 | 19.5 | 21.4 | 7.9 | 14 |
| Valeriani | 11.6 | 15.3 | 83.7 | 80.8 | 4.7 | 3.7 | 43 |
| Streithorst | 0.0 | 0.0 | 81.3 | 34.6 | 18.8 | 6.7 | 16 |
| Briggs | 4.8 | 1.7 | 76.2 | 50.5 | 19.0 | 11.2 | 21 |
| Duke | 0.0 | 0.0 | 72.7 | 12.4 | 27.3 | 6.3 | 11 |
| Total | 3.7 | 169.5 | 85.2 | 2,812.5 | 11.1 | 527.5 | 2,973 |
| **ABC** | | | | | | | |
| Smith | 3.4 | 21.0 | 83.9 | 431.2 | 12.7 | 88.5 | 442 |
| Reasoner | 2.9 | 18.5 | 87.3 | 396.0 | 9.8 | 70.6 | 408 |
| Shoemaker | 9.1 | 2.3 | 63.6 | 15.4 | 27.3 | 6.4 | 11 |
| Shoumacher | 0.0 | 0.0 | 80.0 | 29.5 | 20.0 | 8.4 | 15 |
| Donaldson | 0.0 | 0.0 | 87.0 | 46.9 | 13.0 | 9.3 | 23 |
| Kaplow | 3.7 | 1.8 | 96.3 | 25.9 | 0.0 | 0.0 | 27 |
| Reynolds | 4.5 | 2.3 | 81.8 | 34.0 | 13.6 | 7.0 | 22 |
| Matney | 0.0 | 0.0 | 92.3 | 23.8 | 7.7 | 1.9 | 13 |
| Zimmerman | 5.9 | 1.8 | 76.5 | 32.9 | 17.6 | 7.5 | 17 |
| Collins | 0.0 | 0.0 | 58.3 | 15.3 | 41.7 | 8.7 | 12 |
| Jarriel | 8.5 | 7.4 | 85.1 | 79.9 | 6.4 | 5.8 | 47 |
| Gill | 5.0 | 1.9 | 80.0 | 24.8 | 15.0 | 1.2 | 20 |
| Clark | 0.0 | 0.0 | 66.7 | 14.3 | 33.3 | 9.0 | 12 |
| Giggins | 7.7 | 5.3 | 76.9 | 26.0 | 15.4 | 3.9 | 13 |
| Wordham | 0.1 | 1.9 | 72.7 | 15.8 | 18.2 | 5.6 | 11 |
| Geer | 0.0 | 0.0 | 85.7 | 23.1 | 14.3 | 3.3 | 14 |
| Peterson | 0.0 | 0.0 | 90.0 | 19.5 | 10.0 | 2.4 | 10 |
| Koppel | 5.6 | 5.3 | 83.3 | 32.5 | 11.1 | 7.3 | 18 |
| Total | 3.1 | 115.9 | 85.6 | 2,434.1 | 11.3 | 477.4 | 2,538 |

[a]Each reporter appearing in a story was included in tabulations. Thus totals on which the table is based are substantially greater than totals for other analyses that did not include multiple entries.

John Chancellor devoted the greatest amount of time to favorable and unfavorable issue stories. Smith and Reasoner spent a greater amount of time reporting favorable issue stories than Cronkite, but considerably less time than Cronkite reporting unfavorable issue stories. When Smith and Reasoner's time was combined, the same amount of time was devoted to unfavorable issue coverage as Cronkite; but the ABC anchormen devoted considerably more time to favorable and neutral issue coverage than Cronkite.

Cronkite reported by far the fewest stories (once stories reported by co-anchormen Smith and Reasoner were combined). Cronkite reported only 615 issue stories during the campaign period in comparison with 914 stories reported by Chancellor and 442 stories reported by Smith and 408 by Reasoner (850 issue stories covered by ABC anchormen together).

Thus it was possible that differences in the absolute number of stories that anchormen report might soften contrasts among the anchormen in the time devoted to favorable and unfavorable coverage of issue stories. But these contrasts still were not eliminated once the amount of reporting was taken into account. Chancellor, for instance, reported nearly half again as many stories as Cronkite, but Chancellor also devoted nearly five times as much time to favorable issue coverage as Cronkite and only 15 minutes (of about 173 minutes' total time) more than Cronkite to unfavorable issue coverage. Together, Smith and Reasoner devoted only a little more time (159 minutes) to unfavorable issue coverage than Cronkite (157 minutes), but they devoted more than three times as much time to favorable issue coverage as Cronkite (40 minutes compared with 12 minutes).

Issue coverage by other individual network reporters was generally more unfavorable than favorable. A few exceptions appeared. A slightly larger proportion, for instance, of Collingwood's stories on CBS, Mackin and Valeriani's stories on NBC, and Kaplow and Jarriel's stories on ABC were favorable than were unfavorable. Giggins on ABC, moreover, reported more unfavorable than favorable issue *stories*, but spent more *time* on favorable than unfavorable coverage of issues. In each case all the other reporters mentioned (except Collingwood) devoted more time to favorable than unfavorable issue coverage.

On CBS, Plante and Scheiffer, followed by Morton, Schorr, and Herman, presented issue stories most unfavorably. More than 20 percent of the issue stories that Plante and Scheiffer reported were unfavorable, and more than 15 percent of the stories that Schorr,

169

Herman, and Morton reported were unfavorable. In terms of time devoted to issue stories that were unfavorable, Mudd (43 minutes), Schorr (24 minutes), and Rather (22 minutes) ranked highest among CBS reporters. But it is even more significant that all of the reporters devoted the bulk of their coverage (in terms of time as well as numbers of stories) to stories that were neutral.

Most of the issue coverage on NBC was also devoted to stories that were neutral in terms of both numbers and time. On NBC, for instance, 20 percent or more of the issue stories that were reported by Stern, Lord, and Duke were unfavorable. But in no case did these percentages represent issue coverage that consumed more than twelve minutes of broadcast time during the entire campaign. More than 15 percent of the issue stories reported by Delaney, Nesson, and Streithorst were judged to be unfavorable; but even less broadcast time was devoted to these stories than to the issue stories reported by Stern, Lord, and Duke. Finally, it appeared that NBC reporters were less likely than reporters on other networks to report neutral issue stories.

ABC issue coverage was also far more likely to have been neutral than either favorable or unfavorable. More than 20 percent of the issue stories reported by Shoemaker, Shoumacher, Collins, and Clark were unfavorable. But in no case was more than ten minutes total time devoted to unfavorable stories by any of these reporters. Less than ten minutes' broadcast time, moreover, was devoted to ABC reporters who report favorable issue stories in as much as 5 percent of their coverage (Zimmerman, Jarriel, Koppel, Shoemaker, Gill, Giggins, and Wordham).

Valeriani on NBC was most likely of all the reporters to report stories that had favorable issue implications (about 12 percent). This coverage comprised about fifteen minutes of broadcast time. No other reporter spent as much broadcast time on favorable issue coverage.

### Commentaries

Sharper inter-network differences existed in the way that commentaries were related to issues than in the way that straight news was related to issues (see table 34). Commentaries about issues were much more unfavorable than was straight news coverage, and David Brinkley, the NBC commentator, was by far the most likely to make unfavorable comment. Six of ten issue-oriented commentaries that Brinkley broadcast were unfavorable; none of his issue-oriented commentaries were favorable.

TABLE 34

PERCENTAGES OF STORIES AND TIME DEVOTED TO FAVORABLE, NEUTRAL, AND UNFAVORABLE
COVERAGE OF ISSUES IN COMMENTARIES BY COMMENTATOR AND NETWORK

| Commentator | Favorable | | Neutral | | Unfavorable | | N |
|---|---|---|---|---|---|---|---|
| | % | Time | % | Time | % | Time | |
| CBS Sevareid | 3.4 | 2.3 | 65.5 | 43.5 | 31.0 | 24.7 | 29 |
| NBC Brinkley | 0.0 | 0.0 | 40.0 | 18.7 | 60.0 | 33.6 | 25 |
| ABC Smith | 20.7 | 9.2 | 48.3 | 21.9 | 31.0 | 15.5 | 29 |
| Reasoner | 30.8 | 6.3 | 30.8 | 6.7 | 38.5 | 9.1 | 13 |

About 31 percent of the Sevareid and Smith issue commentaries and about 39 percent of the Reasoner issue commentaries were unfavorable, and less than 5 percent of the comparable Sevareid commentaries were favorable. But nearly 21 percent of the Smith commentaries and nearly 31 percent of the Reasoner commentaries were favorable.

Time spent on favorable and unfavorable commentary roughly paralleled the proportion of program time devoted to commentaries, but this correspondence was far from complete. Brinkley spent nearly thirty-four minutes and Sevareid nearly twenty-five minutes on unfavorable commentaries; this contrasted to sixteen minutes that Smith, and nine minutes that Reasoner, devoted to unfavorable commentaries. Smith and Reasoner, moreover, devoted nine and six minutes, respectively, to favorable issue commentaries, in comparison with less than three minutes for Sevareid and no time for Brinkley.

It is also interesting to note that Reasoner placed the least overall emphasis on neutral commentaries (31 percent and seven minutes), and Sevareid the greatest (66 percent and forty-four minutes). Similarly, Brinkley appeared to be far more acerbic in issue commentaries than were the others, since he devoted the most overall emphasis to commentaries that were unfavorable.

SOME SELECTED ISSUES

Allegations of bias about issues have been at the heart of criticism of network news coverage during the last several years. Yet evaluation of network issue coverage remains elusive for several reasons. First, it is difficult to select issues in an unbiased way that meets the approval of all or even most of those who are concerned with objective news reporting. When issues are placed in exhaustive categorizations so that all issue stories may be included in an analysis (as has been done in earlier portions of this study), crucial distinctions may be masked over and blurred. When specific issues are selected in a purposive way, on the other hand, decisions become open to criticism because some crucial issue has been either omitted from analysis or conceptualized in a different way than a critic might prefer.

Second, as we have discovered, not very many stories about most topics were broadcast during the seventeen-week period of this study. It would appear that effects of news coverage that are based on a great deal of repetition of issue material would not have been great during the 1972 campaign. Any theme concerning a specific issue would not be repeated very frequently; nor would a single reporter cover a specific issue very frequently during a campaign. Without a fair amount of repetition, the impact of news bias concerning issues would not be expected to loom very large in comparison with stories that were more frequently covered.[3]

We tried to select issues that were given some attention in the major-party platforms. Not too many clear-cut instances of outright confrontation became evident when the major-party platforms were scrutinized.[5] Another strategy followed was to include specific issues that were relatively frequently covered in the news itself. Finally, an attempt was made to include issues on which fairly intense popular cleavages were known to exist (based on various opinion polls that were conducted during the campaign as well as on a cross-sectional election survey conducted during the second phase of this project).

Criteria for selecting issues were admittedly somewhat arbitrary. None of the strategies for categorizing issue stories exhausted the possibilities for alternative ways of classifying issues because the strategies were not always mutually exclusive in application to news content. But once a specific issue was selected, all stories emphasizing that issue were included in the analysis.

### Vietnam

Vietnam received more coverage than any other specific issue during the campaign period. This coverage was predominantly neutral or unfavorable; little if anything favorable was said concerning Vietnam or American involvement in Vietnam by most of the anchormen and reporters (see table 35). Reasoner was most unfavorable and Smith most favorable, once the number of stories about Vietnam that each anchorman reported was taken into consideration. Chancellor reported the largest number of Vietnam stories (nearly three hundred) and spent a greater amount of time reporting favorable stories than any other anchorman (about fifteen minutes), although Chancellor and Reasoner devoted the smallest proportion of their Vietnam coverage to favorable stories.

TABLE 35

PERCENTAGES OF STORIES AND TIME DEVOTED TO FAVORABLE, NEUTRAL, AND UNFAVORABLE COVERAGE OF VIETNAM BY NETWORK AND REPORTER

| Network and Reporter | Favorable | | Neutral | | Unfavorable | | N |
|---|---|---|---|---|---|---|---|
| | % | Time | % | Time | % | Time | |
| **CBS** | | | | | | | |
| Cronkite | 3.6 | 5.4 | 85.0 | 153.9 | 11.4 | 27.6 | 140 |
| Collingwood | 0.0 | 0.0 | 96.2 | 29.5 | 3.8 | 0.3 | 26 |
| Kalb | 0.0 | 0.0 | 94.7 | 32.8 | 5.3 | 1.3 | 19 |
| Rather | 0.0 | 0.0 | 86.7 | 14.7 | 13.3 | 4.9 | 15 |
| Mudd | 0.0 | 0.0 | 90.2 | 51.8 | 9.8 | 9.2 | 41 |
| Total | 2.2 | 16.3 | 87.4 | 724.2 | 10.3 | 126.3 | 669 |
| **NBC** | | | | | | | |
| Chancellor | 2.2 | 14.6 | 85.9 | 249.1 | 12.0 | 49.9 | 276 |
| Utley | 0.0 | 0.0 | 91.3 | 21.5 | 8.7 | 4.9 | 23 |
| Jones | 0.0 | 0.0 | 87.5 | 33.0 | 12.5 | 5.3 | 16 |
| Lord | 0.0 | 0.0 | 78.6 | 19.5 | 21.4 | 7.9 | 14 |
| Valeriani | 8.3 | 4.8 | 91.7 | 30.9 | 0.0 | 0.0 | 12 |
| Streithorst | 0.0 | 0.0 | 81.3 | 34.6 | 18.8 | 6.7 | 16 |
| Total | 2.0 | 43.9 | 86.2 | 797.1 | 11.7 | 164.2 | 894 |
| **ABC** | | | | | | | |
| Smith | 3.7 | 9.0 | 82.4 | 93.4 | 13.9 | 18.3 | 108 |
| Reasoner | 1.4 | 3.6 | 82.6 | 112.8 | 15.9 | 32.5 | 138 |
| Collins | 0.0 | 0.0 | 58.3 | 15.3 | 41.7 | 8.7 | 12 |
| Jarriel | 10.0 | 1.5 | 90.0 | 28.6 | 0.0 | 0.0 | 10 |
| Giggins | 9.1 | 5.3 | 81.8 | 23.6 | 9.1 | 2.1 | 11 |
| Koppel | 7.7 | 5.3 | 76.9 | 25.9 | 15.4 | 7.3 | 13 |
| Total | 2.1 | 32.3 | 82.6 | 580.9 | 15.3 | 152.2 | 726 |

Collingwood, Kalb, Rather, and Mudd all reported unfavorable and neutral Vietnam coverage, but failed to report anything favorable. Rather and Mudd were most unfavorable in reporting about Vietnam when both the proportion of stories and time devoted to them was considered. Utley, Jones, Lord, and Streithorst provided exclusively unfavorable or neutral coverage of Vietnam on NBC, and Valeriani (in twelve stories) included one favorable story (and no unfavorable ones) in his coverage. In contrast to coverage on CBS and NBC, Collins was the only ABC reporter to provide exclusively unfavorable or neutral coverage on Vietnam. Jarriel, Giggins, and Koppel all included at least some favorable coverage. It is necessary, however, to point out that the actual number of stories included by the reporters was not very large. Thus the overall impact of favorable and unfavorable coverage was not likely to be over-whelming.

When linkages between news coverage of Vietnam and the Re-publican and Democratic campaigns were considered, it appeared that the Republicans gained more from this coverage than the Democrats. Cronkite, Smith, and Reasoner related Vietnam to the GOP campaign in either favorable or neutral ways, and Chancellor provided more favorable than unfavorable coverage with regard to the Republicans.* Exactly the opposite pattern emerged when the way that these anchormen related Vietnam coverage to the Demo-cratic campaign was studied. Cronkite, Smith, and Reasoner pro-vided either unfavorable or neutral coverage of the issue with re-gard to the Democratic campaign effort (but no favorable coverage), and Chancellor provided more unfavorable than favorable cover-age.

Among the CBS reporters, Collingwood and Kalb reported at least some stories relating Vietnam unfavorably to GOP campaign ef-forts, and Kalb and Rather provided some Vietnam coverage re-lating favorably to the campaign. Utley, Jones, and Lord all reported some coverage tied to the Republican campaign, but only Lord provided coverage that could be classified as favorable or unfavor-able (only one unfavorable story). The picture on ABC, once again, was different. Jarriel, Giggins, and Koppel all reported Vietnam stories that related to the Republican campaign, and this coverage was either favorable or neutral with respect to GOP efforts.

Among all the reporters on the networks, only Chancellor tied a single story about Vietnam to the Democratic campaign in a favor-able way. Kalb and Mudd on CBS and Jarriel and Koppel on ABC linked Vietnam to the Democrats in unfavorable ways in one story. And a few other reporters linked Vietnam to Democratic efforts in a neutral way. But it is also important to emphasize that very few stories by any of the reporters (other than the anchormen) were included in these evaluations.

### Busing and Law and Order

Very few non-neutral stories concerning busing to attain racial balance in the public schools or the issue of law and order were car-ried on network news, although some favorable and unfavorable coverage of each issue was provided by the networks during the campaign period. The analysis was reported in terms of anchormen and all other network reporters on these issues because a very small number of stories about the issues were involved. The lack of stories made inferences concerning the impact of specific reporters uncertain at best and certainly increased the likelihood that a single coding error (no matter how improbable) could greatly distort conclusions about bias in coverage by an individual reporter.

*Busing.* Each anchorman and the reporters on each network reported stories that were either neutral or unfavorable, but not favorable, with regard to busing.* Coverage was predominantly neutral about the issue, with Chancellor and Smith and Reasoner each reporting but one unfavorable story (Cronkite reported only neutral stories about the issue). ABC reporters provided the most unfavorable stories (about 18 percent of the stories), and CBS reporters provided the least unfavorable coverage of this issue (5 percent of the stories and eight minutes of time). NBC reporters devoted the most time to unfavorable coverage (thirteen minutes), but fell between CBS and ABC in terms of the relative number of stories unfavorable to busing (11 percent). On the basis of the few stories that appeared during the campaign, CBS coverage was relatively least unfavorable and ABC coverage relatively most unfavorable.

*Law and Order.* Network coverage of law and order was also predominantly neutral, but, unlike the bussing controversy, some favorable coverage did appear during the campaign. Cronkite and other CBS reporters who covered the issue provided no favorable and some unfavorable coverage. This contrasted with the way the issues was handled on NBC and ABC. Chancellor and Smith and Reasoner included both favorable and unfavorable coverage of the issue, but they reported it in a predominantly neutral way. Chancellor and other NBC reporters included the greatest amount of favorable coverage; Cronkite included the largest proportion of, and devoted the greatest amount of time to, unfavorable stories.

### Conservation

Stories about conservation of natural resources (including environmental problems) constituted yet another area in which the balance of news coverage was unfavorable.* Cronkite reported only neutral or unfavorable stories about the issue, although other CBS reporters contributed some favorable coverage. On NBC coverage of such stories was exactly balanced, with Chancellor providing about the same coverage to stories that were favorable and those that were unfavorable. In all these cases, however, more than 85 percent of the coverage was neutral.

ABC's treatment of the issue was different. Smith was more critical in news stories about conservation and Reasoner more favorable than the other anchormen. About two of five Smith stories were unfavorable, and one in four of the Reasoner stories was favorable. It is important to note, however, that Smith reported only ten stories and Reasoner only four stories on the topic during the campaign.

But the same trend appeared when stories about conservation by all ABC reporters (forty-three) were scrutinized. About 5 percent of the stories on CBS and NBC were favorable, in comparison with 14 percent of the stories on ABC. Similarly, about 10 percent of the stories on CBS and 5 percent of the stories on NBC were unfavorable, in comparison with 36 percent of the stories on ABC. Finally, 50 percent of the stories on ABC were judged to be neutral in coverage. The amount of time devoted to news stories about conservation, moreover, paralleled the percentages of stories quite closely. So few conservation news stories were related to either the Democratic or the Republican presidential campaigns in 1972 that partisan analysis was not meaningful.

### Cost of Living

Economic issues have been important in maintaining and shifting coalitions in American presidential politics. The networks devoted a fairly large amount of attention to the cost of living during the 1972 campaign, although the issue itself was not very often linked to the major-party campaigns in this coverage in either a favorable or unfavorable way.*

Cronkite and Chancellor devoted about the same proportion of stories to favorable and unfavorable coverage of the issue; Smith devoted twice as many stories to unfavorable as to favorable coverage; and all of Reasoner's news stories were neutral. As was true of reporting about conservation, Smith devoted more time to favorable and unfavorable stories and less time to neutral stories about the cost of living than the other anchormen. CBS overall reporting, however, was most likely to be favorable, and NBC overall reporting was most likely to be unfavorable in the proportion of stories broadcast. At the same time, ABC devoted the most time (slightly more than five minutes) to favorable, and NBC the most time (about eighteen minutes) to unfavorable, coverage.

Very little favorable or unfavorable attention was given to the cost-of-living issue in coverage of the major-party campaigns. What little linkage existed was predominantly neutral or unfavorable. Only Smith (in one story) and Kaplow (for a total of five minutes) associated it with the Republican campaign in a favorable way, and none of the sources associated the issue with the Democrats in a favorable way.

Only Cronkite associated the cost of living with the Democratic campaign in an unfavorable way (a little more than four minutes coverage in all). In contrast, some stories unfavorable to the GOP campaign were covered on each network by each anchorman except Reasoner; Cronkite was most likely to report such stories (over 12 percent), and Chancellor least likely (5 percent). Smith, however, devoted more time than the other anchormen to cost-of-living stories that were either favorable or unfavorable to Republican campaign efforts (nearly three minutes of unfavorable and two minutes of favorable coverage). NBC devoted the least time to such stories (under one minute) during the campaign.

### Honesty in Government

The issue of honesty in government received a fair amount of coverage in relation to the Republican but not the Democratic presidential campaign.* The majority of stories were neutral rather than unfavorable, but the predominance of the neutral classification was not as great as it was among the other issue stories. For example, Cronkite devoted 30 percent (almost 13 minutes), Chancellor 33 percent (ten minutes), and Reasoner 25 percent (under two minutes) to unfavorable coverage of the issue.

Smith devoted 17 percent of his coverage (eight minutes) to unfavorable stories; he devoted more coverage (83 percent) to neutral stories than any other anchorman. In all, CBS reporters devoted more time (forty-four minutes) to unfavorable coverage than did ABC (thirty minutes) or NBC (thirty-one minutes) reporters. NBC reporters were more likely to report stories that were unfavorable (33 percent) than either CBS (29 percent) or ABC (19 percent) reporters.

None of the stories concerning honesty in government were related to the Democratic campaign in any except a neutral way, but each network carried a fair amount of coverage that related the issue to GOP campaign efforts in an unfavorable way. These linkages between honesty in government and the Republican campaign, however, did not follow the trends present in evaluations of network issue coverage. CBS reporters (including Cronkite) were substantially less likely to relate stories about the issue to the Republican campaign in an unfavorable way (25 percent or thirty-four minutes) than were NBC reporters (including Chancellor) or ABC reporters (including Smith and Reasoner). NBC devoted about 43 percent of its stories (twenty-nine minutes) to unfavorable coverage, and ABC devoted about 44 percent of its comparable coverage (fifty-five minutes) to unfavorable stories about the topic.

### Government Functioning

During the campaign less coverage was given to the issue of government functioning than to the issue of honesty in government,* and this coverage was considerably more likely to be neutral than was coverage of the latter issue. No favorable or unfavorable coverage of government functioning appeared on ABC—all its stories were neutral. In contrast, about 17 percent of the CBS coverage (twenty-eight minutes) was unfavorable, and about 33 percent of the NBC coverage (eighteen minutes) was unfavorable. Chancellor devoted 25 percent of his stories about the topic to unfavorable coverage, and 17 percent of Cronkite's coverage (nine minutes) was unfavorable. No one reported any favorable stories about government functioning.

A different picture emerged when we focused on how government functioning was related to the partisan campaigns. Cronkite and Chancellor reported some stories linking the issue favorably to the Republican campaign. Cronkite, however, also reported several stories relating it to GOP campaign efforts in an unfavorable way. About 17 percent of Cronkite's coverage (less than one minute) was favorable, whereas 50 percent (over twelve minutes) was unfavorably tied to the Republican presidential campaign. Three long stories were unfavorable, and one very short story was favorable. In all, CBS devoted 17 percent of its coverage to favorable stories (representing under one minute) and a larger percentage (representing thirty-eight minutes) to unfavorable stories. Chancellor on NBC reported one story (25 percent of his stories on the topic, or less than one minute) linking government functioning favorably to the Republican campaign, and none linking the topic unfavorably to the GOP campaign. About 14 percent of the stories (less than one minute) by all NBC reporters were favorable to GOP efforts, and none were unfavorable. All of the ABC coverage of the issue was neutral.

None of the networks carried stories about government functioning related to the Democratic presidential campaign in a favorable way, although in a few stories CBS and NBC linked it to the Democratic efforts in an unfavorable way. Cronkite devoted one story (17 percent, or less than one minute) to coverage that related the issue to the Democratic campaign in an unfavorable way. Chancellor followed suit with a single comparable story (25 percent, or less than one minute). Other CBS and NBC reporters added very few stories that were related unfavorably to Democratic campaign efforts. All of the ABC coverage of this area was neutral.

*Amnesty*

The little coverage of the amnesty issue was neutral as far as the issue itself was concerned.* This was not true of coverage that linked it to the campaigns. Surprisingly little coverage was given to the question on network news throughout the campaign (given the amount of debate and the intense feelings that the subject aroused). The few stories that CBS and NBC reported (ABC reported no stories that emphasized amnesty) linked the issue both favorably and unfavorably to the Republican campaign and unfavorably to the Democratic campaign.

Cronkite reported two stories (of six, for about three minutes) that tied the issue to the GOP efforts in a favorable way. He gave exactly the same amount of coverage to stories that related it to the Democratic campaign in an unfavorable way. One of Chancellor's two stories emphasizing amnesty (less than one minute) tied it to the GOP efforts in a favorable way, but both of Chancellor's stories were neutral with regard to Democratic campaign efforts. Other network coverage paralleled coverage by the respective network anchormen.

*Size and Control of the Military*

A fair amount of attention was given to stories about the size and control of the military during the campaign. This was also a question discussed thoroughly by various partisan groups and another issue on which intense feelings existed. But little if any network news coverage of the subject emphasized linkages between the military and the campaigns.*

CBS reported a few stories (6 percent of its coverage, less than two minutes) that were favorable, but reported no stories that were unfavorable. All of Cronkite's coverage was judged to be neutral. In contrast, both NBC and ABC devoted some coverage to stories about military size and control that were unfavorable, but none that were favorable. About 18 percent (six minutes) of Chancellor's stories in this area were unfavorable, and about 16 percent of all NBC reporters' coverage (seventeen minutes) was unfavorable. One of Smith's five stories about the issue (less than two minutes) was unfavorable, ten of Reasoner's eleven stories were neutral, and 7 percent of all ABC coverage was unfavorable (less than five minutes).

*Taxes, Jobs, and Wages*

Both taxes and employment are key issues in the American political arena. Indeed, the major electoral coalitions clustered about the two major parties have been greatly influenced by such economic questions. In light of these facts, it was surprising to note that network news failed to relate either taxes or jobs and wages to the major-party campaigns during the 1972 election.* Nor was a great deal of attention given to these issues, because the networks broadcast very few stories emphasizing either taxes or jobs and wages.

*Taxes.* One of Smith's two stories about taxes (less than one minute) was favorable, and none of his coverage was unfavorable. None of the stories on the subject on CBS or on NBC was favorable. Two of Cronkite's six stories were unfavorable (less than one minute), and two of Chancellor's ten stories (about four minutes) were unfavorable. Total network coverage of tax issues paralleled coverage by the anchormen. Thus the issue became almost a non-issue in the 1972 campaign.

*Jobs and wages.* Little coverage was given to jobs and wages, and none to stories linking the issue to the partisan campaigns in a favorable or unfavorable way. None of the stories during the campaign were unfavorable to the issue, and almost all were neutral. One of the four stories (about two minutes) that Reasoner reported was favorable, but none of the stories on NBC or that Cronkite reported on CBS were either favorable or unfavorable. About 17 percent (less than seven minutes) of the stories on CBS and 25 percent (about six minutes) of these stories on ABC were favorable.

### Labor

Network news did link organized labor to the partisan political campaigns. Considerably more coverage was devoted to such stories than to stories about taxes or about jobs and wages. Stories that emphasized labor were most favorable on CBS and most unfavorable on NBC.* All Cronkite's six stories (two minutes) were neutral, and about 6 percent of Chancellor's stories (less than one minute) were favorable and 13 percent (four minutes) unfavorable. Seventeen percent of Smith's stories were favorable (less than one minute), and all of Reasoner's stories were neutral (four minutes). CBS devoted about the same proportion of coverage to stories that were favorable and unfavorable, although it spent considerably more time on the latter than on the former (two minutes on favorable and seven minutes on unfavorable coverage). Differences in overall NBC and ABC treatment paralleled that of the respective anchormen.

Organized labor was tied to the Republican campaign in a predominantly neutral or ambiguous way by all the networks, although CBS gave some (about two minutes) attention to aspects of the issue that were unfavorably tied to the GOP campaign. No stories about labor were linked to the Democratic campaign in a favorable way; and although ties between labor and the Democrats were predominantly neutral or ambiguous in most network coverage, all the anchormen and networks devoted at least some coverage to stories that linked the issue to the Democratic campaign in an unfavorable way. Less than one minute was devoted to such stories on CBS, compared with five minutes on NBC and seven minutes on ABC.

### Welfare and Poverty

Slightly less attention overall was devoted to stories about economic welfare and poverty during the campaign than to stories about labor.* But differences in network coverage of the issue did emerge. One of the eight stories that Cronkite reported (less than two minutes) was unfavorable, and none of his coverage was favorable. One of Chancellor's six stories on the topic was favorable (less than one minute) and one was unfavorable (less than three minutes). One of the six stories that Smith reported was unfavorable (less than three minutes), and the other five were neutral; and one of the four stories that Reasoner reported was unfavorable (two minutes), and three were neutral.

In all, nearly four minutes of CBS coverage that emphasized welfare and poverty was unfavorable and none favorable. ABC devoted about thirteen minutes to unfavorable coverage, and NBC devoted one minute to favorable and seven minutes to unfavorable coverage. ABC devoted the greatest amount of time to the issue (thirteen minutes), and CBS the least time (four minutes).

None of the networks emphasized stories about welfare and poverty related to the GOP presidential campaign in either a favorable or unfavorable way. But the issue was related to Democratic campaign efforts in unfavorable ways; one of Cronkite's eight stories (less than two minutes) was unfavorable. All six of Chancellor's stories, all six of Smith's stories, and all four of Reasoner's stories established neither favorable nor unfavorable linkages with Democratic campaign efforts.

Network overall coverage of welfare and poverty did generally parallel coverage by anchormen. All NBC and ABC stories linked the issue to the Democratic campaign in a neutral way; on CBS only one Cronkite story did not.

181

CONCLUSION

Differences appeared in the way that different news personnel covered stories about the administration, major-party campaigns, and issues in the extent of favorable and unfavorable coverage. On some issues these differences were as great when reporters employed by the same network were compared as when reporters for different networks were compared. There was almost as much variation in the implications of news coverage within networks as among networks. And yet, the analysis of specific issues in the latter portion of the chapter suggested that there was also tremendous variation in the extent to which different specific issues were given favorable or unfavorable coverage, at least by anchormen and other network reporters. Most issue coverage was either neutral, balanced (about evenly between favorable and unfavorable content and style of reporting), too ambiguous to classify as either favorable or unfavorable, or simply not relevant to particular topics.

There was a general tendency for Cronkite to be a bit more critical (more unfavorable and less favorable) and for Smith and Reasoner to be less critical (less unfavorable and more favorable). Chancellor covered more stories, and, although he devoted a larger absolute amount of time to favorable and unfavorable stories about issues, the proportion of his time and stories that were favorable or unfavorable generally fell between comparable proportions of Cronkite and Smith and Reasoner coverage.

A similar pattern emerges when issue coverage related to the Democratic and Republican campaigns is scrutinized. Cronkite was most unfavorable in linking issues to the Democratic campaign, and Smith and Reasoner were most favorable in linking issues to both Republican and Democratic campaigns. As far as the network reporters go, however, very little issue content favorable to the Democratic campaign efforts was carried on any of the networks. It thus appeared that the Republicans derived a clear benefit from general issue coverage on all three networks, although this advantage may have been slightly less on ABC than on the other networks.

It was also apparent that good news was driven out by bad, and that both were driven out by neutral issue coverage. Network news was predominantly neutral; but when issue stories could be classified reliably as either favorable or unfavorable, more fell into the latter category than into the former. This was somewhat more likely to occur on CBS and somewhat less likely to occur on ABC than on NBC.

Coverage of thirteen relatively specific issues (Vietnam, busing, law and order, conservation, cost of living, honesty in government, governmental functioning, amnesty, size and control of the military, taxes, jobs and wages, labor, and welfare and poverty) was also subject to analysis. Relatively few stories about particular issues were included in news coverage during the study period; Vietnam was an exception to this rule. Thus coverage by anchormen rather than by all reporters was employed in most of the issue analysis so that more than one or two stories could be used as a basis for judgments about the character of coverage.

Several other major points about network news issue coverage emerged from the analysis. First, Smith and Reasoner did not speak with a single voice. In the case of Vietnam coverage, for instance, Smith's coverage was more likely to be favorable than any other anchorman's reporting, and Reasoner's coverage was more likely to be unfavorable than that of other anchormen. Second, coverage of Vietnam tended to be more favorable to the Republican campaign than to the Democratic campaign. Coverage, no doubt, was particularly influenced by reports of peace initiatives during the last months of the campaign. But even with these peace initiatives, surprisingly little coverage favorable to the Democratic campaign appeared on network television news (given the strongly "dovish" image that was widely attributed to the Democratic challenger).

Third, the networks did not embed issue emphases in campaign coverage, at least in a partisan way; most issue content was related to the major-party campaigns in a neutral or ambiguous way (that is, when related to the campaigns and partisan politics at all).

Fourth, analysis of specific issue coverage showed just how tenuous conclusions based on general issue coverage were, for each of the networks could be classified as most or least favorable with regard to a variety of "liberal" and "conservative" positions on issues; and these classifications were subject to change depending on whether the percentage of stories or the amount of time devoted to stories was employed as an indicator of coverage in some instances.

Generally speaking, CBS was most favorable to jobs and wages (along with ABC), cost of living (along with ABC), labor, and size and control of the military. CBS was most unfavorable in its coverage of law and order, taxes, honesty in government, and government functioning. In contrast, NBC was both most favorable in its coverage of law and order (along with ABC) and welfare and poverty; and NBC was most unfavorable in its coverage of the cost of living, size and control of the military, and labor. ABC was most favorable in its coverage of law and order and jobs and wages (along with

NBC), conservation, cost of living (along with CBS), and taxes. ABC was relatively most unfavorable in its coverage of the Democratic National Convention.

Few issues were systematically associated with the partisan campaigns; however, some linkages were established and should be noted. ABC associated the cost of living most favorably with the Republicans, and ABC and CBS associated the issue most unfavorably with the Democratic campaign. CBS was less likely to link honesty in government to the GOP campaign in an unfavorable way than the other networks; but it tied government functioning most unfavorably to the Republican campaign efforts, and NBC tied it most favorably to the Republican campaign. On the amnesty issue CBS was both most favorable and most unfavorable to the Republicans and most favorable to the Democrats.

CBS linked labor most favorably and most unfavorably to the Republicans, whereas ABC tied labor to the Democratic campaign in the most unfavorable way. On the question of welfare and poverty, CBS was most unfavorable to the Democratic campaign efforts, and each network tied welfare and poverty to the GOP campaign in a neutral way.

Thus it appeared that CBS may have been more critical in coverage of some issue areas, and ABC and NBC less critical. It was also clear that each network's coverage could be defined in a variety of ways if specific issue clusters were isolated. But differences between favorable and unfavorable coverage were slight in most cases. Indeed, the complexity of issue coverage and campaign coverage scrutinized in this chapter once again suggests that political bias, such as may exist, was not systematically present during the 1972 campaign.

* Detailed statistical tabulations are available from the author upon request.

1. Limitations of space preclude a more thorough description of the ways in which issues were linked to the administration and the major-party campaigns. The findings presented in this chapter are quite representative, however, of our findings concerning the relationship between issues and the administration and the major parties.

2. See the debate between CBS and Efron portrayed in Winick, "Critique of *The News Twisters*"; CBS News, "CBS News Comments on 'The News Twisters' " (New York; mimeographed, 1971); Efron, *How CBS Tried to Kill a Book*; and Weaver, "Is News Biased?"

3. Efron, *The News Twisters*.

4. One problem, however, was avoided in the present analysis. All or most of the stories that were aired on weekdays during 10 July to 6 November 1972 were included. Large numbers of stories are therefore not required to make "significant" inferences in a statistical

sense. Although some errors may have occurred in coding operations, no error was due to the sampling of stories in the ordinary sense that error is regarded in sampling problems. Thus any results are statistically "significant," even if results may not necessarily always be practically or theoretically significant.

5. See Paul Anderson and C. Richard Hofstetter, *Television News and the Convention Platforms: A Partisan Baseline, Working Paper Number 11 in the Television Election News Coverage Project (TENCP)* (Columbus: Ohio State University, Polimetrics Laboratory Report No. 23, 1974).

# 8. Campaign 1972 through the Eyes of Television News

INTRODUCTION

It is not possible to make a persuasive case that partisan political bias was present in network television news coverage of the 1972 presidential election campaign. Indeed, based on the evidence in this study, the objective reader would be forced to conclude that partisan bias was not a significant factor in news coverage. This does not mean, of course, that substantial partisan bias has not characterized television news coverage of social and political events prior to, or following, the 1972 campaign. Neither does it mean that other types of bias were absent from the evening news, nor that biases did not have an impact on the campaigns. These conclusions will be elaborated and important caveats outlined in this chapter by describing the form and nature of television news coverage on CBS, NBC, and ABC.

Let us recall the notion of political bias. The most important distinction made in discussions of biased news coverage involves the difference between *political bias* and *structural bias*. All communication is selective: only some aspects and interpretations of situations and events are transmitted. Only a portion of the transmitted information, moreover, is received and cognized by individuals. Thus both production and reception of information are selective and, in this sense, biased.

The same general characteristics of communication are no less true of one specific type of communication, network news programming. Some facts and some interpretations of these facts are selected as relevant by news personnel, and some stories are selected to be broadcast by others. Finally, only some facts included in news stories actually broadcast are perceived by viewers. This never includes "all the facts," or all the interpretations, or all the stories, or all the information. In this sense "purely objective" reporting is impossible.

Selectivity at each stage involves implicit sets of ideas about what is going on (theories) that reporters, news editors, producers, and other news personnel hold. Individuals among the public also hold ideas about reported events. Selectivity is ubiquitous in news reporting (as in other areas of human activity), but this does not mean that questions of bias are irrelevant. One set of ideas about what is happening in the news is by no means as good as any other set of ideas. But the pervasiveness of selectivity does not imply that all news observations boil down into an infinite, relativistic regress. Some versions of what is happening in the social and political world are more appropriate than others by clear, unambiguous standards. The facts I believe to be true, moreover, may not be as accurate as the facts you believe to be true.

Structural bias involves selection of news based on the characteristics of the medium itself. Television has many attributes that facilitate reporting specific kinds of information in specific ways. The same is true of radio, newspapers, and magazine coverage of news events, although the specific structural biases involved depend on the particular characteristics of each medium. Structural biases are, of course, constant for all news programming on television, just as the same structural biases appear in each example of news coverage in the same kind of medium.

The commercial character of network television news, coupled with limited time for news broadcasting, establishes the most important constraint on the evening news. News—like other programming on commercial television—must attract an audience, sponsors, and station affiliates who are willing to broadcast it. In addition it must live within a budget in an area where costs are very high. Newsmen must live with these grim realities as they produce the news. They are also the most important bases for many of the structural biases we found present in the evening news.

Characteristics of particular situations may interact with structural biases arising from characteristics of the television medium. Politics in America—especially electoral politics, with all its conflict, drama, glamour, and moralistic appeal—is exciting. Thus politics is easy to report, and produces news. Audiences are attracted by the showmanship of the campaign. Newsmen's and candidates' interests coincide to ensure that the campaigns receive widespread coverage. Thus a situational component emerges in considerations of structural bias.

Political bias involves selection of news based on political considerations or prejudices. If one faced only a liberal or a conservative news establishment, or a group of news establishments "out to get" or "out to support" the president, then selection of information broadcast on network news might be expected to reflect political prejudices. It would appear clear that news reporters, just like politicians or any other Americans, have an abundance of political prejudices. But this is not the question relating to biased news reporting. The question underlying the furor about news bias involves the extent to which prejudices or preferences are translated in the information-selection process to support or undermine a political position or personality in systematic and consistent ways. Proof to support these assertions must lie in what is actually broadcast and not in the hearts of newsmen.

Ascertaining whether or not political bias is present in programming in an objective and scientific manner is no simple and straightforward matter. To assess news coverage, one must distinguish between structural (whether medium or situationally constrained) and political bias. We have not completely solved the problem in this study (as is true in other studies as well), but we hope that additional light has been shed on the kinds of evidence necessary to support assertions about political bias in televised or other forms of news.

The most vexing problem in studying bias is to discern a baseline for comparisons of news coverage. What measures are needed to determine the presence or absence of political bias as opposed to structural biases in television news? A second problem plaguing this study (and other studies) involves how much difference between standards of bias is required to "be significant." How much can the news depart from standards of "objectivity" (however defined) in order to assert that a meaningful amount of bias exists? The latter question is important, but it pales in significance unless the former question is answered in a decisive way. An adequate baseline must be established if one is to make judgments concerning bias.

At one extreme an objective baseline independent of news programming might be formulated only by a team of impartial experts (or, more realistically, a large number of knowledgeable people with an even larger variety of prejudices). These experts would formulate descriptions of an event included in the news based on their own observations, and the report might then be compared with what had been presented on the evening news. Or perhaps one might observe an event himself and then make an assessment of news coverage by comparing his own impressions with those reported on the news. Clearly, such "solutions" are not reasonable because they are not feasible. In the present study, for instance, 4,349 news stories about events occurring all over the world were included. Quite obviously, it would have been impossible to observe even a small number of these stories in a way independent of the mass media; and in many cases it would have been impossible to observe the events in a way independent of the television medium itself.

Baselines used in evaluating news coverage require that additional assumptions be made about the way news is produced, and criteria about the presence or absence of political bias based on these assumptions are relative rather than absolute in nature. Thus one can be less than certain of his conclusions about this type of bias, even after the most painstaking analyses. First, we cannot simply note that "bad" news tends to drive out "good" news—as we have discovered time and again in this study—and go on to infer that political bias was present. We must also ask if similar patterns of news coverage appeared on each of the networks. Indeed, the nearly identical kinds of news coverage on each network suggest that structural (or situational) bias, not political bias, was inherent in the predominance of "bad" news coverage in television news programming. We would conclude that something inherent in the nature of commercial television news, or in American political campaigning in 1972, produced a negative overtone to the news.

Second, it is important to assume that variation appeared in the views of reporters, news producers, and other news personnel, and that this individual variation occurred despite considerable agreement on what was newsworthy. Professional criteria of newsworthiness did not, however, necessarily imply collusion. It is reasonable to conclude that variations among networks can be used as a criterion for inferring the presence of political bias.[1] By making comparisons of news coverage among members of the same medium, we eliminate structural bias as an explantion for variation. Structural biases that affect CBS surely also affect NBC and ABC, since each is essentially like the others. The same situations, moreover, faced each network during the campaign. Thus it would appear reasonable that differences in the way that Nixon or McGovern were covered on each of the three major networks could be explained as structural (or situational) bias. Imagine that Nixon was covered very favorably and McGovern very unfavorably on CBS; McGovern was covered very favorably and Nixon very unfavorably on NBC; and each was covered in about the same way on ABC. We would conclude that CBS maintained a *relatively* more pro-Nixon and anti-McGovern bias than the other networks; that NBC maintained a *relatively* more pro-McGovern and anti-Nixon bias; and that ABC fell somewhere in between CBS and NBC. But if *each* network devoted more coverage to favorable Nixon stories than to favorable McGovern stories and if this coverage were similar on each network, then our assumptions would not lead us to conclude that political biases were at work. Thus distinguishing political from structural (or situational) bias in news programming involves comparisons of the way the networks cover stories. A sense of statistical equity lies at the center of this concern.[2]

A third major consideration is suggested by the preceding discussion. We are never really in a position to evaluate some kinds of variation in news coverage. In some ambiguous cases it was simply not possible to ascertain what "the facts may be." It may be, for example, that one candidate was the epitome of virtue and his opponent the epitome of vice. If this were true and each candidate were given absolutely equal amounts of favorable and unfavorable news coverage, then one would—erroneously, in this case—conclude that the news was unbiased. The virtuous person received the less favorable coverage and the vicious person more favorable coverage in relation to each candidate's just due. But we are rarely in a position to make these kinds of judgments. Instead, it is necessary to rely on many information sources to reflect the virtues and vices of individuals and groups. It is even more important, therefore, to evaluate the extent to which the three networks agreed or disagreed in how various kinds of stories were reported.

Inferences about political bias are always relative rather than absolute for the same reasons. For example, although we might be able to infer that ABC gave more favorable coverage to the GOP than did CBS, we cannot say in an absolute sense that CBS was biased against the GOP or that ABC was biased in favor of the GOP. At best, we could conclude that, *relative to the other network's coverage*, CBS was biased against, and ABC was biased in favor of, the GOP. But even then, it would be necessary to compare coverage of the GOP with coverage of the Democratic party on CBS and ABC. Conclusions might quickly be reversed if the Democratic party fared better on ABC but far worse on CBS than the Republican party.

GENERAL DIMENSIONS OF POLITICAL NEWS COVERAGE

Exactly what was the outline of network news coverage during the 1972 campaign? Several general conclusions about the way in which the news was reported appear evident from the analyses presented in the earlier chapters.

1. Network television news was by no means dominated by election coverage, even during the height of a national campaign for the presidency. Issue reporting dominated the news, but only about one issue story of five gave a major emphasis to a presidential candidate, a major political party, or the campaign for the presidency.

191

2. It was useful to classify news stories into candidate, issue, and party (and campaign) categories according to their predominant emphases. About four of five news stories could be classified in this way. The tripartite classification, moreover, corresponded to a major conceptual framework widely used to classify individual attitudes and beliefs about politics during election campaigns. But the scheme was useful to categorize news only if combinations of candidate, issue, and party emphases characterized stories.

3. Not many stories were exclusively about either major party or major party candidate. When stories emphasized a candidate, party, or issue, they generally also emphasized at least one other subject as well. Thus the political news reported was multifaceted in nature, tying at least candidates, issues, and political parties together.

4. Networks varied in some specific mechanics of news reporting. ABC news coverage included the fewest stories and the least broadcast time. NBC reported many more, but shorter, news stories than the other networks; but NBC consumed less total air time than CBS in broadcasting politically relevant stories than either NBC or ABC, but covered many fewer stories than NBC. Thus the average time devoted to each political story was greater on CBS than on NBC.

5. Despite differences in mechanics resulting in different quantitative characteristics of stories, network news coverage about politics was amazingly similar in profile. The overall patterns of news reporting were parallel once the differences in numbers of stories and lengths of stories had been converted into proportions of stories and time consumed by stories. If more time was devoted to issue coverage on CBS, for instance, more time was also devoted to comparable coverage on NBC and ABC in comparison with the way time was devoted to candidate or party stories on the networks. If proportionately fewer stories were carried about political issues in relation to other coverage on CBS (and less time devoted to these stories), then an identical pattern emerged in NBC and ABC coverage. We assume that these similarities were due to the nature of television news (structural biases), or to the character of the 1972 campaign (situational factors), rather than to conspiratorial activities. A closer look at these findings is presented below.

6. The amount of political coverage on each network did not necessarily correspond to patterns of political activity or to the orderly development of the campaign. Rather than devoting a steadily increasing amount of attention to political news between the earliest major-party convention and the election, a great deal of attention was given to "nomination politics" surrounding the national conventions and to campaign politics during the last weeks of the campaign. But very little network political reporting was broadcast during September, the month that traditionally signified the beginning of the presidential campaign. Studies of television news coverage should make every effort to include extensive consideration of the pre–Labor Day portion of political campaigns.

7. The lot of minor-party candidates was not eased by attention they received on network news. Very little coverage concerned minor-party candidates during the 1972 campaign, and what little appeared was dominated by the AIP candidate, John Schmitz. This coverage contrasted with that afforded AIP standard-bearer George Wallace during the 1968 campaign.

8. Major-party candidates for president received the bulk of attention during the campaign. Over 80 percent of the stories and time about candidates were devoted to either Nixon or McGovern. In these stories Nixon received less exposure than McGovern, but Agnew received more coverage than Shriver. In other network coverage Democratic candidates for other offices received substantially more coverage then Republican candidates for comparable offices.

9. Political news was dramatized in network coverage much more than other kinds of news. A large amount of film was broadcast in action settings in political news, no doubt adding to the drama and excitement of the campaign. This was made possible by a variety of factors. Advance scheduling of campaign events, for instance, made the campaigns more accessible to television news personnel; scheduling also facilitated pictures and action coverage.

10. Surprisingly little use of non-network sources of information for stories was apparent in the news. The viewer might have expected an explicit demonstration that more thorough background investigation for important news stories had occurred. Yet network reporters were portrayed as the only

sources of information in a majority of news stories. No interviewing or checking of details was explicitly present in these stories. In fact, only about one story of five included explicitly partisan (Democratic or Republican) sources during the campaign. In this regard ABC included the most political sources and NBC the fewest.

11. Corroboration rather than conflict in content information was introduced by the additional sources that the news stories did include. When several different reported sources were juxtaposed in a story, each source was more likely to be portrayed as substantiating what the other source said than questioning what the other source said or introducing new and different information. Clearly, juxtaposition of reported sources was not a widely used technique for providing the public with differing information about what was going on in the political world. An "adversary" view of presenting differing information in televised news does not make a great deal of sense in this regard. Conflicting facts do not appear to speak for themselves or to appear very often on network news, at least when non-reporter sources are present in stories.

DIMENSIONS OF POLITICAL BIAS AND COVERAGE IN STORIES
ABOUT CANDIDATES AND PARTIES

To assert that political bias is present in news coverage, one must find consistently more favorable or consistently less favorable coverage of one candidate by a network in comparison with coverage of the same candidate by other networks. Thus if our analysis revealed that one candidate had consistently been treated more favorably by CBS than by NBC or ABC, an initial basis for inferring bias in coverage would have been present. This "residual" notion of bias is far from satisfactory, since it has been alleged that all networks may have the *same* biases, but the notion is explicit and a starting point for analysis.

But it would also have been necessary to show that one side not only had been treated less favorably by a network in comparison with that side's treatment by the other networks but that the one side had been treated less favorably by a network *in comparison with the treatment the network had accorded the opposition.* If we were to assert, for instance, that ABC had an anti-Nixon flavor in its coverage, it would be crucial to know whether ABC *also* had an anti-McGovern flavor and, if so, whether the anti-McGovern flavor was more pronounced than the anti-Nixon flavor. If the latter was true, then ABC would have a pro-Nixon bias *relative to its coverage of McGovern*. If we could also demonstrate that CBS and NBC were relatively more favorable to McGovern than was ABC, this would increase our confidence in the correctness of the interpretation.

The massive collection of statistics on which this report was based revealed a mosaic of conclusions. The key to this mosaic is not a total lack of inequity in the way that the news treated candidates, parties, and issues; rather, the key to understanding these statistics is to note the lack of a *consistent* pattern in statistical inequities and the ubiquitous degree of *parallelism* in the way that all three networks reported political news. The remainder of this section is devoted to a review of some of these very complex findings.

Very few clear-cut instances of partisan bias in network news coverage appeared. The instances that we can clearly define, moreover, were neither consistent nor very significant in terms of the portion of network time consumed. The following were illustrative of the narrowly constrained set of instances:

1. ABC presented stories about Nixon in which sources were more supportive than sources in comparable stories about McGovern. The opposite pattern appeared in CBS coverage of Nixon and McGovern.

2. In terms of evaluative aspects of news coverage, ABC was slightly more unfavorable to McGovern, and CBS was slightly more unfavorable to Nixon. What little sarcasm, for instance, appeared in stories about the candidates was a bit more unfavorable to Nixon on CBS and unfavorable to McGovern on ABC. On CBS, coverage was also more favorable to the Republican than to the Democratic campaign. In this regard ABC was most favorable to the Republicans (in terms of gaining support), and NBC was most favorable to the Democrats (in terms of losing support less than on the other networks).

3. Ratings of stories about candidates revealed a similar picture. Specific instances of inequity appear; but most differences in ratings were parallel on the three networks. CBS portrayed Nixon in a more corrosive, simplified, and unfavorable way. But CBS Nixon coverage was also most interesting and CBS most critical in its McGovern coverage. CBS Republican stories were most unfavorable, and comparable ABC stories were most favorable. None of these differences, however, was very large.

4.  In terms of themes that appeared in news stories, a very slight trend for the GOP to receive more unfavorable coverage on CBS appeared, but the Republicans tended to receive more favorable coverage on CBS than on NBC or ABC.

5.  Small differences in the way in which the networks handled several issues also appeared. These relative differences are summarized in table 36. Two observations are vital to interpretation of the table: (1) evaluations relate to the issue in question and not necessarily to government policy about the issue; and (2) all differences among networks are relative and rarely are very large.

TABLE 36

RELATIVE FAVORABLE AND UNFAVORABLE CONTENT OF ISSUE STORIES
BY NETWORK AND ISSUE

| NETWORK | STORY RELATIVITY [a] | |
| | Favorable | Unfavorable |
| --- | --- | --- |
| CBS | Size and control of military<br>Jobs and wages[b]<br>Labor | Law and order<br>Honesty in government[c]<br>Government functioning[d]<br>Jobs and wages<br>Welfare and poverty<br>Taxes |
| NBC | Vietnam[e]<br>Law and order<br>Welfare and poverty | Vietnam[e]<br>Cost living<br>Size and control of military<br>Labor<br>Busing[f]<br>Treatment of criminals |
| ABC | Law and order<br>Conservation<br>Cost of living<br>Taxes<br>Treatment of criminals | Welfare and poverty<br>Conservation |

[a]Based on amount of time devoted to favorable and unfavorable coverage on each network, from the analysis of specific issues in chapter 7.

[b]No network devoted unfavorable coverage to the jobs and wages issue.

[c]No network devoted favorable coverage to the honesty in government issue.

[d]No network devoted favorable coverage to the government functioning issue.

[e]NBC devoted the most favorable and the most unfavorable attention to the Vietnam issue.

[f]No network devoted favorable coverage to the busing issue.

6.  In assessing specific sources, Cronkite was very slightly more unfavorable and less favorable in the way he related issues to the administration, and Smith and Reasoner proved to be very slightly more favorable and less unfavorable in this regard. But these differences were slight at best. Smith and Reasoner,

moreover, by no means spoke with a single voice, and Cronkite was least favorable to both parties and campaigns.

Thus very little support for accusations of bias appeared in our analysis. The above findings were gleaned from literally thousands of comparisons. Differences in most instances, moreover, proved to be slight when they did appear. Much more significant were our conclusions concerning structural and situational biases that emerged in campaign coverage by the networks.

## STRUCTURAL AND SITUATIONAL BIASES IN NEWS COVERAGE

If very little evidence was found to establish the presence of partisan bias in network coverage of the 1972 presidential campaign, our analysis did establish substantial and consistent differences in the way in which political objects—candidates, parties, and issues—were covered. We assume that these differences were due to structural or situational biases because their profiles were nearly identical on all three networks. An overview is presented below.

1.  The McGovern candidacy, the Democratic party, and Democratic campaign efforts received more coverage than the Nixon candidacy, the Republican party, and Republican campaign efforts. Coverage did, however, become more statistically equitable toward the end of the campaign. Parallel patterns appeared on the major networks in terms of these differences in total candidate and campaign exposure. Thus a structural (and perhaps situational) bias existed that favored McGovern and the Democrats because they received more exposure than their opponents.

Let us look more specifically at what was involved in the advantage that the Democrats and the McGovern candidacy enjoyed in their greater overall exposure during the campaign. Candidate McGovern maintained an advantage over candidate Nixon in positional emphasis (McGovern stories were more likely to appear early in a broadcast), more direct quotations from the candidate or his associates, more film, and a greater propensity to be found in action settings. McGovern was also more likely to be associated with crowds, to be shown as part of an ongoing scene, and to be associated with favorable crowds. This included unorganized as well as organized crowds that frequently appeared during the campaigns. Somewhat more time was devoted, moreover, to reported Democratic sources in McGovern stories than to reported Republican sources in Nixon stories. Cited secondary sources (juxtaposed sources) were more likely to be supportive of primary (the initial) sources in McGovern than in Nixon stories (except on ABC). But all of these observations were true in the news programming of *each* network.

The Democrats (and the Democratic campaign) received comparable advantages in exposure in political reporting on each network. In comparison with the GOP, the Democrats received coverage in more stories that consumed more time. They received more film coverage in action settings, a greater amount of coverage in closeups and flashbacks, and a greater positional emphasis (Democratic stories were more likely to appear early in a news program). Many of these advantages diminished during the campaign—they were most pronounced during the national nominating convention months of July and August—but the net advantages were nonetheless clear and explicit.

Democrats also received an advantage in terms of the tendency to include active and larger crowds in their news stories (although the level of explicit supporter enthusiasm was about the same for each party) and the portrayal of greater antagonism toward the opposition. Republicans probably received some advantage in being consulted as secondary sources for stories about Democrats more frequently than Democrats were consulted in stories about the Republicans. Not unexpectedly, Democrats were also somewhat more likely to receive a greater degree of support from secondary sources than their opposition.

Little consistent variation in the way the networks handled Nixon and McGovern stories, and Republican and Democratic stories, was evident, although some differences did occur. CBS was generally more critical in its juxtaposition of sources in stories about *both* of the parties, and NBC was generally less critical in its juxtaposition of sources in stories about *both* of the parties (ABC had an intermediary position in this regard). A style of reporting was evident clearly enough; but this style did not work to the partisan advantage of either the Democrats or the Republicans in a clear way. The slight differences that occurred in candidate and party coverage that may qualify as evidence for partisan bias were not very consistent nor did they represent very large differences in terms of either time or number of stories.

These observations were based on what might be called "raw," quantitative indicators of exposure. They were important in assessing potential impact of coverage, because the amount of coverage—regardless of qualitative aspects of it to some extent at least—control a person's impressions about the source. But it was also important to inspect more refined, evaluative aspects of television coverage.

The relative advantages of each type were in opposite directions in the case of news coverage of the 1972 campaign.

2.   An opposite advantage existed in some of the more qualitative aspects of candidate and party coverage. Nixon, but not the Republican party (and campaign), was more likely to receive favorable coverage, and McGovern, but not the Democratic party (and campaign), was more likely to receive unfavorable coverage. The Republican and Democratic parties received comparable favorable and unfavorable coverage on each network. Although Nixon received coverage that was favorable more often than McGovern on each network, some inter-network differences did occur. Candidates were associated with a variety of groups on each network, but Nixon generally benefited from favorable group associations more than McGovern.

Network coverage of the Nixon campaign (if not the GOP) was more favorable than network coverage of the McGovern campaign (if not the Democratic party). This tendency was strongest on CBS, although CBS was also most critical of both campaigns. Network coverage of the Democrats was considerably more polarized—i.e., more favorable or unfavorable, rather than neutral—than coverage of the GOP. The networks also portrayed the Democrats as losing support more often than the GOP, and nearly all stories suggested that the GOP was maintaining its support. Thus the Democratic camp was seen as being rife with conflict, and the Republicans were seen as tranquilly advancing toward the election.

The networks also contributed somewhat to maintaining partisan coalitions. The Democrats were associated with non-whites, blue-collar workers, union members, and non-party supporters. But these groups were also associated with the GOP nearly as much in network news stories. The GOP, moreover, was portrayed as cutting into the traditional Democratic support from southerners and young people. Finally, the fact that greater emphasis was given to associations of Democrats with national figures in their party may imply a broader base of support for the Democrats.

Reported network sources of stories (usually anchormen) were either judged to be neutral or unfavorable more often than favorable, and the respective partisan sources that were mentioned were predominantly favorable, as might well be anticipated. Institutional sources cited were more unfavorable, and experts more favorable, to the GOP than to the Democrats. But the most important differences in candidate and party coverage were parallel on each network's news programming. Indeed, differential coverage by networks provided meager advantage to one side or the other.

199

3.   The preceding conclusions were drawn from research on coding of videotaped material according to a well-elaborated set of rules and conventions. In most instances they represent fairly straightforward classification of content in standard ways. Counts of the number of stories, and the amount of time measured in minutes, was the metric of comparison used to formulate conclusions. Confidence in our interpretation of these data increased when we found that the results of other methods (with other sources of possible error independent of errors that might exist in the preceding measures) of classifying the content of network news broadcasts supported these findings.

All stories, for instance, were rated on a variety of rating scales designed to evaluate the substance or content of stories with regard to candidates, issues, and parties and campaigns, and to evaluate the way that stories were presented on television. Analysis of these rating scales revealed that each candidate fared better than his opponent in some respects, so that neither received an unequivocal advantage. The same finding emerged with respect to the parties.

Generally speaking, candidate Nixon fared somewhat better than candidate McGovern, although this conclusion depended on what specific dimensions of news programming were considered to be good or bad. Nixon was portrayed as being more efficient, competent, milder, and more passive; but Nixon stories were presented in a way judged to be less interesting than McGovern stories. In contrast, McGovern was portrayed as more likable, sincere, honest, kind, unselfish and active; and McGovern stories were judged more interesting than Nixon stories. Nixon stories were also generally presented in a more favorable, less corrosive, less critical, and simpler way than McGovern stories. McGovern coverage became more favorable and Nixon coverage less favorable toward the end of the campaign; but, McGovern coverage was initially relatively unfavorable and Nixon coverage initially relatively favorable.

Candidate coverage was rated as relatively impartial on each network, despite some network differences in other ratings. ABC and CBS, for instance, portrayed both candidates in a more critical way than NBC, and NBC stories were judged to be least interesting. CBS stories concerning both candidates were rated as being most complex and interesting. Differences in story content and presentation were neither large nor overwhelmingly favorable to one side.

The GOP was portrayed as the most efficient, successful, strong, and the least good and honest party. Republicans were portrayed in a relatively unfavorable and boring way. Again, CBS presented party stories in the most critical, complex, interesting, but also the most favorable way in comparison with the other networks. Differences among networks in average (mean) ratings were very slight in nearly all instances.

Indeed, if formal tests of statistical significance were calculated, most of the differences in ratings would not be statistically significant. Nor was much variance in the rating scales explained by either the candidate or the party emphasis of news stories. (The logic of significance testing is inapplicable when probability sampling is not employed, as it was not in this study.) The entire universe of possible observations was included.

A further check on the adequacy of the first two classification techniques of news story content was employed in this study. All stories were broken down into component thematic parts, and the evaluative implications were scrutinized for the candidates, parties (and campaigns), and issues. Once again, support was provided for our findings that little partisan bias was apparent in network news during the 1972 campaign.

Candidate Nixon, for instance, received more favorable mention than candidate McGovern. Nixon also received more unfavorable mention as well. Although the disparity between Nixon and McGovern in the amount of unfavorable coverage was not as great as the disparity in the favorable coverage (which gave Nixon a net advantage), the patterns of advantage and disadvantage were similar on all networks.

Minor differences occurred, but even they were mixed. CBS was quite polarized in its coverage of candidates, including more favorable thematic content than the other networks. NBC was least polarized, containing the least favorable and unfavorable thematic content in candidate stories. Although more candidate stories appeared near the conclusion of the campaign, the average number of candidate themes did not increase. This may imply that the news was not becoming increasingly politicized in content, even though a larger portion of attention was turned toward the electoral struggle.

Similar conclusions emerged when one inspected themes about the major parties. CBS again provided the greatest number of coverage themes about parties. Republicans generally benefited by receiving more favorable thematic coverage on each network; Democrats generally received more unfavorable coverage. Despite some irregularities, the GOP received some advantages in thematic coverage during the campaign. But the disparities in network coverage—were vastly outweighed by similarities in network coverage. Conclusions of political bias are improbable at best.

201

4. Issue coverage is central to many discussions of network news bias. Even if political bias was difficult to discern, could it still have intruded in issue coverage? Such bias might, conceivably, have worked to favor the more liberal party's standard-bearer, or to favor the more conservative party's candidate, depending on its character.

The question of bias in issue coverage, however, was considerably more complex and ambiguous than might be thought at first glance. Parties did not always take clearly antagonistic, opposing sides on many issues. Furthermore, situational constraints often outweighed "liberal" or "conservative" positions on many policies. Nor did large segments of the American public weigh issue alternatives in explicitly liberal or conservative terms. Thus categorizing issue positions as "liberal" or "conservative" was neither very straightforward nor useful.

To evaluate political bias in issue coverage, we scrutinized the way in which issues were linked to candidates, parties, and campaigns. It was possible to circumscribe issue topics (Vietnam, law and order, honesty in government, and so on) without necessarily labeling positions as either liberal or conservative. The logic of this analysis involved determining to what extent one of the networks consistently treated a set of issues differently than the other networks, and to what extent the treatment could be related to partisan concerns. If both conditions were discovered, then some evidence would exist to assert that biased coverage was involved.

Very little political issue bias was present in network news reporting when we compared the way networks handled specific issue areas with the way networks related issues to major party campaign efforts. The predominant issue treatment was neutral, as had been repeatedly found true in other news coverage. There was also more unfavorable than favorable issue coverage in the evening news on each network. Relatively little attention was paid to most topics included under the "issue" rubric, at least when some specificity was used to define issue areas. A large and diverse number of specific issues were included, but not much consistent coverage was devoted to single topics throughout the campaign. Party politics, Vietnam, the economy, government functioning, and a few other issues became almost "institutionalized" in the sense that large amounts of attention were regularly devoted to them. But in comparison with these issues, few other issue concerns received much air time.

As in the case of other news coverage, network reporters proved to be by far the most important observable source (i.e., the only observable source) of issue stories. This pattern was most common in NBC coverage and least common in CBS coverage. Institutional sources were most frequently cited for issue stories outside of news personnel on each network. CBS was more likely to use opposing juxtaposition of sources, and was most critical in issue coverage. All three networks cited Democratic more than Republican sources in issue coverage, and Democrats received less critical juxtaposition of sources in issue stories related to them on each network. ABC most frequently reported Democratic sources, and CBS most frequently reported Republican sources.

Although the mosaic in table 36 may produce some evidence for a case of political bias in network issue coverage, this material is weak and contradictory at best. Discrepancies in issue reporting could be due in large part to the kinds of assignments individual reporters received and the kind of access they had in reporting a story. Most issue reporting was neutral or ambiguous. Large differences emerged in the way in which any of the networks' personnel reported the same story and the way in which that network personnel reported different kinds of stories. Cronkite, for instance, was relatively critical and Smith less critical in comparison with their anchormen colleagues. But many exceptions to this generalization occurred. Cronkite was most unfavorable when relating issue stories to the Democratic camp, and Smith and Reasoner were most favorable in linking issue stories to both partisan camps. There was very little issue content favorable to the Democrats; this resulted in a net Republican advantage. However, trends in coverage were parallel on all three networks so that a case for political bias on these grounds is tenable only if one concludes that they all had the same bias.

Inspection of ratings and thematic analyses reinforced these conclusions. Few differences emerged in either content or presentation from the evaluative ratings of issue linkages to candidates and partisan campaigns. If anything, the issues related to McGovern in a slightly unfavorable way, although McGovern's issue ratings became more favorable and Nixon's more unfavorable as the campaign neared its conclusion in October and early November. Differences were slight in thematic content of issue stories, although a tendency appeared to favor Nixon rather than McGovern. Even in this regard, more unfavorable thematic issue content also appeared in Nixon stories.

CONCLUSION

We conclude that news coverage of the 1972 campaign was not biased in a political way. Some weaknesses, however, do not allow us to accept this conclusion in an unequivocal manner.

*Some Caveats and Comments*

Perhaps the greatest problem in assessing bias was to establish an objective baseline. This study's major criterion for political bias has been differences among the networks in coverage of the same thing. But what if the networks are all biased in the same partisan way? Actual instances of political bias would be interpreted as structural or situational because statistical similarities would be misleading. Indeed, this is the Achilles heel of the argument presented here. Our assumptions concerning evidence of structural or situational bias may well have been much too strong, but no viable alternatives were present that withstand conceptual analysis better than the alternative that was employed.

We attempted to establish baselines that were independent of television news. These studies were not reported in detail because of space limitations, but it is worthwhile to summarize some conclusions. Associated Press wire stories,[3] Democratic and Republican political advertisements (partisan spots),[4] major-party platforms,[5] and campaign coverage from the *Chicago Tribune* and the *Washington Post*[6] were all analyzed. Each study tried to establish a baseline subject to limitations different from those on televised news. News stories were then compared with wire stories, spots, and platforms to gauge the possible extent of confusion between structural and partisan bias contained in this study.

Preliminary analysis of wire stories, political spots, and convention platforms led to identical conclusions. No basis was present for asserting political bias in network news coverage of the 1972 campaign. But the different media clearly had varying structural requirements.

It is possible that news program characteristics may not have measured what we assumed they did, and were therefore invalid. Invalidity can stem from unreliability and poor conceptualization of a problem.

Reliability in coding media content is reasonably straightforward to establish. However, very limited theoretical development in the area of media processes and effects requires that any study of media bias make special efforts to establish the validity of measures.

Satisfactory reliability levels were found for most measures included in the study, and reliability was regularly and rigorously checked.

Two separate validity studies were made. In one study, small groups of intense liberals, conservatives, Republicans, and Democrats coded a number of stories selected to represent major analysis categories.[7] These "known groups" coded materials in very similar ways, suggesting that coding was not a simple product of coder ideology and supporting the validity of our measures.

The second study employed a multitrait-multimethod approach to validity.[8] Different *kinds* of measures (classification, rating, and thematic) were interrelated, supporting the convergent validity more than the discriminant validity of the measures. Although questions were raised in this validity study about the thematic measures in particular, the study supported the validity of most measures to some extent.

Another problem of selectivity, discussed extensively in chapter one above, was apparent at this point. We focused on statistical patterns rather than on individual instances of news coverage in this study. It is possible that a single story (insignificant as a percentage of the total of 4,349 stories) might have had tremendous impact on viewers and set a theme for the entire campaign. Thus a second phase of this project will scrutinize viewer impact and perceptions of network news. It might be that content analysis and survey research are not sufficiently developed to uncover effects of single instances or more subtle kinds of political biases in news coverage.

The 1972 election may have been a particularly poor time to study political bias because a unique set of election characteristics outweighed "normal" news coverage. But each presidential election has been unique in many respects. The bias question, moreover, was hotly debated during this time, and analysis had to begin at some point.[9] Finally, structural factors in news coverage have been duly noted.

The fact remains, however, that *replications* of this study during other elections or conducted under different conditions are absolutely *essential* for more confident conclusions about news programming. This study analyzed only the 1972 campaign news coverage. Interpreting its findings is, therefore, particularly hazardous because of rapid changes in the nation's social and political climate and changes in the television news industry.

It is also important to note that the effects of structural bias may be far from neutral on the fortunes of a candidate and party. Indeed, coverage that makes "good news" may be devastating on a campaign. A major difference between structural (and situational) kinds of bias on the one hand and political bias on the other is that astute campaigners may find the former considerably easier to manipulate to their own advantage than the latter. At least, most candidates have an opportunity to exploit the structural characteristics of television for many purposes. But the debate has too often failed to make the basic distinction that we have tried to clarify here.

To reiterate once again, the interpretation of all the findings in this report is contingent on our view of the effects of television exposure on citizens. This must be true to at least some extent, although it is clearly legitimate to argue that political and structural biases may be less than desirable in and of themselves. Two very general alternative views appear to underlie much of the debate: (1) a rationalist view that seems to imply that many people are exposed to television news and that small biases have considerable impact on their view of the world; (2) an individual differences model that argues that the same coverage may have a variety of effects on viewers contingent on their psychological and sociological constitution and on the situation in which viewing occurs. In general, the second model assumes that effects—even of major kinds of biases in news coverage—would usually be minimal. Few would unequivocally accept the conclusions of either model in an unqualified way. Nonetheless, which set of assumptions are accepted makes a considerable difference in how the minor differences in coverage that were discerned in this study are interpreted. Questions of impact and imagery will be more thoroughly investigated in a second report.[10]

### A Final Word

Differences in network coverage of candidates, parties, and issues were too muted to provide a basis for allegations of either political or structural bias. Differences among networks were slight when they occurred in systematic ways. Most coverage was neutral or ambiguous rather than favorable or unfavorable. One party's advantages were generally offset by the other's in selected aspects of news programming. Although structural and situational biases existed on all three networks, perhaps favoring the Democrats more than the Republicans, these biases generally reflected sheer quantity of coverage, *not* evaluative aspects of the coverage.

A plausible explanation for the structural biases is readily at hand. An incumbent president faced a non-incumbent challenger in the 1972 election. The challenger was an underdog, and the president did relatively little personal campaigning. The challenger had to vigorously attack the incumbent, and thereby maximize his news exposure. It was easier to gain access to the challenger's campaign than the incumbent's. Finally, differences in 1972 campaign coverage may have been at least partially due to a badly split, factionalized Democratic party facing a relatively united, tranquil opposition that conducted a low-profile campaign.

The failure to find political bias during the 1972 campaign should not be interpreted as suggesting that substantial political bias has been absent at other times. The notion of bias in the news remains an empirical question. We hope this study has shown the kinds of evidence needed to support such allegations and, therefore, elevated the level of rational debate. Perhaps in the future, opponents and proponents alike will pursue questions of network coverage even more systematically.

1. Westerstahl, "Objective News Reporting," chaps. 1-2. Ernest W. Lefever, *TV and National Defense: An Analysis of CBS News, 1972-1973* (Washington, D.C.: Institute for American Strategy Press, 1974), confuses this distinction to some extent in his analysis.

2. Ibid.

3. C. Richard Hofstetter and Gary D. Malaney, *The Campaign through the Eyes of the Associated Press Wire Reports: A Non-Video Baseline, Working Paper Number 9 in the Television Election News Coverage Project (TENCP)* (Columbus: Ohio State University, Polimetrics Laboratory Report No. 22, 1976).

4. Cliff Zukin and C. Richard Hofstetter, *Campaign Attributes Reflected in Nixon and McGovern Advertisements: A Propagandistic Baseline, Working Paper Number 10 in the Television Election News Coverage Project (TENCP)* (Columbus: Ohio State University, Polimetrics Laboratory Report No. 23, 1974).

5. Anderson and Hofstetter, *Television News and Convention Platforms.*

6. C. Richard Hofstetter, "Biased News in the 1972 Campaign: A Multi-Media Analysis," paper presented at the International Communication Association, Division VI, Political Communication, 14-17 April 1976, at Portland, Oregon.

7. C. Richard Hofstetter and Tamara House Juba, *A Validation of Content Codes by Known Groups, Working Paper Number 6 in the Television Election News Coverage Project (TENCP)* (Columbus: Ohio State University, Polimetrics Laboratory Report No. 19, 1974).

8. Paul Strand and C. Richard Hofstetter, *Convergent and Discriminant Validity of Selected Indicators, Working Paper Number 7 in the Television Election News Coverage Project (TENCP)* (Columbus: Ohio State University, Polimetrics Laboratory Report No. 20, 1974).

9. Jack Wichita and C. Richard Hofstetter, *The Television Issue Context of the 1972 Presidential Election, Working Paper Number 12 in the Television Election News Coverage Project (TENCP)* (Columbus: Ohio State University, Polimetrics Laboratory Report No. 25, 1974).

10. Hofstetter, *Television and Civic Education.*

# Index